Vices and Virtues

PART II

EARLY ENGLISH TEXT SOCIETY

Original Series, No. 159

1921 (for 1920), reprinted 1967

PRICE 25s.

Vices and Virtues

BEING

A Soul's Confession of its Sins

with

Reason's Description of the Virtues

A MIDDLE-ENGLISH DIALOGUE

OF ABOUT 1200 A.D.

EDITED, WITH AN INTRODUCTION, TRANSLATION, NOTES,
AND GLOSSARY, FROM THE STOWE MS. 240

EDITED BY

F. HOLTHAUSEN

PART II

NOTES AND GLOSSARY

Published for
THE EARLY ENGLISH TEXT SOCIETY
by the
OXFORD UNIVERSITY PRESS
LONDON   NEW YORK   TORONTO

OXFORD
UNIVERSITY PRESS

Great Clarendon Street, Oxford OX2 6DP
United Kingdom

Oxford University Press is a department of the University of Oxford.
It furthers the University's objective of excellence in research, scholarship,
and education by publishing worldwide. Oxford is a registered trade mark of
Oxford University Press in the UK and in certain other countries

© The Early English Text Society 1921

The moral rights of the authors have been asserted

Database right Oxford University Press (maker)

First Edition published in 1921
Reprinted 1967

All rights reserved. No part of this publication may be reproduced,
stored in a retrieval system, or transmitted, in any form or by any means,
without the prior permission in writing of Oxford University Press,
or as expressly permitted by law, or under terms agreed with the appropriate
reprographics rights organization. Enquiries concerning reproduction
outside the scope of the above should be sent to the Rights Department,
Oxford University Press, at the address above

You must not circulate this book in any other form
and you must impose this same condition on any acquirer

Published in the United States of America by Oxford University Press
198 Madison Avenue, New York, NY 10016, United States of America

British Library Cataloguing in Publication Data
Data available

Library of Congress Cataloging in Publication Data
Data available

Original Series, 159

ISBN 978-0-19-722159-4

NOTES TO "VICES AND VIRTUES."

Page 3, l. 2. Although the beginning of this division is lost, there can be no doubt that it treated on *wrath* (*anger, ire*). This is clear as well from the biblical passage, quoted in l. 3, which is taken from Matth. v. 24, as from the order of the capital sins, generally arranged so that *wrath* precedes *sorrow*. Cf. e.g. Wulfstán's Hom. xlvii (ed. by Napier, p. 245), *se ðridda is ira, þæt is yrre. se feorða is tristitia, þæt is unrótnes.*—Ælfric's sermon on Dominica in media quadragesime (Homilies of Æ., ed. by Thorpe, vol. ii. p. 218), *feorða wéamet, fífta unrótnys.*—' De octo viciis et de duodecim abusivis hujus seculi' (Old Engl. Homilies, ed. by Morris, i. 103), *þeo feorð[e] sunne is ihatan ira, þet is on englisc wemodnesse . . . þeo fifte sunne is tristicia, þet is þissere worlde sarinesse*.

on godes awene muðe, On *own,* which in our text is frequently used as an emphasizing of the possessive relation (e.g. p. 7/1, 9/7, 11/19, 13/27, 19/28, 23/1, 12, 14, 17, 18, 23/28, &c.), cf. Mätzner, Engl. Gr.³ iii. p. 241 ϵ; Koch, Histor. Gr.² ii. p. 253, § 323.

10. Quoted from 2 Cor. vii. 10, *Saeculi autem tristitia mortem operatur.* As the words stand, they are probably taken from the context of some other source, where they occurred in the middle of a sentence as an ablat. absol.

12. *Ðes awerȝede gast, hie makeð.* On this repetition of the subject by a pronoun cf. Kölbing, Sir Tristrem, p. 92, note 13 f.; Mätzner, Engl. Gr.³ ii. p. 19 *b* seq. Further examples below are *hie,* 5/18, *he* 15/6, *we* 15/23, &c.

ðane religiuse man means a man who is bound by monastic vows, a monk or friar; cf. *cloðes of religiun,* p. 5/33 and note.—*religiun,* p. 43/3.

13. *sari & drieri & heui.* Cf. Mätzner, Wörterbuch, i. p. 672 : *sœri & an heorte druri,* Laȝ. ii. 184; ii. p. 491 : *ðat swinc heui & sor,* Gen. & Ex. 2565.

17. *oðer halȝe to sechen,* refers to pilgrims who travel to visit churches and relics of a saint. See Chaucer's Leg. of good Women, Dido, 384, *Dido She seketh halwes, and doothe sacrifise.*—Cant. Tales, Prologue, 12 seq., *Thanne longen folk to gon on pilgrimages, And palmers for to seeken straunge strondes, To ferne halwes, kouthe in sondry londes.*—Ib. 17, *The holy blisful martir for to seeke.* Cf. also Zupitza's notes to Guy of Warwick (E.E.T.S., E.S. xxvi), p. 425/8394, and in our text p. 35/5.

20. It is unnecessary to supply *don.* Cf. Cant. Tales, The Parson's Tale, *De Accidia* (Chaucer ed. by Morris, iii. p. 323 seq.), *but accidie doth noon such diligence. He doth alle thing with anoy, and with wraweness, slaknes, and excusacioun, and with ydelnes and unlust,* &c. The translation on p. 2 ought to be, accordingly " or do them " instead of " or cause them to be done."

22. As the virtues (see note to 29/31) so the vices too are represented as sisters.

26 seq. Cf. Ancren Riwle, p. 268 seq.

27. *be daiȝe and be nihte.* Cf. Rich. M. Meyer, Die altgerm. Poesie, p. 285, where instances of the formula *dæges and nihtes, dæg and niht* from OE. are given; for ME. specimens see Mätzner, i. p. 581: *daies & nihtes,* Laȝ. i. 230.—*deies & nihtes,* OEH. p. 7.—*dei ne naht,* ib. p. 57.—*dei & niht,* ib. p. 65.—*dai & nighte,* Ps. lxxiii. 18.—*ba bi daie & bi nith,* Laȝ. i. 88. Cf. also Wissmann, King Horn, p. 85/263; Caro, Engl. Stud. xii. 347.

28. *Swilch hit,* &c. I am not quite certain about the meaning of this sentence.

P. 5, l. 1. *þat is þe ænde . . . ðat hie wolde.* On this change of tenses cf. Mätzner, Engl. Gr.³ ii. p. 110 seq.

2. On *man* as an indef. pron. cf. Koch, ii. p. 307, § 377; Zupitza, Guy, p. 454, note to 11472, where it is also followed by *he.*

3. *his lif ladde.* Cf. Fuhrmann, Die alliterierenden Sprachformeln, &c. (dissert. of Kiel), Hamburg, 1886, p. 64.

8. *Hie was anȝinn of alle sennes.* Cf. Sirach x. 15, *Initium omnis peccati est superbia.*

8 seq. alludes to the doctrine of Lucifer's fall, founded on Job iv. 18; Is. xiv. 12-15; 2 Pet. ii. 4; Jude 6, and known to the modern English reader from Milton's Paradise Lost, books i, v, and vi. I add, from Defensor's Liber Scintillarum (Migne, Patrol. lat. tom. 88, col. 639), *Superbia ex angelis daemonia fecit.* Ambrosius.—*Superbia de coelis deposuit archangelum.* Vitae patrum.

9. *heuene heinesse.* Cf. Fuhrmann, p. 48, sub "*hyȝe in heuen.*"

10. *Deus superbis resistit* = 1 Pet. v. 5; James iv. 6.

11. *modi mannen.* Cf. Fuhrmann, p. 41.

12. *Godd seið,* &c. Cf. Matth. xxiii. 12, *Qui autem se exaltaverit, humiliabitur.*—Luke xiv. 11, *Quia omnis, qui se exaltat, humiliabitur* (= xviii. 14).

14. *michel ilaten of me seluen.* Cf. 24, *he latt ðe bet of him seluen.*—7/2, *Sume læteð wel of hem seluen.*—55/29, *michel læteð of hem seluen.*—57/20, *he læte vers of him seluen.*—65/19, *he latt wel of him seluen.*—109/23, *ne latt tu herfore non ðe unwurþere.* Cf. Sohrauer, Kleine Beitr. z. altengl. Gramm., Berlin (dissert.), 1886, p. 10, § 3, 5; Schröer, Winteney-Version d. Reg. St. Benedicti, p. 152, note to 31/15.

16. *scolde . . . nolde* is a rhyme!

17 seq. *Ðies ilche modinesse . . . naðelæs hie haueð.* Cf. note to 3/12 and Schleich, Ywain & Gawain, p. 108/302.

26. *bewop* ought to have been converted into *bewepð* (cf. the foot-note), and accordingly the translation would be "weeps."

27. *halȝen te seken.* Cf. note to 3/17.

28 seq. Cf. OEH. ii. 83/19, *hie giuen here tigeðe noht for to hauen heuene blisse, ac for to hauen here þe hereword of eorðliche richeise; hie giuen here elmesse noht for godes luue, ac for neheboreden, oðer for kinraden, oðer for onur to hauen, oðer ne mai elles for shame, oðer for þonc to hauen, oðer for hereword to hauen.*

30. = Matth. vi. 2.

32 seq. Cf. p. 3/12 seq.

33. On *religiun* and *order* cf. Konrath, Beitr. z. Erklärung u. Textkritik des Will. v. Schorham, Berlin, 1878, p. 32/54.

P. 7, l. 1. *aȝene*. Cf. note to 3/2.

On *ne* = "neither . . . nor" cf. Kaluza, Engl. Stud. xiv. p. 178/119. In our text it occurs p. 27/6, *ðu ne namann.*—33/4, *te golde ne to seluer.*

3. *ȝif he bie* ought to be *bieð*, as *ȝif* is connected with the indicative mood of the other verbs. The occurrence of *he*, "he," and *hie*, "they," side by side is remarkable.

Is *menstre* = "minster" or "ministry"?

6. *ic am becnawe* means "I confess." See Mätzner, i. p. 224/5; New Engl. Diction. i. p. 778/4.

7. *idon* had better been translated "induced."

12. = Wisd. ii. 24. The Vulgate reads, *Invidia autem diaboli mors introivit in orbem terrarum.*

16 seq. See 5/8 seq. and note.

17-21. Cf. Rom. v. 19, *Sicut enim per inobedientiam unius hominis peccatores constituti sunt multi: ita et per unius obedientiam justi constituentur multi.*

18. *Adam, ure forme fader.* Mätzner gives (ii. p. 178) the following quotations for it: OEH. ii. 101.—*Of our forme fader Adam*, Hamp. 482.—*A. oure form fader dere*, Holy Rood, p. 62.—*oure formere f. A.*, Maund. p. 2 ; i. 608 : *ure forme fader*, OEH. ii. 35 ; cf. ib. ii. 63/3 : *oure firste f. A.*, R. of Gl. p. 9.

19. Cf. Rom. v. 12, *Propterea sicut per unum hominem peccatum in hunc mundum intravit, et per peccatum mors; et ita in omnes homines mors pertransiit, &c.*

20. *ma ðanne fíf ðusend wintre.* Cf. the Evangelium Nicodemi, part ii. (Descensus Christi ad inferos), c. 3 (Tischendorf, Evang. Apocr.[2] p. 394), where Seth relates the words of Michael, ". . . *quando completi fuerint quinque millia et quingenti anni : tunc veniet super terram amantissimus dei filius ad resuscitandum corpus Adae . . . Tunc descendens in terras amantissimus dei filius Christus Iesus introducet patrem nostrum Adam in paradisum ad arborem misericordiae.*" The same is said by Annas and Caiphas to Pilate, c. xii. p. 410, "*Et invenimus in libro primo de Septuaginta, ubi locutus est Michael archangelus ad tertium filium Adae primi hominis de quinque millibus et quingentis annis, in quibus venturus esset de coelis dilectissimus dei filius Christus: . . . quia in quinque et semis millibus annorum venturus esset Iesus Christus*" . . . ; ib. p. 412, "*Qui fuerunt simul anni V millia quingenti, sicut invenimus scriptum in bibliotheca praenuntiasse Michael archangelum ad tertium filium Adae Seth, in quinque et semis millibus annorum advenisse Christum.*" . . . .—The same source relates how Adam was delivered by Christ out of hell, a story afterwards frequently represented as the "Harrowing of Hell" in the Miracle Plays, &c.

On *winter* = "year" cf. Zupitza, Engl. Stud. xiii. p. 354/67.

27. See Gen. ii. 17.

32. *ure lauerd Crist, ðe was hersum his fader anon to ðe deaðe.* Cf. Philip. ii. 8, *factus obediens usque ad mortem.*

P. 9, l. 1. *.ðis scorte lif*, = 59/26, 61/25, 75/15. Other expressions for "life" are : *on ðese scorte time*, 23/2.—*on ðese arme liue*, 21/14, 89/34.—*on ðese liue*, 35/27, 53/3, 61/34.—*hier on liue*, 57/4.—*hier on ðese liue*, 57/8.—*hier*, 35/8, 55/7, 103/27.—I add the paraphrases for "to live": *ða litle hwile* ðe wer her wuniʒið, 19/19.—ðis scorte lif her laden, 21/23.—ðar hwile ðe ic on ðese wrecche lichame am wuniende, 47/16.—he was her on ðese liue wuniʒende, 51/5.—On ða time ðe hie was hier on liue libbende, 55/1.—ðo litle hwile ðe ðu art mid him her on ðise weiʒe, 75/14.—ðe hwile ðe ðu art on ðine wrecche lichame ʒebunden, 85/31.—All ðare hwile ðe ðu art on ðese earme liue, 89/33. —þe litle hwile ðe we tegedere wunieð, 97/14.—Ne biest ðu naht hier lange wuniʒende, 103/20.

þat ... ðat. Cf. Mätzner, Engl. Gr.³ iii. p. 436/3 seq.

8. *wisen* ought to have been supplied after *a manies kennes*. Cf. Mätzner, i. p. 521 seq.: *on ælches cunnes wise*, Laʒ. i. 344.—*O whillcess kinness wise*, Orm. 5283.—*on this kin wise*, Amadace, st. 29.—*On feole cunne wisen*, Laʒ. i. 73.—*a vele kunne wise*, OE. Misc., p. 39.—*A þre cunne wise*, p. 38.—*On alle kinne wise*, Orm. 850.—In our text occur: *on alles kennes wisen*, 25/17.—*an hwilches kennes wise*, 29/6 seq.—*alles kennes wisen*, 49/16.—*on manies kennes wisen*, 149/18. Cf. Zupitza, Notes to Guy, p. 395/4346.

11 seq.=James v. 12, *Nolite jurare, neque per coelum, neque per terram, neque aliud quodcunque juramentum. Sit autem sermo vester: Est, est! Non, non!* (=Matth. v. 37).

13 seq. *Al þat we more sweriʒeð*, &c. Cf. Matth. v. 37, *Quod autem his abundantius est, a malo est.*

14 seq. *sacleas of ðessere senne*. See Fuhrmann, l.c. p. 33 on top.

16. *soð te seggen.* See ib. p. 52 seq.

24. *mid rihte*=9/25, 51/34, 53/25, 69/24, 133/7, 139/27.—*þe gode rihte*, 97/1.—*mid gode rihte*, 99/26, 115/11.—*mid michel rihte*, 115/22. Cf. Schröer, Winteney-Vers., p. 158, note to 95/13, 14.

Crist ..., ðe is ... icleped soðh (=l. 32) Cf. 1 John v. 6, ... *Et spiritus est, qui testificatur, quoniam Christus est veritas.*

25. *dieuel is icleped ... fader of leasinge.* Cf. John viii. 44, ... *cum loquitur mendacium, ex propriis loquitur, quia mendax est et pater ejus.*

26.=Is. xiv. 14, the words of the king of Babylon as quoted by the inhabitants of hell when he came down to them. He was taken as the representative of Satan by the Fathers; cf. e. g. Hieronymus, Comment. in Isaiam proph. lib. vi. c. 14 (Migne, 24/226 seq.); Haymo, Com. in Is. lib. ii (ib. 116/791 seq.), *Possumus et ista referre allegorice ad diabolum, qui mane, i. e. in exordio mundi ortus, vel elevatus est inter caeteros angelos, sed cecidit de coelo. Juxta quod Dominus dicit Luc. X: "Videbant Satanam sicut fulgur cadentem de coelo." Qui antequam corrueret, dicebat talia cogitando, vel postquam corruit. Sed antequam corrueret, cum esset in firmamento, cupiebat in coelum ascendere, ubi solium Domini est. Sed postquam correptus per verba arrogantiae est sicut est ille, gloriatur ascendere super angelos in coelum, et super nubes, vel super corda electorum*, &c. "*Verumtamen—laci*," (ib. 792). *Nab. vel diabolus qui per superbiam dixerat: " In coelum conscendam, ero similis Altissimo," non solum ad infernum corruit de solio gloriae, sed ad ultimas partes inferni lapsus est*, &c. Cf. also York Plays, p. 4/91.

29. *Đu me þencst wel to wreiʒen*, &c. Cf. 75/18-21. The devil was believed to accuse the departed souls before God's judgment. Cf. e. g. The Pricke of Conscience, p. 149/5480,—

  Alswa devels sal accuse þam þar
   of alle þair syns, bathe les and mar, &c.

and the legends in Anglia, iii. p. 321, No. 2; p. 347, l. 12 seq.

P. 11, l. 5. *Sedens*, &c. = Ps. xlix. 20 (Heb. l. 20), which continues, *et adversus filium matris tuae ponebas scandalum.*
8. *pater noster*, the beginning of the Lord's Prayer (Matth. vi. 9).
9. *Đus ðu dedest*, &c. = Ps. xlix. 21 (l. 21), *Haec fecisti, et tacui. Existimasti inique, quod ero tui similis.*
11. *Ac ðu scalt stonden*, &c. = Ib.: *arguam te, et statuam contra faciem tuam.*
13 seq. *Dilexisti*, &c. = Ps. li. 5 (lii. 3), continuing, *iniquitatem magis, quam loqui aequitatem.*
16. *forði ðe scal god . . . forliesen.* Cf. ib. 7 (5), *Propterea Deus destruet te in finem.*
16 seq. *baðe lichame & saule.* Cf. Meyer, p. 286 : *líces & sáwle* in OE.
17. *Ga awei*, &c. Cf. Matth. vii. 23, *Discedite a me, qui operamini iniquitatem!*—Id. xxv. 41, *Discedite a me, maledicti! in ignem aeternum, qui paratus est diabolo.*—Luke xiii. 27, *Discedite a me, omnes operarii iniquitatis!*
20. *forbod te brekene.* Cf. OE. Dan. 299, *brǽcon bebodo.*
26. *bouhte oðer him sealde.* On this frequent combination cf. Kölbing, Ipomedon, p. 453/8851.
26 seq. *þat ic biȝate & he forlure.* Cf. Kölbing, l. c. p. 424/5221.
27 seq. Cf. Lev. xix. 35, *Nolite facere iniquum aliquid in judicio, in regula, in pondere, in mensura*; ib. 36, *Statera justa, et aequa sint pondera, justus modius, aequusque sextarius.*—Deut. xxv. 13, *Non habebis in sacculo diversa pondera, majus et minus*; ib. 14, *nec erit in domo tua modius major et minor.*—Prov. xi. 1, *Statera dolosa, abominatio est apud Dominum.*—Ib. xx. 10, *Pondus et pondus, mensura et mensura; utrumque abominabile est apud Deum.*—Ib. 23, *Abominatio est apud Dominum pondus et pondus; statera dolosa non est bona.*—On the use of *ne* after *forbett* and similar verbs, cf. Zupitza, Engl. Stud. xiii. p. 411/765. In our text cf. 27/11, 55/5, 65/28, 87/31.
28 seq. *ac ðat we sculen . . . leanen, wið-uten erðliche mede.* Usury was forbidden as a sin, cf. p. 77/19 seq., and Skeat's Notes to Piers Plowman, p. 121/239; 404/111. Cf. Ælfric's Hom. ii. 554, *Se Ælmihtiga God forbéad þurh his witegan, þæt nán ðæra manna þe rihtwis béon wile, ne sceal syllan his feoh tó gafole.*—See also note to p. 77/19.
31. *Soþ to seggen.* Cf. Fuhrmann, l. c. p. 52 seq.

P. 13, l. 1. *oðer of wordes oðer of weorkes* is a frequent allit. formula. Cf. O. Hoffmann, Reimformeln im Westgerm. (dissert. of Freiburg), Darmstadt, 1885, p. 60.
4 seq. = 1 Cor. vi. 10, *. . . neque maledici, neque rapaces, regnum Dei possidebunt.*—The interpunction of the text, l. 5, ought to be: "*possidebunt. Ðat bieð ða . . .*," and in l. 7 : "*muȝen, for.*" Accordingly, the translation is to be altered: "*possidebunt.* That are the . . . Heaven, because."
7. *godes handiwerc* is a biblical expression. Cf. Ps. cxxxvii. 8 (cxxxviii. 8), *Opera manuum tuarum ne despicias.* Further examples see below, pp. 21/22, 115/5, and in Mätzner, ii. p. 420.
7 seq. *ðꝭ he hafð iblesced.* See Gen. i. 28, *Benedixitque illis Deus.*
9. *ȝe hodede ȝe leawede* = *hadede* and *leeavede*, 79/17. Cf. Wulfstán, 234/7, *ǽgðer ge gehádodum mannum ge lǽwedum.*—272/20, *gehádede* and *lǽwede.*—OEH. i. 131, xiii, *eiðer ihadede & ileawede.*—*Ihadede & lewede* (= ii. 153, xxvi).

sibbe & framde. Cf. Engl. Stud. viii. p. 449, v. 93, *To sibbe & fremde ek.*—
Cf. Lewin, Poema morale, p. 74/34, and Mätzner, ii. p. 205 : *þe fremede & þe sibbe*, OE. Misc. p. 59.—*with fremid & sibbe*, Polit. Songs, p. 202.—*þe fræmden & þo sibbe*, Mor. Ode, st. 17.—*þe fremde ne þe sibbe*, K. H. 63.—*fremde & sybbe*, R. of Gl. p. 346.—*sibbe & fremde*, Havel. 2275.

13. *benemð* ought to have been translated : " bereaves, deprives."

17. = Matth. v. 39, *Sed si quis te percusserit in dexteram maxillam tuam, praebe illi et alteram.*—Luke vi. 29, *Et qui te percutit in maxillam, praebe et alteram.*

19. *Gif he ðe werejede*, &c. Cf. Luke vi. 28, *Benedicite maledicentibus vobis.*

21. *swinge* (after Dr. Morris's emendation) ought to have been translated: "stroke, blow."

24. *ac hadde.* The subject *he* is left out. Some specimens of this use are given by Mätzner, Engl. Gr.³ ii. p. 32 ; Zupitza, Notes to Guy of Warwick, p. 345 seq. In our text it occurs on p. 37/4 (*hie*), 55/6 (*she*), 57/21 (*he*), 67/20 (*he*), 69/22 (*je*), 119/18 (*he*), 123/16 (*he*), 127/5 (*he*).

25. *mine i-liche.* Cf. Zupitza, Engl. Stud. xiii. p. 349, No. 33. In our text cf. 15/23.

25 seq. = Ps. lxxx. 13 (lxxxi. 12).

P. 15, l. 2. *ær ðane he of ðese liue fare.* Cf. Mätzner, ii. p. 77: *þan he sal of þesse liue faren*, OEH. ii. 27.—*farenn ut off life*, Orm. 8359.—*þo heo schulde hunne fare*, St. Edm. Conf. 124.—*Ear we faren hennen*, Leg. St. Kath. 1393.—Ib. ii. 474 : *þet we moten heonene feren to þan eche blisse*, OEH. i. 11.—*til þei fare hennus*, Alex. & Dindim. 373.—In our text we find the following paraphrases for "to die": *þat tu fram ðine lichame scoldest skelien*, 17/24.—*ðanne he henen farð*, ib. 29.—*ær ðanne hie of ðese liue faren*, 55/31.—*ær ðu fram ðine lichame scelie*, 57/10.—*ðanne ðu art itwamd fram ðine lichame*, 75/17.—*jif hie bien ðar mide jenomene*, 79/10.—*ðat ani man deað þolije*, 105/31.—Cf. Sievers, Heliand, p. 448, seq. under "*sterben*," and Meyer, l. c. p. 139.

5 seq. This is certainly not a biblical quotation, but I am unable to say what is meant by the "*hali write.*"

8 seq. = John vi. 38, *quia descendi de coelo, non ut faciam voluntatem meam, sed voluntatem ejus, qui misit me*; ib. 39, *haec est autem voluntas ejus, qui misit me, Patris* : . . . .

11 seq. See Luke ii. 13, *Et subito facta est cum angelo multitudo militiae coelestis laudantium Deum, et dicentium*: ib. 14, " *Gloria in altissimis Deo! et in terra pax hominibus bonae voluntatis !* "

21. *ne on speches ne on dades.* Cf. OE. *spréca & dǽda*, Gŭðlác, 225. Mätzner, i. p. 595 gives: *ne on dade ne on speche*, OEH. ii. 187.

23 seq. Cf. Matth. xxiii. 27, *quia similes estis sepulcris dealbatis, quae a foris parent hominibus speciosa, intus vero plena sunt ossibus mortuorum, et omni spurcitia.*—On *þruh* cf. Zupitza, Guy, p. 447/10707.

24. *wiðuten . . . and wiðinne.* See Fuhrmann, p. 36.

25. *Mea culpa* occurs in the liturgic confession of sins (beginning *Confiteor Deo omnipotenti*), which is used e. g. in the Introitus of the mass, at the holy communion, the extreme unction, the general absolution, and is daily prayed in the compline of the breviary office ; see Wetzer und Welte's Kirchenlexikon², iii. 882 seq. ; Skeat, Notes to Piers Plowman, p. 106/64.

30. *rimen ne tellen.* Cf. Orm. 17686, *and tald and rimedd*.

33. *are & forȝiu[en]esse.* Cf. Mätzner, i. p. 103: *Forrȝifenesse & are*, Orm. 5695. Ib. ii. 172 : *ore ne forȝieuenesse*, OEH. ii. 229.

P. 17, l. 5. *gildenene* is probably a clerical error for *gildene.* For the phrase "*golden Bezants*" cf. Zupitza, Engl. Stud. xiii. p. 379, note 312. The *Bezant* was, after Murray's authority, "A gold coin first struck at Byzantium or Constantinople, and seemingly identical with the Roman *solidus* or *aureus*, but afterwards varying in value between the English sovereign and halfsovereign, or less. It was current in Europe from the ninth century, and in England till superseded by the noble, a coin of Edw. III."

6 seq. The parable of the five talents, see Matth. xxv. 14 seq., *Sicut enim homo peregre proficiscens, vocavit servos suos, et tradidit illis bona sua*; ib. 15, *et uni dedit quinque talenta, . . .*; ib. 16, *Abiit autem, qui quinque talenta acceperat, et operatus est in eis, et lucratus est alia quinque.* Ib. 21, *Ait illi dominus ejus :* "*Euge ! serve bone et fidelis ; quia super pauca fuisti fidelis, super multa te constituam ; intra in gaudium domini tui !*" (= 23).—This allegorical application to the five senses comes from Hieronymus, Comment. in Evang. Matth. lib. iv. cap. xxv. vers. 14, 15 (Migne, 26/193 seq.), *In quinque, et duobus, et uno talento vel diversas gratias intelligamus, qua unicuique traditae sunt, vel in primo, omnes sensus examinatos ; in secundo, intelligentiam et opera ; in tertio, rationem, qua homines a bestiis separamur.*— Idem, Expositio in Evang. Matth. cap. xxv. vers. 14 seq. (Migne, 30/577), *Quinque talenta, id est, quinque sensus—visus, auditus, odoratus, gustus et tactus. . . .*—Gregorius, Hom. in Evang. lib. i. hom. ix (Migne, 76/1106 seq.), *Quinque etenim sunt corporis sensus, videlicet visus, auditus, gustus, odoratus et tactus. Quinque ergo talentis donum quinque sensuum, id est exteriorum scientia, exprimitur.* —Beda, Expos. in Matth. Evang. lib. iv. cap. xxv (Migne, 92/108 A), *Quinque igitur talentis donum quinque sensuum exprimitur.*—Christianus Druthmarus, Expos. in Matth. cap. lvi (Migne, 106/1465 D), *. . . vel in quinque talentis donum quinque sensuum, id est, exteriorum scientia exprimitur, viz. visus, . . . Quia satis abundeque honoratur, qui in his V sensibus vigere permittitur.*—It is also found in Ælfric's Hom. ii. 550, *Sé eádiga Gregorius pápa trahtnode þis godspel, and cwæð :* "*. . . Sé mennisca Crist dǽlde his gód his ðéowum, forðan þe hé forgeaf his geleáffullum þá gástlican gife . . . þá fíf pund getácniað þá fíf andgitu úre(s) líchaman, þæt is, gesihð and hlyst, swæcc and stenc and hrepung. Ðás fíf pund underféhð ǽlc þǽra þe ðá fíf lichamlican andgitu ansúnde hæfð.*"

12 seq. *Ælche dai me cumeð sonden*, &c. On the different meanings of *sonde* see Zupitza, Guy, p. 445/10477; the idea itself may be illustrated by a comparison with ch. 13, lib. iv of the book "*De Anima*," wrongly ascribed to Hugo of St. Victor (Migne, 177/185 seq.), *His ita dispositis introducere debet* [viz. into the house of Conscience] *Prudentia aliquos nuntios, qui aliqua narrent quae ad exercitationem valeant. Itaque nuntius mortis ingressum postulans admittitur. Qui rogatus ut dicat qui sit, unde veniat, . . . sic incipit :* "*Ego sum timor mortis, et mortem robis venire nuntio*," &c.— The homily "Sawles Warde" in OEH. i. 245 seq. as well as the appendix to Dan Michel's Ayenbite of Inwyt, p. 263, are translations of this Latin text; cf. Vollhardt, Einfluss der lat. geistl. Litteratur, &c., Leipzig, 1888, p. 26 seq., and Konrath, Engl. Stud. xii. p. 459 seq.—For poems on the Messengers of Death cf. Engl. Stud. xiv. p. 182 seq.; Anglia, xiii. p. 359/11.

24. *earme saule* = 63/31, 103/16. Cf. *his erme saule*, OEH. i. 27/29, and in our text: *on ðese arme liue*, 21/14 (=89/34).

forðsiðe. Synonyms for "death" are collected by Sievers, Heliand, p. 452 seq., Meyer, l. c. p. 140. Cf. Mätzner, ii. p. 188 seq. sub *forðfare*, *-faren, -wenden*.

26 seq. The end of the above-cited parable, Matth. xxv. 30, "*Et inutilem servum ejicite in tenebras exteriores!*" is combined with the simile of the King's marriage feast (ib. xxii.), where the corresponding passage (verse 13) runs, *Tunc dixit Rex ministris: "Ligatis manibus et pedibus ejus, mittite eum in tenebras exteriores; . . ."* (cf. viii. 12).

28 seq. Cf. Gregorius, Hom. in Ev. lib. i. hom. ix (Migne, 76, 1109/6), *Per poenam quippe in exteriores tenebras cadit, qui per culpam suam sponte in interiores tenebras cecidit; et illic coactus patitur tenebras ultionis, qui hic libenter sustinuit tenebras voluptatis.*—Christianus Druthmarus, Expos. in Matth. c. 56 (Migne, 106/1469), *Superius dixi quia tenebras interiores caecitas mentis appellatur; exteriores tenebrae erunt in inferno, ubi neque Deus, neque sol ei lucebit.*—Ælfric, Hom. i. 530, *þá inran þéostru sind þǽre heortan blindnys, þá yttran þ. is séo swearte niht þǽre écan geniðerunge.*—Id. ii. 556, *Se unhólda ðéowa wearð ðá áworpen on þám yttrum þéostrum, forðan ðe hé ðolode ðurh wite þá yttran blindnysse seðe ǽr, ðurh his gylt, on ðám inrum þéostrum befeoll. Ðǽr hé ðolað néadunge þéostra ðurh wráce, seðe ǽr lustlice forbær his unlustes þéostra.*—Haymo, Hom. de Temp. 135 (Migne, 118/725), *Quia tenebrae interiores caecitas est mentis, exteriores vero poena infernalis.*

29. *hwider he scal.* In the older English (as still in Modern German) a verb of motion may be left out after an auxiliary. See Mätzner, Engl. Gr.[3] ii. p. 49 seq.; Zupitza, Guy, p. 361/855; Zielke, Sir Orfeo, p. 120/94. In our text cf. 25/29, 103/25.

30 seq. are based on the so-called "Descensus Christi ad inferos," the second part of the apocryphical Evangelium Nicodemi. The Latin A-text has (Tischendorf, Evang. Apocr.[2] p. 391 seq.) cap. ii, *Nos autem cum essemus cum omnibus patribus nostris positi in profundo in caligine tenebrarum, subito factus est aureus solis calor purpureaque regalis lux illustrans super nos. Statimque omnis generis humani pater cum omnibus patriarchis et prophetis exultaverunt dicentes: "Lux ista autor luminis sempiterni est, quae nobis promisit transmittere lumen coaeternum." Et exclamavit Esaias et dixit: "Haec est lux patris, filius dei, sicut praedixi. . . . Et nunc advenit et illuxit nobis in morte sedentibus." Et cum exultaremus omnes in lumine quod superluxit nobis, supervenit nobis genitor noster Simeon, et exultans dixit nobis: "Glorificate dominum Jesum Christum filium dei. . ."*—Ib. cap. v (p. 398 seq.), *Haec dicente David ad inferum supervenit in forma hominis dominus maiestatis, et aeternas tenebras illustravit et indissolubilia vincula disrupit: et invictae virtutis auxilium visitavit nos sedentes in profundis tenebris delictorum et in umbra mortis peccatorum.*—Ib. cap. viii (p. 402), *Et extendens dominus manum suam dixit: "Venite ad me, sancti mei omnes, qui habetis imaginem et similitudinem meam. . . ."*—The B-text has, cap. ii (p. 422 seq.), *Cum igitur essemus in tenebris et umbra mortis detenti apud inferos, subito illuxit nobis lux magna, . . . Et audita est vox filii patris altissimi ". . . rex gloriae Christus dominus intraturus adveniet." . . .*—Ib. cap. viii (p. 429), *Et ecce dominus Jesus Christus veniens in claritate excelsi luminis mansuetus*, &c.—

Ib. cap. ix. (p. 430), *Tunc salvator perscrutans de omnibus . . . partem secum reduxit ad superos.*

32. *ðar is wop and woninge,* &c. See Matth. xiii. 42, *Ibi erit fletus, et stridor dentium* (=xxii. 13, xxiv. 51, xxv. 30). The fire is mentioned, ib. xiii. 42, *Et mittent eos in caminum ignis. Ibi erit,* &c. (=50).—Cf. the similar description of hell on p. 63/31 seq., and Pricke of Conscience, p. 177 seq. and p. 252 seq.

wop and woninge. Cf. *wóp and wánung,* Wulfstán, 139/3 = Be dómes dæȝe, 201.—*þar is wop and wonynge,* OE. Misc. p. 74/55.—*waning and wop,* Poema morale (ed. Lewin), vers 233.

P. 19, l. 1. *chiueringe of toðen = stridor dentium,* cf. note to 17/32. That the pains of hell consisted also in sudden changes of heat and cold is very often told; cf. e. g. OEH. i. 251, and Poema morale, l. c. seq.

2. *sorwȝe and sarinesse.* Cf. Hoffmann, l. c. p. 55 seq.

5 seq. The same idea occurs OEH. i. 271 seq.: *. . . alle þe ahefulle deueles of helle, þat hwuch of ham swa is lest laðeliche and grureful, mihte he, swuch as he is, to monkin him scheawe, al þe world were offeard him ane to bihalde, for ne mihte na mon him seo and in his wit wunie, bute ȝif þe grace and te strengðe of Crist baldede his heorte.*—Cf. also Pricke of Consc. p. 63/2298 seq.:—

> *Bot a gret payne þan til us sal þis be*
> *þe sight of þam when we þam se;*
> *For þai er swa grisely, als says þe buke,*
> *And swa blak and foule on to loke,*
> *þat al þe men here of mydlerd*
> *Of þat sight mught be aferd;*
> *For al þe men here of þis lyfe*
> *Swa grysely a sight couth noght descryfe,*
> *Ne thurgh wyt ymagyn ne deme,* &c.

* * * *

p. 64/2312:—

> *For in þis lif here may na man*
> *Se þam in þe fourme þat þai haf þan,*
> *For if þai had swa large powere,*
> *In swilk forme to shew þam here,*
> *Out of witte þan þai shuld men flay,*
> *Swa orrible and swa foul er þai;*
> *For-why swa hardy man here es nane*
> *Ne þat ever was liffand in flesshe and bane,*
> *þat saghe a devel in his fygur right,*
> *þat he ne for ferdnes of þat sight*
> *Shuld dighe, or at þe leste tyn his witt,*
> *Als son after als he had sene it.*

The same idea is repeated on p. 185/6841 seq.

8 seq. *mid muðe seggen.* See the same phrase 55/31, 121/31; and cf. Zupitza, Engl. Stud. xiii. p. 392/458.

9 seq. *Wa hem ðatt hie,* &c. Cf. 63/20 and 113/15. See Wulfstán, 297/24, *forþan wá éow, þæt gé áfre gewurdon men.*—OE. Misc. p. 172/87, *Awai þat þu euere to manne ischape were!*—Cf. Zupitza, Engl. Stud. xiii. p. 386/387.

13 seq. = Ezek. xviii. 30, *Convertimini, et agite poenitentiam ab omnibus iniquitatibus vestris.*

15. *scrift* is defined OEH. ii. 129/1, *and clepede hem to shrifte, þat is, to reusende and to forleten and to beten here sinnes, for þat is shrift.*

16 seq. Cf. 1 Thess. v. 2, *Ipsi enim diligenter scitis, quia dies Domini, sicut fur in nocte, ita veniet.*—Ib. 4, *Vos autem, fratres! non estis in tenebris, ut vos dies illa, tamquam fur, comprehendat.* Cf. also 2 Pet. iii. 10.

17. *Fasteð & wakieð.* Cf. 1 Thess. v. 6, *Igitur non dormiamus sicut et caeteri, sed vigilemus, et sobrii simus.*

18. *buȝeð fram euele & doð god.* Cf. 65/13, *hu ðu scalt fram ðan euele buȝen, & hu ðu scalt gode werkes don.* It is a translation of Ps. xxxiii. 15 (xxxiv. 14), *Diverte a malo, et fac bonum.*

wepeð & wanið (= 34). Cf. Wulfstán, 183/2, *wépað & wániað.*—Orm. 5653, *wepenn wiþþ skill and wanenn.*—Ib. 8128, *to wepenn & to wanenn.*—Laȝ. 25827, *wepen & weinen (woni).*

23. = Ps. cxviii. 21 (cxix. 21).

24. *behode* is a misprint for *bebode.*

25 seq. relate to the Roman breviary prayer. Cf. Horstmann, Altengl. Legenden, Neue Folge, Heilbronn, 1881, p. iii seq.

28. *erres of ðare laczste.* Cf. Mätzner under *erles* and *ernes* (ii. p. 49): *þis ure lauerd ȝiueð ham as on erles of þe eche mede þat schal cume þrafter,* Hali Meid. p. 7.—*That is a wed, or eernes, of ȝoure heritage,* Ephes. i. 14, Oxf. —In our text, 31/28, we find a further example, *earres of ðare eche blisse.*

29. = Matth. xxv. 41, *Tunc dicet et his, qui a sinistris erunt: "Discedite a me, maledicti! in ignem aeternum, qui paratus est diabolo, et angelis ejus."*

P. 21, l. 3. *He hit wat ðe wat alle þing.* Cf. 75/2, 95/26.

5. *Moder of mildce* = *mater misericordiae,* as St. Mary is called in the famous antiphona *Salve regina.* See similar expressions in Fuhrmann, p. 41.

6 seq. *besieke . . . to Jesu Criste.* Cf. Mätzner, Engl. Gr.³ ii. pp. 300 seq.

10. *are and mildze.* Cf. Mätzner, i. p. 103: *are & millce,* Orm. 1476.—*milce & ore,* OEH. 195; St. Edm. Conf. 362; Rob. of Gl. p. 340.—*milse & ore,* Owl & Night. 1083, 1404.—*his milce & his ore,* St. Edm. Conf. 448.—I add, *Wiþþ soþfasst millce & are,* Orm. 5699.

11. On the preterites *underfenge* and *wære* after the present *ilieue,* l. 10, cf. Mätzner, Engl. Gr.³ ii. p. 112 seq.

12 seq. *to alle ðo halȝen . . . ðe is an ȝeu, ðat ȝie,* &c. This changing from the third to the second person occurs in invocations to God and the Saints. Cf. Kaluza, Engl. Stud. xiv. p. 177/4.

15 seq. *ðar ðe wei is slider and we . . ., and fele unwines. . . .* On this ellipsis of *are* cf. Mätzner, Engl. Gr.³ ii. pp. 165 seq.; Koch, Histor. Gr.² ii. p. 55. Cf. Owl & Night. ed. Stratmann, 956.

16. *teforen & baften.* Cf. *biuoren & bihinden,* OEH. i. 251/11, and Fuhrmann, p. 34.

23. *mid his hali grace.* A great number of similar phrases are collected by Zupitza, Engl. Stud. xiii. p. 353, notes 58 and 64. Cf. in our text, *ðurh godes grace,* 21/27, 23/29, and see *grace* in the glossary. Almost the same is, *mid godes fultume,* 23/31.

26. *senfulle saule.* See Fuhrmann, p. 42.

27. *wissedest and warnedest.* Cf. Wulfstán, 132/11, *wissode and warnode.*

NOTES (19/13-25/15).

28. *yielde þe godd!* See Mätzner, ii. p. 348 for more specimens. Cf. the German '*Vergelt's Gott!*'
bien icnawe of ought to have been translated " confess."
P. 23, l. 3 seq. *me ðin uncuðe name me.* MS.—*me* after *name* may be a mere clerical repetition; but cf. Zupitza, Guy, p. 383/2893-4, where several instances of double pronouns are given, and in our text 35/30 (*him*).
7. = Ps. lxxvi. 11 (lxxvii. 10).
9 seq. *godes anlicnesse ðe was iscapen on ðe.* Cf. Gen. i. 26, "*Faciamus hominem ad imaginem et similitudinem nostram!*" . . . ; ib. 27, *et creavit Deus hominem ad imaginem suam.*—Cf. Sigewulfi Interrogationes in Genesin, Angl. vii. p. 19, *In quo est homo conditoris sui imago?* R. *In interiori homine.* (Cf. also the notes!)
16. *wanten awei.* See Fuhrmann, p. 55 seq.
20. *lare liernin.* Cf. Mätzner, iii. p. 43: *nefde ileorned . . . nane lare*, Laȝ. ii. 130.—*Of swuche larespel þu haues leaue ileorned*, Leg. St. Kath. 385.
20-28 may be an allusion to Matth. xii. 43-45, *Cum autem immundus spiritus exierit ab homine, ambulat per loca arida, quaerens requiem, et non invenit;* ib. 44, *tunc dicit: " Revertar in domum meam, unde exivi;" et veniens invenit eam vacantem, scopis mundatam, et ornatam;* ib. 45, *tunc vadit, et assumit septem alios spiritus secum nequiores se, et intrantes habitant ibi. . . .* (Cf. Luke xi. 24-26.)
22 seq. *idele saule & amti.* Cf. Mätzner, ii. p. 24: *idele & emti of gode*, Leg. St. Kath. 392.
28. *iwelt after here aȝene wille.* Cf. Fuhrmann, p. 55, "*welde at wylle.*"
30. *hwat hie bien, þese mihtes.* Cf. Mätzner, Engl. Gr.[3] ii. p. 18/2 seq.
31. *scilden fram.* The same construction see 87/3, 103/1, 107/6. Cf. Schleich, Ywain & Gawain, p. 103/2.
32. *ham to ðin earde*, &c. Paradise or heaven is meant. See Engl. Stud. vi. pp. 23 seq.
P. 25, l. 8. *hie iliefð ðat hie næure niseih* = Hebr. xi. 1, *Est autem fides sperandarum substantia rerum, argumentum non apparentium.*
9 seq. *Eadi bieð*, &c. = John xx. 29, *Beati qui non viderunt, et crediderunt.*
10-29 are based on the so-called Athanasian Creed (Symbolum St. Athanasii), *Fides autem catholica haec est, ut unum Deum in Trinitate, et Trinitatem in unitate veneremur. . . . Sed Patris, et Filii, et Spiritus Sancti una est divinitas: aequalis gloria, coaeterna majestas.*
13 seq. Ib., *Pater a nullo est factus: nec creatus, nec genitus. Filius a Patre solo est: non factus, nec creatus, sed genitus.*
14. *al swa his wisedom.* Cf. 1 Cor. i. 24, *Christum Dei virtutem, et Dei sapientiam.*—Ib. 30, . . . *In Christo Jesu, qui factus est nobis sapientia a Deo.*
14 seq. *on heuene wiðuten moder, and on ierðe wiðuten fader.* Cf. 117/4 seq. and Alcuin, Interrog. Sigewulfi in Genes. Angl. vii. p. 45, *Quia Christus sine matre in coelis et sine patre in terris.* . . .—Ib. p. 57, *Unde et bis genitus dicitur, sive quia Pater eum genuit sine matre in aeternitate, sive quia mater sine Patre in tempore.* Ælfric repeats the same in his Homilies, i. 24, and ii. 6.
15 seq. Cf. the Athanasian Creed, *Spiritus Sanctus a Patre et Filio : non factus, nec creatus, nec genitus, sed procedens.*

16. *al swa here beire lune.* The Holy Ghost was frequently explained as the Love of the Father and the Son by the scholastic theologians of the twelfth century. In English literature I find this idea (from a Latin original) in Ælfric's Hom. ii. 42, *se hálga gást is lufu and willa þæs fæder and þæs suna.* —Ib. 604, *hé is heora bégra willa and lufu.* And in his translation of Alcuin's Sigewulfi Interrog. in Genesin, Anglia, vii. p. 54/522, *sepe is witodlice heora willa and lufu him bám gemǽne . . . cymð of him bám swá swá lufu and willa.* Cf. also the notes of the editor to ll. 511 and 519; further on p. 56/530 seq. and note. Einenkel, The Life of St. Katherine, p. 87/1772, *and te hali gast, hare beire luue.* Cf. in our text p. 37/2:

16 seq. Cf. the Athanasian Creed, *Sed totae tres personae coaeternae sibi sunt et coaequales.*

emliche on ielde. Cf. Orm. 18572, *all off efenn elde.*

20 seq. Cf. John iii. 16, *Sic enim Deus dilexit mundum, ut Filium suum unigenitum daret.*—1 John iv. 9, *In hoc apparuit caritas Dei in nobis, quoniam Filium suum unigenitum misit Deus in mundum, &c.*

21 seq. Cf. the Athanasian Creed, *Quia Dominus noster J. Chr. Dei filius, Deus et homo est. . . . Perfectus Deus, perfectus homo : ex anima rationali, et humana carne subsistens.*

23 seq. Cf. the Apostles' Creed, *Qui conceptus est de Spiritu Sancto, natus ex Maria virgine.*

24 seq. Cf. the Athanasian Creed, *Qui passus est . . . tertia die resurrexit a mortuis. Ascendit ad coelos, sedet ad dexteram Dei Patris omnipotentis: inde venturus est judicare vivos et mortuos.*

27 seq. The quotation is from the next to the last verse of the same Creed.

29 seq. On *sculen* without an infinitive (go, walk, &c.), cf. note to 17/29.

32 seq. = Matth. xvi. 16, 17.

P. 27, l. 1 seq. = Ib. 17, *Quia caro et sanguis non revelavit tibi, sed Pater meus, qui in coelis est.*

3 seq. = Ib. 18, *Et ego dico tibi, quia tu es Petrus, et super hanc petram aedificabo Ecclesiam meam.* The interpretation of this passage is found in the Fathers very frequently; cf. e. g. Hieronymus, Comment. in Evang. Matth. lib. iii. cap. xvi (Migne, 26/121 seq.), . . . *Ita et Simoni, qui credebat in petram Christum, Petri largitus est nomen. At secundum metaphoram petrae, recte dicitur ei: Aedificabo Ecclesiam meam super te.*—Beda, Expos. in Matth. Evang. lib. iii. cap. xvi (Migne, 92/78), *Metaphorice ei dicitur : Super hanc petram, id est, Salvatorem, quem confessus est, aedificatur Ecclesia, qui fideli confessori sui nominis participium donavit.*—Id. Homilies, lib. ii. hom. xvi (Migne, 94/222), *Et supra hanc petram, id est super Dominum Salvatorem, qui fideli suo cognitori, amatori, confessori participium sui nominis donavit, ut viz. a petra Petrus vocaretur : supra quam aedificatur Ecclesia, quia non nisi per fidem et dilectionem Christi, per susceptionem sacramentorum Christi, per observantiam mandatorum Christi, ad sortem electorum et aeternam pertingitur vitam,* etc.—Haymo, Hom. de Sanctis, hom. iii (Migne, 118/762), *Utrumque autem nomen ab illa petra derivatur, de qua ait Apostolus: "Petra autem erat Christus* (1 Cor. x.)*"; quod autem ait: "Et super, &c.," tale est ac si diceret, super hanc fidem, id est super me, quem tu confessus es, aedificabo Ecclesiam meam. "Fundamentum enim aliud," ait Apostolus, &c.* (1 Cor. iii.).—Paschasius Radbertus, Expos. in Matth. lib. viii.

cap. xvi (Migne, 120/560), *Quia tu es Petrus, quod a petra derivatum est nomen, id est, a me super quem aedificatur omnis Ecclesia. Non enim, ut quidam male putant, Petrus fundamentum totius Ecclesiae est: "Quia fundamentum nemo aliud potest ponere,"* &c. (1 Cor. iii. 11). *Licet super eodem fundamento primus, . . . tamen in ea petra, de qua nomen sibi ex dono traxit, et super eam tota construitur et constabilitur illa coelestis Jerusalem, id est, supra Christum, ut firma permaneat in sempiternum.*—Anselmus Laudunensis, Enarrationes in Matth. cap. xvi (Migne, 162/1396), *Et super hanc petram, id est super me, aedificabo Ecclesiam meam. Quasi dicat: Sic es Petrus a me petra, ut tamen mihi reservetur fundamenti dignitas. Sed tu, cui ego ut amatori et confessori meo participium mei nominis dedi, super me fundamentum, mundos lapides ordinabis, et reprobos removebis, et portae inferi, id est, peccata, vel haeretici . . . non praevalebunt adv. eam Ecclesiam. Qui enim intimo amore cordis fidem Christi perceperit, facile quidquid extra ingruerit, vincet.*—Ælfric, Hom. ii. 390, refers to St. Austin, *Augustinus tractavit, quod Petrus in figura significat ecclesiam, quia Christus petra, Petrus populus christianus. . . . Crist is gecweden " petra," þæt is " stán," . . . Crist cwæð: "þú eart stǽnen, and ofer ðisne stán, þæt is, ofer ðám geleáfan þe ðú nú andettest, ic getimbrige mine cyrcan." Ofer mé sylfne ic getimbrige mine cyrcan, . , . Ic eóm séo trumnyss ðe ðé healdan sceal, and ealle ðá getimbrunge cristenre gelaðunge.*

5. *hie sculen bien mine lemen, and ich here heaued.* Cf. 1 Cor. vi. 15, *Nescitis, quoniam corpora vestra membra sunt Christi?*—Ib. xi. 3, *Volo autem vos scire quod omnis viri caput Christus est.*—Ephes. i. 22, . . . *et ipsum dedit caput supra omnem Ecclesiam.*—Ib. iv. 15, . . . *crescamus in illo per omnia, qui est caput Christus.*—Ib. v. 23, . . . *sicut Chr. caput est Ecclesiae.*—Ib. 30, *Quia membra sumus corporis ejus, de carne ejus et de ossibus ejus.*—Col. i. 18, *Et ipse est caput corporis Ecclesiae.*—Cf. 131/26; also Ælfric, Hom. i. 272, *forðon þe hé úre heáfod, and wé sýnd his lima.*

7. = Matth. xvi. 18.

9. This interpretation is very old. Cf. Ambrosius, Expos. in Luc. lib. vi. (Migne, 15/1781), *Quae autem sunt portae mortis, hoc est, portae inferi, nisi singula quaeque peccata?*—Hieronymus, Comment in Evang. Matth. lib. iii. c. xvi (Migne, 26/122), *Ego portas inferi reor vitia atque peccata : vel certe haereticorum doctrinas, per quas illecti homines ducuntur ad tartarum.*—Beda, Expos. in Matth. Evang. lib. iii. c. xvi (Migne, 92/79), *Portas inferi haereticam pravitatem nominat, sive vitia et peccata, unde mors ad animam venit.*—Id. Homil. lib. ii. hom. xvi (Migne, 94/222), *Sed et prava infidelium opera ineptaque colloquia portae utique sunt inferi, in quantum suis vel fautoribus vel sequacibus iter perditionis ostendunt. . . . Multae sunt itaque portae inferi, sed harum nulla Ecclesiae, quae supra petram fundata est, praevalet, quia qui fidem Christi intimo cordis amore perceperit, omne quidquid exterius periculi tentantis ingruerit, facillime contemnit.*—Haymo, Hom. de Sanctis, hom. iii (Migne, 118/762), *Aliter portas inferi, vitia et peccata intelligere possumus, qualia Apost. commemorat, dicens: "Manifesta, &c."* (Gal. v. 19), *quae recte portae inferi nominantur, quia in se perseverantes ad infernum dimergunt, &c.*—Paschasius Radbertus, Expos. in Matth. lib. viii. c. xvi (Migne, 120/561), *Novimus quia portae inferorum vitia sunt et peccata ; nam unumquodque peccatum per quod descenditur ad inferos, porta est inferorum,* &c.

11. *sune ne* ought to have been left in the text, because of the precedent

negative sentence. Cf. Blickl. Hom. 37/15, *Ne gelýfe þæs nǽnig mon þæt him ne genihtsumige þæt fæsten.*—Ælfric, Hom. ii. 230/1, *þá wiðsóc Crist . . . þæt hé déofol on him næfde.* See Zupitza, Engl. Stud. xiii. p. 411/765.

15 seq. *Credo in Deum* is the beginning of the Apostolic, *Quicunque vult* of the so-called Athanasian Creed.

20 seq. = Gal. iv. 11, *Timeo (vos), ne forte sine causa laboraverim in vobis.*

22 seq. = Ib. 10, *Dies observatis, et menses, et tempora, et annos.* Cf. also Ælfric, Hom. i. 100, *Nú wígliað stunte men menigfealde wigelunga on ðisum dæge, mid micclum gedwýlde, æfter háðenum gewunan, ongéan heora cristendóm, swylce hí magon heora líf gelengan, oþþe heora gesúndfulnysse, mid þám ðe hí gremiað þone ælmihtigan scyppend. Sind éac manega mid swá micclum gedwýlde befangene, þæt hí cépað be ðám mónan heora fær, and heora dǽda be dagum, and nellað heora ðing wanian on mónan-dæg, for anginne ðǽre wucan,* . . . p. 102 (after quoting the same scriptural passage as V. & V. 27/20, and 29), *Is hwæðere æfter gecýnde on gesceapennysse álc líchamlíce gesceaft ðe eorðe dcenð fulre and mægenfæstre on fullum mónan þonne on gewanedum. Swá éac tréowa, gif hí béoð on fullum mónan geháewene, hí béoð heardran and langfærran tó getimbrunge, and swíðost, gif hí béoð unsǽpige geworhte. Nis ðis nán wiglung, ac is gecýndelic ðincg þurh gesceapenysse.*—Cf. also Ælfric's[1] treatise, ' De temporibus,' in Cockayne's Leechdoms, vol. iii. p. 266, *ne sceal nán cristen mann nán þincg be ðám mónan wiglian, gyf hé hit déð, his geléafa ne bið náht.*—Ib. p. 268, *Hit is gecýndelic þæt ealle eorðlice líchaman béoð fulran on weaxendum mónan þonne on wanigendum. Éac þá tréowa þe béoð dhéawene on fullum mónan béoð heardran wið wyrmǽtan and lengfærran þonne þá ðe béoð on niwum mónan dhéawene.*—Superstitions and rules concerning moons and days are collected in the same vol., pp. 150-168, 176-196, 224.

29 seq. = Colos. iii. 17, *Omne, quodcumque facitis in verbo, aut in opere, omnia in nomine Domini Jesu Christi,* . . .

33. *neiðer ne euel ne god.* Cf. OE. *gódes and yfeles*, Gen. 465, Dom. 43, 107, Wid. 51, Fæd. 45, Sal. 362, and, vice versa, Gen. 480 (Rich. M. Meyer, Die altgerm. Poesie, Berlin, 1889, p. 287).—Mätzner, ii. p. 289, has: *After vuele cumeð god*, Laȝ. i. 153.—*goed after yuil*, OE. Misc. p. 111.—*Sundren god from vuele*, Ancr. R. p. 270.—*Forbue iuel, and do god*, OEH. ii. 63.—*þat vuel he al forlette, þat gode he imette*, Laȝ. i. 288.—*to halde gude or ille*, Hamp. 78.

P. 29, l. 1. *ne on wele ne on wauȝhe.* Cf. OE. *welan and wáwan*, Gen. 466; see Fuhrmann, p. 36.

ne on hale ne on unhale. I collect the following specimens from Mätzner, ii. p. 400: *ȝho . . . warrþ hal off hire unnhæle*, Orm. 15519.—*Ic mac unhale men al hale*, Metr. Homil. p. 35.

ne ðurh fier ne ðurh water. Cf. OE. *fýr and wæter*, Metra 11/43.

8 seq. Concerning this popular superstition, cf. J. Grimm, Deutsche Mythologie, 4. ed. vol. ii. p. 937 seq. He calls it "*Angang*," and shows how it was a common belief in the middle ages that any one meeting a monk or priest on the way would have ill consequences. Reginald Scott, in his Witchcraft, p. 114 (quoted l. c. p. 942), says: "*If any hunters, as they were a-hunting, chanced to meet a frier or a priest, they thought it so ill luck, as they would couple up their hounds and go home, being in dispair of any*

---

[1] On his authorship and the sources of the work, cf. Anglia, x. 457 seq.

NOTES (27/11–31/1).   167

further sport that day."—Other examples are given in vol. iii. 323 seq. of Grimm's work.—On *foot* = "man," cf. Mätzner, ii. p. 194 a, who quotes : *euch fot*, Leg. St. Kath. 1369; 2271, and *euerilk fot*, Havel. 2430.

10. *gode handsselle.* On this superstition cf. OEH. ii. 11/11, *and þat is liðer custume þat man leueð get, and þat is after-clepenge . . . and handselne.*—Middleton, Your Five Gallants (ed. Bullen, vol. iii. p. 219/62), act iv. sc. 8, has, *Surely a merchant's wife gives lucky handsel.* Later on, we have the testimony of J. Aubrey, in his "Remaines of Gentilisme and Judaisme" (1686–87), ed. in the Publications of the Folk-Lore Soc. iv. London, 1881, p. 80, "*Spittle.* 'Tis *a common use in London, and perhaps over great part of England, for Apple-woemen, Oyster-woemen, &c., & some Butchers, to spitt on the money w*ᶜʰ *they first recieve in the morning, w*ᶜʰ *they call good handsell."*

15 seq. = Mark ix. 22.

18 seq. See Matth. xvii. 19, *Dixit illis Jesus :* " . . . *Amen quippe dico vobis: Si habueritis fidem, sicut granum sinapis, . . .*" and Luke xvii. 6, *Dixit autem Dominus : " Si habueritis fidem, sicut granum sinapis,"* &c.

19 seq. For this explanation cf. Ambrosius, Expos. in Luc. lib. vii. 178 (Migne, 15/1837), *Nunc ex natura sinapis, quae virtus comparationis sit aestimemus. Granum ejus certe res est vilis et simplex: si teri coeperit, vim suam fundit. Etiam fides primo simplex videtur: sed si teratur adversis, gratiam suae virtutis effundit.*—Maximus, Episcopus Taurinensis, Hom. cix. " De grano sinapis I" (Migne, 57/507), *Sicut enim granum sinapis prima fronte specie sui est parvum, vile, despectum, non saporem praestans, non odorem circumferens, non indicans suavitatem : at ubi teri coeperit, statim odorem suum acrimonia exhibet, cibum flammei saporis exhalat, et tanto fervoris calore succenditur, ut mirum sit in tam frivolis granis tantum ignem fuisse conclusum : . . .* (508), *Ita ergo et fides Christiana prima fronte videtur esse parva, vilis et tenuis ; non potentiam suam ostendens, non superbiam praeferens, non gratiam subministrans. At ubi diversis tentationibus teri coeperit, statim vigorem suum prodit, acrimoniam indicat, calorem dominicae credulitatis aspirat, et tanto divini ignis ardore jactatur, ut et ipsa ferveat et participantem sibi ardere compellat,* &c.—Beda, in Luc. Ev. Expos. lib. v. c. xvii (Migne, 92/540), *Fidem perfectam grano sinapis comparat, quae sit viz. et ad faciem humilis, et in pectore fervens, vilis quidem passim contuentibus, nullarumque virium apparens, sed pressuris attrita, quid perfectionis intus gerat ostendens. . . . Sic profecto fides tentationum pistillo probata,* &c.

24. James ii. 20, 26.

25 seq. = Tit. i. 16, *Confitentur se nosse Deum, factis autem negant.*

26 seq. Allusion to James ii. 19, *Et daemones credunt, et contremiscunt*(?).

31. *hire suster, ðe rihte ȝeleaue.* The virtues were allegorically represented as sisters. Cf. Skeat, Notes to Piers Plowman, p. 152/270; Vollhardt, Einfluss der lat. geistl. Litter. &c. p. 34.

34. *on ðare swikele woreld* = 41/10. Cf. *of ðare beswikene w.* 49/6.—*on ðese lease w.*, 41/4.—*on ðare l. w.*, 65/27.—*of ð. l. w.*, 73/2.—*on ðessere swinkfulle world*, 33/9.—*of ðare bitere woreld*, 45/9.—*on ðessere woreld*, 35/12.—*on ðesse worlde*, 43/6.—*hier on world*, 123/13.—*of ðessere michele wrecchade*, 21/17.

P. 31, l. 1. *ne telþ hie*, etc. Cf. Philip. iii. 8, *Verumtamen existimo omnia detrimentum esse, propter eminentem scientiam Jesu Christi Domini mei, propter quem omnia detrimentum feci, et arbitror ut stercora, ut Christum lucrifaciam.*

1 seq. *hie* refers to *spes* (*hope*), and ought to have been translated "she" or "it."

2. *michele merhþe.* Cf. Fuhrmann, p. 42.

4 seq. = Tit. ii. 11–14, *Apparuit enim gratia Dei Salvatoris nostri omnibus hominibus;* ib. 12, *erudiens nos, ut abnegantes impietatem et saecularia desideria, sobrie et juste, et pie vivamus in hoc saeculo;* ib. 13, *exspectantes beatam spem, et adventum gloriae magni Dei, et Salvatoris nostri Jesu Christi.*

5. *godes grace.* Cf. Fuhrmann, p. 72.

7. *woreldliches* is a clerical error for *woreldliche.* Cf. note to 43/5.

9. *Cristes* is a blunder for *Criste*, probably caused by the correction of the following *gode* to *godes.*

11. *alle ðo behotes ðe he us behiet.* Cf. Fuhrmann, p. 13; Engl. Stud. vii. p. 464/20.

11 seq. Cf. Philip. iii. 20; *Nostra autem conversatio in coelis est, unde etiam salvatorem exspectamus Dominum nostrum Jesum Christum;* ib. 21, *qui reformabit corpus humilitatis nostrae, configuratum corpori claritatis suae*, &c.—And Matth. xiii. 43, *Tunc justi fulgebunt sicut sol in regno Patris eorum.*

16. = Ps. iv. 6.

19. *werdles wele.* Cf. Fuhrmann, p. 43.—*warldes w.*, Engl. Stud. vii. pp. 116/267, 117/397.

21 seq. = Ps. iv. 7.

23. *all* is here adverb and ought to have been translated "quite."

26. = Ps. iv. 7.

31. *niht ne dai.* Mätzner, i. p. 581 has: *niht & dai*, Hali Meid. p. 15.— For further examples cf. Engl. Stud. xii. p. 347.

32 seq. = Ps. xliv. 8 (xlv. 7).

P. 33, l. 3 seq. The first quality of oil is already mentioned by Augustinus in Joh. Evang. Tract. vii. cap. i. 20 (Migne, 35/1435), *Quomodo enim oleum a nullo humore premitur, sed disruptis omnibus exsilit et supereminet: sic et charitas non potest premi in ima*, &c.—Id. sermo 93, cap. iv (Migne, 38/575), *Ipsa est supereminens via, id est, charitas, quae merito oleo significatur. Omnibus enim humoribus oleum supereminet.*—Ælfric, Hom. ii. 564 says, *Se ele getácnað þá sóðan lufe, séoðe næfre ne ateorað. Eles gecýnd is þæt hé wile oferstigan ælcne wætan.*—Cf. also OEH. i. 83, at the bottom, *Oli haueð huppen him lihtnesse and softnesse and hele. Alse þu scalt habben hwenne þu hauest idon þi scrift of þine misdede; þenne þu scalt habbe lihtnesse and sóftnesse and* (p. 85) *hele. þis is þet oli, þe muchele mede þet þu scalt habben hwenne þu hauest ibet þine misdeden.*—Cf. also Walafrid Strabo, Glossa ordinaria, Ev. Matth. xxi. 1 (Migne 114/152), *Olei natura lucis ministra est, et laborum et dolorum solamen, et excellit caeteris liquoribus.*

5. *bernen brihte.* Cf. Mätzner, i. p. 211, *beorninde briht*, St. Marher. p. 19.—*se briht as þa he bearnde*, St. Juliana, p. 69.—From the New Engl. Dict. I take: *That byrnyd bryght as anny glase*, Torrent of Portyngale (ed. Adam), 553.—*bright-burning Troy*, Shakesp. Tit. Andr. iii. 1/69. Cf. Launfal, 513.

11 = Ps. cxlv. 4 (cxlvi. 4).

14. *te golde ne to seluer.* See the OE. instances in Meyer, p. 286. I add from the Blickl. Hom., *ne bæd goldes, ne seolfres*, 21/5.—*goldes & seolfres*, 99/28.—*ne mid golde, ne mid seolfre*, 125/35.—*mid golde & mid seolfre*, 127/7.—*ne his goldes, ne his seolfres*, 195/4.—Mätzner, ii. 293 gives: *nouþer*

gold ne seoluer, OEH. i. 9.—*of gold oðer of seluer*, Leg. St. Kath. 267.—*of gold other of siluer*, Trevisa, ii. 313.—I add from Owl & Night. 1366, *gold & seolver*. Cf. Engl. Stud. vii. pp. 103/25, 120/114, xii. p. 349, l. 12 seq. *nones* had better been retained in the text. Cf. *alles* and *nanes woreldes*, 31/27 and 29.

15 seq.=Jer. xvii. 5.

25.=Matth. xvi. 24, *Si quis vult post me venire, abneget semet ipsum, et tollat*, &c. (=Mark viii. 34 and Luke ix. 23).

28 seq. *Rode tacnieð pine*, &c. Cf. Gregorius M., Hom. in Evang. lib. ii. hom. xxxii (Migne, 76/1234), *Duobus etenim modis crux tollitur, cum aut per abstinentiam afficitur corpus, aut per compassionem proximi affligitur animus.*—Beda says quite the same in his Commentaries to Matthew, Mark, and Luke; Rabanus Maurus, ditto to Matth.—Walafrid Strabo, Glossa ordinaria Evang. Marci, cap. viii (Migne, 114/212), *Vel per abstinentiam macerando corpus, vel per compassionem animum.*—Bruno Astensis, Comm. in Matth. pars iii. cap. xvi (Migne, 165/215), *Crucem enim suam tollit, qui carnem suam cum vitiis et concupiscentiis cruciat et affligit.*—Godefridus, Abbas Admontensis, Homil. festivales, hom. xxi (Migne, 174/715) says, after having quoted St. Gregory, *Ubi enim homo seipsum abnegaverit, ubi per abstinentiam dignisque poenitentiae cruciatibus pro peccatis suis Deo perfecte satisfecerit, potest etiam Christum sequi, quod est tollere crucem Christi, potest, inquam, ad exemplum Christi, qui pro alienis peccatis crucem sustinuit, cruciatibus suis, jejuniis viz., orationibus et vigiliis, alienis apud Deum subvenire errantibus.*—See also OEH. i. 147/34, *Ac he munegeð us an oðer rode to berene, þet is inemned carnis maceratio, fleises lensing. Mon lenseð his fleis hwenne he him ȝefeð lutel to etene and lesse to drinke*, &c.

P. 35, 2 seq. *munekes, . . . ancres, and eremites.* On the difference between these cf. the Rule of St. Benet, cap. i, *Monachorum IV genera esse manifestum est. Primum coenobitarum, hoc est monasteriale, militans sub regula vel abbate; Deinde secundum genus est anachoretarum, id est heremitarum, qui non conversionis fervore novitio, sed monasterii probatione diuturna, didicerunt contra diabolum multorum solatio jam docti pugnare, et bene instructi fraterna ex acie ad singularem pugnam heremi securi jam sine consolatione alterius sola manu vel brachio contra vitia carnis vel cogitationum Deo auxiliante pugnare sufficiunt.*—Isidorus Hispal., De Ecclesiasticis Officiis, lib. ii. cap. xvi (Schröer, Die Ags. Prosabearbeitungen der Benedict. Regel, p. 230), *Sex autem sunt genera monachorum, , . . Primum genus est coenobitarum, id est, in commune viventium, . . . Secundum genus eremitarum, qui, procul ab hominibus recedentes, deserta loca et vastas solitudines sequi atque habitare perhibentur, ad imitationem scil. Eliae et Joannis Baptistae, . . . Hi quippe incredibili mundi contemptu sola solitudine delectantur, herbis tantum agrestibus victitantes, aut pane solo vel aqua contenti, quod eis per certa intervalla defertur, sicque secretissimi penitus et ab omni hominum conspectu remoti, divino tantum colloquio perfruuntur, cui puris mentibus inhaeserunt, . . . Tertium genus est anachoretarum, qui jam coenobiali conversatione perfecti, includunt semetipsos in cellulis, procul ab hominum conspectu remoti, nulli ad se praebentes accessum, sed in sola contemplatione Dei viventes [perseverant. Sed isti de examine coenobiorum probati in omnibus disciplinis monasterii per XXX annos ad hanc contemplationem per obedientiam eliguntur].*—Cf. besides p. 73/24 seq. of our text, and Skeat's

Notes to Piers Plowman, pp. 164/146, 192/188. He gives also an explanation of *kanunekes*, p. 97/171.

3. *fader and moder.* Cf. Meyer, p. 285; Mätzner, ii. 62 seq.: *þine uader and þine moder*, Ayenb. p. 8.—*þin feder and þin moder*, OEH. 13.—*baðe faderles & moderles*, Leg. St. Kath. 77.—I add, *Vor uader & uor moder*, Ayenb. p. 262/11.

4. *wif and children.* Orm. 1608, *and wif and child and hus and ham.*— Gower, i. 115, *Forth with his children & his wife.*

hus and ham. Cf. Hoffmann, p. 52; Fuhrmann, p. 21. The whole passage occurs again on p. 67/18 seq.

5. Cf. note to p. 3/17.

8 seq. See 1 Cor. xiii. 13, *Nunc autem manent fides, spes, charitas, tria haec. Major autem horum est charitas.*

11. *For ðan hie*, &c. Cf. ib. 8, *Charitas nunquam excidit.*

15. *forðan ðe godd*, &c. See 1 John iv. 8, *quoniam Deus charitas est.*— Ib. 16, *Deus charitas est.*

16. *þat is, godes luue and mannes.* Cf. 19/34.

21 seq. *mid ða flere*, &c. Cf. Luke xii. 49, *Ignem veni mittere in terram, et quid volo, nisi ut accendatur?*

24 seq. = John i. 9.

27. *He is icleped godes wisdom.* See note to p. 25/14.

29 seq. On the repetition of *him* cf. notes to pp. 23/3 and 57/7.

31. See Acts ii.—Cf. Gregorius, Hom. in Evang. lib. ii. 30 (Migne, 76/1223 D), *Spiritus sanctus et in igne monstratus est, quia omnes, quos repleverit, simplices et ardentes fecit, simplices puritate, ardentes aemulatione.*

P. 37, l. 2. *ðane hali gast, ðe is here beire luue.* See note to p. 25/16.

7 seq. = John xiv. 23, but before *et mansionem* the words *et ad eum veniemus* are left out.

12. = 1 John iv. 16.

15. *to eten and to drinken.* Cf. Mätzner, i. 677: *eten and drinken*, OEH. ii. 31; Havel. 800.—*eteð & drinkeð*, OEH. ii. 99.—*ete & dranc*, Curs. Mundi, 3551.—*æt & dronc*, Laȝ. ii. 353.—*ne ete ne dronk*, Ch. Tr. a. Cr. 5/1441.— *etenn þære & drunnkenn*, Orm. 4794-7.—*heo æten heo drunken*, Laȝ. ii. 173.— *eten . . . & afterward dronken*, Will. 1906.—*eeten & drank*, Rich. C. de L. 113.—*had eyton & dronkon also*, Amadas, 293.—*etest & drinkest*, OEH. ii. 31.—*eth my uless & dringþ my blod*, Ayenb. p. 95.—*ner eteþþ ne ne drinnkeþþ*, Orm. 16579.—Ib. 678: *etere & drynkere*, Trevisa, iv. 297.—*etingge & dringkinge*, OEH. ii. 39.—*eting & drinking*, ib. 63.—*on etinge & on drinkinge*, ib. 37.—*in etyng & drinkyng*, Wycl. Sel. W. iii. 160.—*inn etinng & inn drinnkinng*, Orm. 19059.—Ib. ii. p. 54 seq.: *selde eten & lesse drinken*, OEH. ii. 95.—*eoten & drinken*, ib. i. 45.—*eoten meokeliche & druncken meokeluker*, St. Marher. p. 14.—*eth & drink*, Ayenb. p. 54.—*I ete & drynke*, Wycl. Luke xvii. 8, Oxf.—*I ette or I drynk*, Hamp. 4675.—*et & dranc*, OEH. 233.—*men ete & drank*, Hamp. 4848.—*etynge & drynkynge*, Maund. p. 253.—*etinge & druncunge*, OEH. 19.—*inn etinng & inn drinnkinng*, Orm. 19063.—The opposite arrangement is much rarer, cf. l. c. i. 677 seq.: *drink & ete*, Curs. Mundi, 1685.—*thai dronke & ete*, Seuyn Sag. 272.—*drinkeres & eteres*, Ayenb. p. 47.—Ib. ii. 55: *drank & eet*, Metr. Hom. p. 39.

18 seq. are the words of the Lord to Cain (Gen. iv. 7), after the Itala. The LXX have: οὐκ ἂν ὀρθῶς προσενέγκῃς, ὀρθῶς δὲ μὴ διέλῃς, ἥμαρτες; Sabatier,

Bibl. Sacr. Lat. Verss. Antiq., gives, *Nonne si recte offeras, recte autem non dividas, peccasti?*

22 seq. seems to contain an allusion to Matth. xvi. 26, *Quid enim prodest homini, si mundum universum lucretur, animae vero suae detrimentum patiatur?* (= Mark viii. 36; Luke ix. 25).

26 seq. = Ps. x. 6 (xi. 5).

33 seq. *a boke finden iwriten.* I do not know what source this means. P. 39, l. 4. *auht* is here adv., meaning "possibly, anyhow" as on p. 53/18, 61/13. Cf. Zupitza, Engl. Stud. xiii. p. 358/97.

7. *mihte and strengþe* = OE. *miht and strengðo*, Gen. 950, Sat. 2.

11. *þat he æure bie þin sceld*, &c. Cf. 2 Sam. xxii. 3, *Deus fortis meus, sperabo in eum; scutum meum, et cornu salutis meae; elevator meus, et refugium meum; salvator meus, de iniquitate liberabis me.*—Ib. 31, *Deus ... scutum est omnium sperantium in se.*—Prov. xxx. 5, ... *clypeus est sperantibus in se.*

12 seq. Cf. 1 John iv. 21, *Et hoc mandatum habemus a Deo: ut qui diligit Deum, diligat et fratrem suum.*

16. = 1 Cor. xiii. 3, *Et si distribuero in cibos pauperum omnes facultates meas, et si tradidero corpus meum ita, ut ardeam, caritatem autem non habuero, nihil mihi prodest.*

21. See St. Gregory, Hom. in Evang. lib. ii. hom. xxxviii, on Matth. xxii. 1-13 (Migne, 76, 1288/10), *Sciendum vero est quia sicut in duobus lignis, superiore videlicet et inferiore, vestis texitur, ita in duobus praeceptis charitas habetur, in dilectione scilicet Dei, et proximi.*

24 seq. Cf. Haymo, Hom. de Tempore, hom. cxxxv (Migne, 118/723 seq.), *Vel certe aliter per vestem nuptialem recte charitas figuratur, quia sicut vestis plurimis filis contexitur, sic charitas diversis virtutibus adornatur.*

34. *gylt forȝifst.* Cf. Fuhrmann, p. 63.

P. 41, l. 5. *berþ ȝewitnesse.* More examples of this phrase are given by Mätzner, i. 206/3. Cf. in our text 59/16, 97/19, 101/25, 141/5.

6 seq. = 1 John ii. 15, *Si quis diligit*, &c.

9. *swa swiðe wittes bedæld.* Cf. Laȝ. ii. 3, *na man ne wurðe swa wod ne witte bidæled þat.* ...—Orm. 4676, *þatt tu narrt rihht wod & all wittess bidæledd* (Mätzner, i. 226).

11. *of ðe liuiȝende lande. Terra viventium* occurs in Ps. xxvi. 13, li. 7, cxli. 6; Is. xxxviii. 11, liii. 8; Jer. xi. 19; Ezek. xxxii. 23, 24, 26, 27, 32; and is often explained by the Fathers, cf. Hilarius, Tractatus in Ps. li. (Migne, 9/318), 17, De Christi regno. *Avulsus autem de tabernaculo, eradicabitur et de viventium terra. Qui enim non manebit in Christo, regni Christi incola non erit. ... Eradicatur ergo de viventium terra, quae in beata regione sanctis Domino conregnantibus praeparatur: cujus ipse in Evangelio meminit, dicens: "Beati mansueti, quoniam ipsi haereditabunt terram"* (*Matth.* v. 4); *et hic idem propheta: "Et placebo Domino in regione viventium"* (*Ps.* cxiv. 9).—Ib. 18, *Terra viventium: et quod mortui Deo vivant. Vivorum autem idcirco terra est, quia omnis fidelis in Domino, licet mortuus sit, Deo tamen vivit*, &c.—Id. Tract. in Ps. cxlii. 5 (l. c. p. 835), *Pars ejus in t. v. est, cum latroni die eodem incolatum paradisi promittit, id est, sortem et regnum haereditatis suae*, &c.—Hieronymus, Breviarium in Psalmos, Ps. xxvi. (Migne 26/952), "*In terra viventium*," *quia pignus nostrum illuc sursum habemus, quod est Christus. Ille accepit de nostra terra mortale corpus, et nos ab ipso*

accepimus spem et fidem, et per spem et fidem credentes, perveniemus in terram viventium,in qua sancti capient haereditatem regni coelorum.—Id. in Ps. li. (Migne, 26/1035), *Quia exterminabuntur a consortio claritatis ejus, ac de beatae sedis habitaculo, vel de viventium terra quam sancti haereditabunt.*— Id. in Ps. cxli. (Migne, 26/1313), "*Portio mea in t. v.*" *In sanctis, qui in eam transferuntur, sicut et latroni ait :* "*Amen dico tibi,*" &c.—Augustinus, Enarr. in Ps. cxli. (Migne, 37/1840), *Portio autem mea, non hic, sed in terra viventium. Dat Deus portionem in t. v.; sed non aliquid a se, extra se. Quid dabit amanti se, nisi se?*—Cassiodorus, Expos. in Psalterium, Ps. xxvi. (Migne, 70/192), *In t. v. id est in futura vita, ubi bona sunt sempiterna.*—Id. in Ps. cxli. (Migne, l. c. 1006), *Paradisus est enim terra viventium, quam soli beati feliciter introibunt, qui sub aeternitate et securitate victuri sunt.*—Ælfric, Hom. i. 550, *þára lybbendra eorðe is séo staðelfæstnyss þæs écan eardes, on ðám gerest séo sáwul swá swá sé lichama on eorðan. Sé eard is rest and lif gecorenra hálgena.*—Ib. 576, *tó staðolfæstnysse lybbendra eorðan, þæt is, tó ðám écan éðle,* &c.—Our text has, 61/16, *ðat liuiende land, þat is, ðat eche lif.*

12. *ȝeseðh oðer ȝeherð.* Cf. Mätzner, ii. 344 seq.: *he ihereð & isihð*, Ancr. R. p. 90.—*misseien mid eȝen, mid min eren iherd*, OEH. 189.—Ib. ii. 365 seq.: *ihereð oðer iseoð*, Ancr. R. p. 196.—*iseien oðer iherd*, ib. p. 92. Cf. to the following, 77/4 seq.

14. *ðat hali writt.* Not the Bible, but some source of the author's, which I have not been able to trace.

16. *mid weddede wiue.* Cf. Zupitza, Engl. Stud. xiii. p. 352, no. 46; Sarrazin, Octavian, p. 174/1267.

17. *ðane rihtwise and onfald Job,* = Job i. 1, *Vir erat in terra Hus, nomine Job, et erat vir ille simplex, et rectus, ac timens Deum, et recedens a malo.*

20. *mid michele wele* cannot be right, and we ought probably to read *wole,* "pestilence," instead of *wele.* Cf. Ettmüller, Lex. Anglo-Sax. p. 78, vôl, -*es*, Schade, Altdeutsches Wörterb.[2] 1214, *wuol.*—*nafte* belongs to OE. *næftig,* "poor."

24. *godes luue ne mannes.* This *ne* instead of *and* originates from the negation in the precedent sentence. Cf. Schleich, Ywain & Gawain, p. 113/955.

26. *modi menn.* Cf. Fuhrmann, p. 41.

33. *lif luuiȝen.* Cf. ib. p. 65.

P. **43**, l. 3. *on religiun.* Cf. note to p. 5/33. The same expression occurs 3/12, 5/33.

4. *þe is icleped uir desideriorum.* See Dan. ix. 23. The following description of the prophet's character is based on chap. i. 5–16.

5. *ðe flesliches lustes* is the same error as *woreldliches,* 31/7.

7. *was* ought not to have been altered, as after *ðára þe* the singular of the verb is used. Cf. Dietrich, Haupt's Zeitschr. xi. 444 seq.

10. *of metes and of drenches.* Cf. OE. *mettas ne drincas,* Metra, 8/9.—Orm. 5680, *Nohht affterr mete, naffterr drinnch.*—Mätzner, i. 677 has: *non mete ne drynke,* Rob. of Gl. p. 389.—*Mete & drinke,* Gow. ii. 140.—*met & drynk,* Seven Sag. 1821.—*mete or drink,* Wycl. Sel. Works, iii. 155.—*þane mete & þane drinke,* Ayenb. p. 29.—*mete oþer drinke,* ib. p. 9.—*wiþouten mete, wiþouten drink,* Gregorleg. 945.—*þe estmetes & drinkes,* OEH. ii. 37.—*metes & drinkes,* ib. 179; Wycl. Sel. Works, iii. 158.—*metes & drinches,* La3. i. 151.—Ib. p. 683: *of mete & of drunc,* Ancr. R. p. 14.—*of mete & of drunche,* ib. p. 342.—*of metes*

& *of drunches*, ib. p. 364. For the opposite order I find only, *þene drinc & þene mete*, La3. i. 55 (Mätzner, i. 677).

12. *ifedd and 3efostred*. Cf. *þe poure lefdi of heouene uostrede & fedde hine*, Ancr. R. p. 260.—*& fosstrenn hemm & fedenn*, Orm. 2077.—*to feden ant to fostrin*, St. Marher. p. 2.—*Wale þat ich þe uedde, þat ich þe uostredde*, La3. iii. 26.—*Haues he ben fed and fostred ay*, Havel. 2236 (Mätzner, ii. 86 and 193).—*fostered & ifedde*, Ch. Court of L. 974 (ib. iii. 25).

12 seq. See Dan. i. 12, "*Tenta nos, obsecro, servos tuos diebus decem, et dentur nobis legumina ad vescendum, et aqua ad bibendum.* Ib. 16, *Porro Malasar tollebat cibaria, et vinum potus eorum ; dabatque eis legumina.*

14. On *sondes* cf. Zupitza, Guy, p. 445/10477.

21. *ðo ðe bieð ute* are those wo have left the world. (Cf. l. 2 seq.)

21 seq. Cf. Gen. vi. 8-9, *Noë vero invenit gratiam coram Domino*. ... *Noë vir justus atque perfectus fuit in generationibus suis, cum Deo ambulavit.* This combination of Job, Daniel, and Noah as moral and typical examples is due to Ezek. xiv. 14-20, *Et si fuerint tres viri isti in medio ejus, Noë, Daniel, et Job: ipsi justitia sua liberabunt animas suas, ait Dominus exercituum*, &c. Cf. Augustinus, Enarr. in Ps. cxxxii. (Migne, 37, 1731/5), *Sic dicit et Ezechiel de tribus personis, in quibus non absurde tria haec genera intelligimus:* ... *Jam illi olim liberati sunt, sed in istis tribus nominibus tria genera quaedam significavit. Noë significat rectores Ecclesiae, quia ipse arcam in diluvio gubernavit. Daniel autem vitam quietam elegit, in coelibatu servire Deo, id est, uxorem non quaerens. Erat vir sanctus, in desideriis coelestibus vitam gerens ; tentatus in multis, et inventus aurum obrizum.* ... *Ergo in nomine Danielis, qui etiam VIR DESIDERIORUM est appellatus, sed utique castorum atque sanctorum, significantur servi Dei,* ... *In nomine Job significatur una illa de molendino quae assumetur. Habebat enim uxorem, habebat filios, habebat multas divitias;* ... *Amissis itaque omnibus repentina afflictione et tentatione, amissa haereditate, amissis haeredibus, sola conjuge sibi relicta,* ... *ait quod nostis: "Dominus dedit,"* &c. *Impletum est in eo quod quotidie cantamus, si et moribus consonemus: "Benedicam Dominum,"* &c. (Ps. xxxiii. 2). *Ergo in istis tribus nominibus significata sunt tria genera hominum, et in illis tribus rursus in Evangelio, quae commemoravi.*

23. *mani3e wintres swanc*, &c. Cf. Gen. v. 31, *Noë vero cum quingentorum esset annorum, genuit Sem, Cham, et Japheth*.—Ib. vii. 5-6, *Fecit ergo Noë omnia, quae mandaverat ei Dominus. Eratque sexcentorum annorum, quando diluvii aquae inundaverunt super terram.* Cf. also York Plays, p. 43/114:

> *A hundereth wyntres away is wente,*
> *Sen I began þis werk, full grathely talde.*

and p. 49/133:

> *A hundereth wyntyr, I watte wele,*
> *Is wente sen I þis werke had wrought.*

26. *to liue & to londe*. Cf. Hoffmann, p. 53 (*lif and land*).

28. *ða arche of ðe hali cherche*. Cf. *saule bote*, l. 32 ; *scipes borde*, l. 33 ; *scip*, 45/3. This comparison of the Church with Noah's ark or a ship is old, and very frequent in the Fathers. Cf. e. g. Hilarius, Comment. in Matth. vii. 9 (Migne, 9/957), *Ecclesia enim instar est navis, et plurimis locis ita nuncupata est: quae diversissimi generis et gentis vectore suscepto, subjecta est omnibus et ventorum flatibus et maris motibus. Atque ita illa et saeculi et immundorum spirituum vexatur incursibus. Propositis enim periculorum omnium*

motibus, Christi navem, i. e. Ecclesiam introimus : scientes nos mari ventoque jactandos.—Maximus Taurinensis, Sermo xciv, "De Mirabilibus" (Migne, 57/722), *Hanc igitur solam Ecclesiae navem ascendit Dominus, . . . Quae navis in altum saeculi hujus ita natat, ut pereunte mundo, omnes quos suscipit, servet illaesos. Cujus figuram jam in Veteri videmus Testamento; sicut enim Noe arca, naufragante mundo, cunctos quos susceperat, incolumes reservavit; ita et Petri Ecclesia, conflagrante saeculo, omnes quos amplectitur, repraesentabit illaesos.*—Ælfric, Hom. i. 536, *forðan ðe Noes arc on ȝþum ðæs micclan flódes hæfde getácnunge þyssere gelaðunge.*—Id. ii. 60, *Gif wé gléawlíce, æfter gástlicum andgite, tócnáwað þæt sé swymmenda arc getácnode Godes gelaðunge.*—Id. ii. 388, . . . *swincð þæt scip, þæt is, séo gelaðung on ðám déopum ȝðum þyssere worulde. Séo gelaðung mæg béon gedréfed on ðám sǽlicum ȝðum ðyssere worulde . . . þeah þéos woruld wéde, and windige éhtnysse ástyrige ongéan Cristes gelaðunge, ne bið héo swáðéah besenced.*—OEH. ii. 43/4, *þe beð on þis shipe, þat is holi chirche, in þis watere þat ich of speke, þat is þis wreche wuereld; and is mid storme faste bistonden, þo beð ure fule synnes, and fele oðre wosiðes.* Cf. also Skeat, Notes to Piers Plowman, p. 210, and the following notes.

28 seq. *ne lichame ne saule.* Cf. Meyer, 286, *lices & sáwle.*

29 seq. This comparison of temptations with winds and storms of the sea is very common in the Fathers. Cf. e. g. Haymo, Hom. xx (Migne, 118/154 A), "*et surgens imperavit ventis et mari,*" *quando tentamenta diaboli contra mentem viri sancti insurgentia conquiescere facit,* &c. See also note to l. 28.

P. 45, l. 2. *ðe liuie de lande*=*terra viventium.* Cf. note to 41/11.

4.=Luke x. 16, *Qui vos audit, me audit; et qui vos spernit, me spernit* . . . .

8.=Ps. ciii. 25 (civ. 25). The allegorical explanation of the sea as the world was given earlier by Hieronymus, Breviarium in Psalmos (Migne, 26/1202 D), "*Illic naves pertransibunt.*" *Quis ex nobis est navis fortis, qui possit istud saeculum fugere et non submergatur aut offendat in petram,* &c. Cf. also OEH. ii. 143/2, *Mundus nomine maris appellatur, tum propter procellas adversitatum, tum propter affluentiam copiae, tum propter refluentiam inopiae, tum quia extra navem in mari non est fiducia salutis.*—Ib. 161/6, *Mundus mari comparatur, quia fluctus erigit* [et] *naves obruit; ita mundus effluit, dum opes confert: refluit, dum aufert; turbine, id est, ultione divina vel fraude diabolica, turbatur. Discordiarum motus concitat, ecclesiarum pacem perturbat.* Cf. also notes to 43/28 seq.

10.=Ps. cvi. 26 (cvii. 26). Cf. Hieronymus, l. c. (p. 1217), "*Qui descendunt mare.*" *Id est saeculum. In navibus. In Ecclesiis quae Christum portant, et a fluctibus hujus mundi tunduntur.* "*Facientes operationem in aquis multis.*" *In populis.* . . . But his allegorical explanation of verse 26 is quite different from ours. Only in Honorius Augustodunensis, Comment. in Psal. (Migne, 194/671) I find an exposition like that of our text: vers. 26, *Praelati, sicut sunt episcopi, dicuntur naves, quae de mundo vehunt ad coelestia plebes.* . . . *Cum procellae et fluctus exaltantur, praelati mente ascendunt usque ad coelos, id est, ad sublimatos virtutibus; et descendunt usque ad abyssos, hoc est, ex altera parte respiciunt ad sorditatem et profunditatem vitiorum,* &c.

12. *ðe michele merhðe.* See Fuhrmann, p. 42 (*much myrþe*).

17. *nielnesse.* The marginal gloss "*abissos*" shows that the word had already become obsolete. Stratmann,[3] p. 419, sub *niwelnisse,* quotes only OEH. i. 225 and 233.

18. *of ðe harde hierte.* Cf. Mätzner, ii. 426 : *Hæpenn follkess herrte iss harrd,* Orm. 9878.—*So harde an herte,* Gow. i. 210.—*O herte hard,* id. ii. 122.—*þe king hert wex herd,* Curs. Mundi, 5903 Cott. This as well as l. 21, *for his herte hardnesse,* is a biblical expression. Cf. e. g. Exod. vii. 3, *Sed ego indurabo cor ejus,* . . . Ib. 13, *Induratumque est cor Pharaonis,* &c.

23 seq. A similar warning against almsgiving is quoted among the devil's instigations in OEH. ii. 29/33, *To þe narewe-herted man on his þonke he seið :* " *Witte wel hwat þu hauest ; walte hwat þe tide, and cun*[n]*e sume meðe þenne þu almesse makest. Đu hauest eðeliche bi aihte to helpen þine kenne,* &c.

26. *Hie wolden forsweljen all ðe woreld, jif hie mihten.* One is reminded of Mephistopheles' words in Goethe's Faust:

> *Die Kirche hat einen guten Magen,*
> *Hat ganze Länder aufgefressen.*

32. *Carite sprat his bowes.* We should expect *hire,* as *Carite* is else treated as a fem.

on bræde and on lengðe. Cf. Mätzner, i. 335 ; the phrase means extension to all sides : *The wide worlde in brede & length,* Gow. ii. 317.—*Al his viage bothe in breede & lengthe,* Lydg. M. P. p. 98.—Also the opposite order occurs, see Mätzner, l. c.

P. 47, l. 14. *ic ðe beseche & bidde.* Cf. Mätzner, i. 262 : *bidde & bezeche,* Ayenb. p. 194.—*Ich bide þe, & biseche þe,* OEH. i. 205.—*bydde & bezeche,* Ayenb. p. 98.—*bed tus & bisohte,* St. Juliana, p. 53.—Ib. p. 226 : *ich bidde & biseche þe,* St. Marher. p. 20.—*bisechen þene king & bidden,* Laȝ. ii. 87.

22. = John viii. 47.

24. = Gregorii Magni în vii Psalm. poenit. Expositio : Ps. xxxvii (Migne, 79/569 C), *Qui sine humilitate virtutes congregat, quasi in ventum pulverem portat.*

P. 49, l. 3. *Đe hali apostel,* &c. See 2 Cor. xii. 9, *Libenter igitur gloriabor in infirmitatibus meis, ut inhabitet in me virtus Christi.*

8. = Matth. xi. 29.

13. = Philip. ii. 6, 7, *Qui cum in forma Dei esset, non rapinam arbitratus est esse se aequalem Deo ; sed semet ipsum exinanivit, formam servi accipiens, in similitudinem hominum factus, et habitu inventus ut homo.*

15 seq. *was jelich godd his fader on ielde & on mihte.* Cf. 25/16 seq. and note.

18. *bar ðat liht,* &c. Cf. John i. 4, *In ipso vita erat, et vita erat lux hominum.*—Ib. 9, *Erat lux vera, quae illuminat omnem hominem venientem in hunc mundum.*—Ib. viii. 12, *Iterum ergo locutus est eis Jesus, dicens :* " *Ego sum lux mundi ! qui sequitur me, non ambulat in tenebris, sed habebit lumen vitae.*"—Ib. ix. 5, *Quamdiu sum in mundo, lux sum mundi.*—Ib. xii. 46, *Ego lux in mundum veni ; ut omnis, qui credit in me, in tenebris non maneat.*

22. *Wa mai bien ðe blinde,* &c. Cf. Orm. 18979 seq.,

> *All all swa summ þe sunnebæm*
> *bishineþþ all þe blinde,*
> *& himm ne cumeþþ rihht na god*
> *off þatt itt onn himm shineþþ,*

which is taken from Beda, Opp. iii. 639, *veluti si quilibet caecus jubare solis offundatur, nec tamen ipse solem, cujus lumine perfundatur, aspiciat* (see Sarrazin, Engl. Stud. vi. 20).

25. *heuene & ierðe.* Cf. Meyer, p. 285 ; Mätzner, ii. 44 seq., 472.

28 seq. *he lai bewunden on fiteres,* &c. Cf. Luke ii. 7, *et pannis eum involvit.*—Cf. also Wulfstán's Hom. 16/20 seq., *ðá hé cild wæs, eall hine man*

fédde, swá man óðre cild fédeð ; hé læg on cradole bewúnden, ealswá óðre cild dóð, . . .

29. mid swaðelbonde ibunden. Cf. Mätzner, i. 196 : ybounde mid bende, Ayenb. p. 220.—vnbint of licames bende, Mor. Ode, str. 198.—binden mid irene bænde, Laȝ. ii. 350.—Ure bendes he unbond, Mor. Ode, str. 95.—Ibunden mid . . . brode þicke bendes, Ancr. R. p. 382.—Ib. 254 : wið þe bondes . . . bind him, St. Juliana, p. 37.—me wið bale bondes bitterliche bindest, St. Marher. p. 13.—Murray gives (i. 646) : band himn wiþþ irrene band, Orm. 19821.— A bande . . . to bynde his hande, Towneley Myst. 217.—binde wele wiþ balk & bandes, Curs. M. 1671.—Bunden faste with bandes of syn, Hamp. Pr. of Consc. 3207, &c.—Cf. also ib. bind and bond.

30. alle wittes & ælle wisdomes. Cf. Fuhrmann, p. 17.

31. ðe nan god ne cann, " that knows not what to do." Cf. 81/19, ðe non god ne cunnen ; ib. 20, ðe non god ne cann.—See Kölbing, Amis & Amiloun, 242/1019 ; id. Ipomedon, 456/506 ; Adam, Torrent of Portyngale, 112/ 2636.—For a similar passage see Orm. 3662 seq.

P. 51, l. 3. He ðat alle cnewes to cnelið. Cf. Philip. ii. 10, Ut in nomine Jesu omne genu flectatur.—Cf. 145/9 and Zupitza, Engl. Stud. xiii. p. 377/277.

3 seq. he was buhsum, &c. See Luke ii. 51, et erat subditus illis.—Cf. Ancr. R. p. 78/5, . . . beih him to one monne, to one smiðe, & to ane wummone, & foluwede ham, &c.

5. he was her . . . wuniȝende 33¼ wintre. Cf. The Harrowing of Hell, ed. Mall, p. 23/45,

þritti winter and þridde half ȝer
Haui woned in londe her.

8. and hersum was his fader. Cf. Philip. ii. 8, factus obediens usque ad mortem.

10. att and dranc, &c. Cf. Ælfric's Hom. i. 151/6, Hé ǽt, and dranc, and slép, and wéox on géarum, and wæs þeah-hwæðere eal his líf bútan synnum.— Cf. also Wulfstán's Hom. 17/4, hine þyrste hwýlum and hwílum hingrode, hé ǽt and dranc, and ǽgðer hé þolode ge cyle ge hǽtan. eall séo menniscnes þolode, þæt menn tó gebyrede, &c.

& reste & sliep. Cf. to ligge & resti & slepe, Ayenb., p. 31/28.

11. wiðuten sennen ane. Cf. Wulfstán, 16/18, þæt hé þurh éadmétta on his menniscnesse eal ádréah, þæt mann déð, bútan synne ánre.

For ði warð dieuel beswiken, &c. Cf. Ambrosius, Expos. in Lucam, lib. ii (Migne, 15/1634), Fallendi autem principis mundi fuisse consilium, ipsius Domini verba declarant, cum apostoli jubentur tacere de Christo (Matth. xvi. 20), cum sanati prohibentur gloriari de remedio (Matth. viii. 4), cum daemones praecipiuntur silere de Dei Filio (Luc. iv. 35).—Fallendi, ut dixi principis mundi fuisse consilium etiam Apostolus declaravit dicens : " Sed loquimur Dei sapientiam in mysterio absconditam . . . quam nemo principum istius saeculi cognovit. Si enim cognovissent, nunquam Dominum majestatis crucifixissent " (1 Cor. ii. 7, 8), hoc est, nunquam me redimi Domini morte fecissent. Fefellit ergo pro nobis, fefellit ut vinceret, fefellit diabolum cum tentaretur, cum rogaretur, cum Dei Filius diceretur, ut nusquam divinitatem propriam fateretur. Sed tamen magis fefellit principem saeculi : diabolus enim etsi aliquando dubitavit, cum diceret : " Si Filius Dei es, mitte te deorsum " (Matth. iv. 6), tamen vel sero cognovit, et discessit ab eo . . . Principes autem saeculi non cognovisse, quo majore possumus quam apos-

tolicae sententiae probare documento : " *Si enim cognovissent*, &c." *Daemonum enim malitia facile etiam occulta deprehendit ; at vero qui saecularibus vanitatibus occupantur, scire divina non possunt.*

13. *forđemden to deaðe.* Cf. Fuhrmann, p. 45.

16. *ðe scames & ðe bismeres.* Cf. Mätzner, i. 266 : *schome & bismer*(*e*), OEH. 279, 283.—*to schome & to bismere*, Hali Meid. p. 17.

17 seq. Cf. St. Bernhardus, Super " missus est," Homiliae, hom. ii (Migne, 183/67). *Oportebat autem a principe mundi aliquandiu celari divini consilii sacramentum : non quod Deus, si palam opus suum facere vellet, impediri posse ab illo metueret : sed quia ipse, qui non solum potenter, sed etiam sapienter quaecunque voluit fecit, sicut in omnibus operibus suis quasdam rerum vel temporum congruentias propter ordinis pulchritudinem servare consuevit, ita in hoc quoque tam magnifico opere suo, nostrae viz. reparationis, non tantum potentiam suam, sed etiam prudentiam ostendere voluit* . . . *placuit ei tamen eo potius et modo, et ordine hominem sibi reconciliare, quo noverat cecidisse : ut, sicut diabolus prius seduxit feminam, et postmodum virum per feminam vicit, ita prius a femina virgine seduceretur, et post a viro Christo aperte debellaretur : quatenus malitiae fraudi dum ars pietatis illuderet, ac maligni fortitudinem Christi virtus contereret, diabolo Deus et potentior appareret et fortior.*

19 seq. *ut of paradise hine ne brohte.* On *bringen out of* cf. Zupitza, Engl. Stud. xiii. p. 344/3 ; Kaluza, Libeaus Desconus, p. 147/276. In our text it occurs on p. 21/17 with *of* only : *of ðessere* (*michele*) *wrecchade ibroht.*

22. = Gen. ii. 17.

25 seq. *ðe trewe ðe stant*, &c. Cf. Gen. ii. 9, *lignum etiam vitae in medio paradisi, lignumque scientiae boni et mali.*—Ib. iii. 3, *de fructu vero ligni, quod est in medio paradisi, praecepit nobis Deus, ne comederemus.*

26 seqq. On the comparisons and relations between the trees of life and knowledge on one side, and the cross on the other side, cf. F. Piper's essay, " Der Baum des Lebens," in the Evangelisches Jahrbuch für 1863, pp. 43 & 54 seq. ; Mussafia, " Sulla leggenda del legno della Croce " in the Sitzungsberichte der philos.-histor. Classe der kaiserl. Akademie der Wissenschaften, 63. Band, Wien, 1870, p. 165.

31. *forȝiuen ðe gelt.* Cf. Fuhrmann, p. 63.

33. *bileueð on ðessere soðe beleaue.* Cf. Mätzner, i. 248 : *ȝoure bileue þat ȝeo an bilefeþ*, Laȝ. ii. 156 (y. T.).

P. 53, ll. 8-15. Cf. 1 Cor. xi. 27 seq., *Itaque quicunque manducaverit panem hunc, vel biberit calicem Domini indigne, reus erit corporis et sanguinis Domini.*—Ib. 29, *Qui enim manducat et bibit indigne, judicium sibi manducat et bibit, non dijudicans corpus Domini.*

15-18. See a similar expression on p. 47/1.

21 seq. Cf. Altdeutsche Predigten, ed. Schönbach, i. 141/5, *die othmûticheit daz ist ein vil groz tûgint, custos est omnium virtutum, sie ist ein hûte aller tûginde. swo die tûgint ist, da ist alliz daz behalden daz man gûtis getût, und swa sie niht enist, da ist iz alliz vorlorn.*

22. *habben ne healden.* Cf. Hoffmann, p. 69 ; Fuhrmann, p. 28.

26. = Luke i. 28.

28. = Ib. 31, *ecce ! concipies in utero, et paries filium*; ib. 32, *Hic erit magnus, et Filius Altissimi vocabitur ;* . . .

31 seq. = Ib. 38.

33 seq. ȝe ðe telleð swa wel of ȝeu seluen, þat me clepeð ȝeu lafdies. Cf. Einenkel, The Life of Saint Katherine (E.E.T.S. 80), p. 7/88, and beon icleopet lefdi, þat feole telleð wel to.

P. 55, l. 1. on liue libbende. Cf. Zupitza, Engl. Stud. xiii. p. 408/695.

2. Cf. De Nativitate Mariae, cap. ii (Evang. Apocr. ed. Tischendorf[2], p. 114), ... scriptura dicente maledictum omnem esse qui non genuisset masculum in Israel.—Cf. also Notes to Piers Plowman, p. 381/224.

3 seq. Hie ðe child nolden beren, &c. Cf. the words of Elizabeth, Luke i. 25, " Quia sic fecit mihi Dominus in diebus, quibus respexit auferre opprobrium meum inter homines."

5 seq. Cf. Pseudo-Matthaei Evang. cap. vii (Evang. Apocr. ed. Tischendorf[2], p. 65), Haec ego didici in templo Dei ab infantia mea, quod Deo cara esse possit virgo. Ideo hoc statui in corde meo ut virum penitus non cognoscam. Cf. also De Nativitate Mariae, cap. vii (l. c. p. 118), ... sola virgo Domini Maria hoc se facere non posse respondit, dicens se quidem et parentes suos Domini servitio mancipasse, et insuper se ipsam Domino virginitatem vovisse, quam numquam viro aliquo commixtionis more cognito violare vellet.

8 seq. = Luke i. 48. For a similar paraphrase of the Magnificat see Blickl. Hom. 159.

13. wapmannes imone. Cf. Wulfstán, 144/33, bútan ǽlces weres gemánan.— Ib. 150/26, þe náfre náhte w. g.—Ælfric, Hom. ii. 8, Marían, þe næfde w. g.— Ib. 606, of Scē Marían, búton w. g.—OEH. i. 275/10, wiðuten meane of wepmon.—Mätzner, ii. 353 : buton weres gemanan, OEH. 227.—Nabbe ich of wepmonne nones kunnes ymone, OE. Misc. p. 85.—Monnes imone, ib. p. 100.— wythoute mannes ymone, Shoreh. p. 118.—of monnes imeane, Hali Meid. p. 25.

16. sonde, ðe he me sante. Cf. Fuhrmann, p. 15 ; Engl. Stud. xii. 353/160, 355/316.

19. = Luke i. 49, Quia fecit mihi magna, qui potens est ; et sanctum nomen ejus!
20. = Ib. 50.
28. = Ib. 51 seq., Deposuit potentes de sede, et ex.

30 seq. The translation, or rather paraphrase, of St. Mary's words is here combined with the author's.

P. 57, l. 1. ðe wolde him seluen herȝen. Cf. notes to pp. 5/8 seq. and 9/26.

1 seq. Cf. Blickl. Hom. 159, Deposuit : & hé dsette þá mihtigan of heora setle, & þæt wæs Satands mid his déoflum, 'þá hé wæs on heofena ríce, & hé þá for his oferhygdum & his déoflu mid him wurdon dworpene on helle gránd.

3. = Luke i. 52.

7 seq. ðat hie occurs twice, separated by an adverbial expression. Cf. notes to pp. 23/3 and 35/29. See another instance of the doubling of a pronoun in Schröer's Winteney-Version d. Reg. St. Benedicti, p. 137/1 seq., & þeo ȝeferreden þæs mid ȝesceade & mid eadmodnesse þæs ȝewylniȝe.

13. The insertion of is was not necessary. Cf. Ward, OE. Drama, Select Plays (Marlowe and Greene), 2nd ed. Oxford, 1887, p. 126/28.

18. frieurenesses & blisses. Cf. Mätzner, ii. 216 : Folkes froure & engles blis, OEH. ii. 255.

31. godes þearuen. Cf. g. wrecchen, 69/2, and Wulfstán, 171/16, godes þearfan.—Ib. 287/6, g. þearfum.

P. 59, l. 2. ðe dom ðe hie . . . fordemden. See Mätzner, i. 606 : I deme domes, P. Pl. 9639.—demde þe hehe burh domes, St. Jul. p. 21.—þe dom was demd, Havel. 2488, 2838.—minne dom þet ich demde mon to, Ancr. R. p. 306.

4. *harmes & scames.* See Mätzner, ii. 431 : *hearm & scheome baðe,* St. Jul. p. 19.—*from hearm & scome,* OEH. 59.
8. I have not been able to find the source of this sentence.
13 seq. See 53/20–22.
19 seq. Cf. Prov. i. 7, *Timor Domini principium sapientiae.*—Ib. ix. 10, *Principium sapientiae timor Domini.*—Jesus Sirach i. 16, *Initium sapientiae, timor Domini* (= Ps. cx. 10).
21 seq. = Ps. xxxiii. 12 (xxxiv. 11).
24. = Ib. 13 (12), where the rest of the verse runs, *diligit dies videre bonos ?*
26 seq. *mid herte oðer mid muðe.* See Mätzner, ii. 476: *mid heorte ne myd muþe,* OE. Misc. p. 81.
29. = Ps. xxxiii. 14 (xxxiv. 13), which continues, *et labia tua ne loquantur dolum.*
30 seq. = Ib. 15 (14), with the conclusion, *Inquire pacem, et persequere eam.*
P. 61, l. 4. Instead of *forlies* there ought to stand the subj. *forliese.*
4 seq. are the translation of Ps. xxxiii. 16 (xxxiv. 15), *Oculi Domini super justos; et aures ejus in preces eorum.*
10 seq. = Ib. 17 (16). The Vulgate has *perdat.*
14 seq. *ðe hie on wunieð & ... luuiȝeð.* The rel. *ðe* is here construed ἀπὸ κοινοῦ as on p. 121/25.
16. *ðat liuiende land.* Cf. note to 41/11.
19 seq. = Prov. xxviii. 14, where the Vulgate has, *Beatus homo, qui semper est pavidus; qui vero mentis est durae, corruet in malum.*
27 seq. = Matth. x. 28. The Vulgate only deviates in *occidunt corpus,* and goes on, *sed potius timete eum, qui potest et animam et corpus perdere in gehennam.*
32. = Eccles. xii. 13. Our author makes a mistake in ascribing this sentence to the Book of Wisdom (Liber Sapientiae).

P. 63, l. 2. *timor sanctus* occurs in Ps. xviii. 10 (xix. 9), *Timor Domini sanctus, permanens in saeculum saeculi;* ... Cf. Hieronymus, Breviarium in Ps., Ps. xviii. (Migne, 26/926), *Timor cum charitate : Unde dixit :* " *Perfecta charitas foras mittit timorem*" (1 John iv. 18). *Timeat non timore gehennae, aut timore poenae, sed timore sancto : sic timeat, ut quem amat non perdat per negligentiam.*—Augustinus, Enarr. in Ps. xviii. (Migne, 36/161), *Timor Domini : non servilis, sed castus ; gratis amans, non puniri timens ab eo quem tremit, sed separari ab eo quem diligit.*
3. *on worelde world* is a translation of the Latin phrase *in saecula saeculorum.*
8. = Eccles. vii. 19.
16. = Ps. xliv. 6 (xlv. 5). l. 18 seq. seem to be derived from the following words of the biblical text, *Populi sub te cadent, in corda inimicorum regis.*
19. *upe ðare bare ierðe.* Cf. OEH. ii. 139/15, *bare eorðe to bedde.*
23. *habben reuhðe of him seluen.* Cf. 65/7 and Ayenbite, p. 197/14, ' *Yef þou wilt kueme god : haue uerst reuþe & merci of þine zaule. Uor huo þet is kuead & ontrewe to him : to huam ssel he bi guod & trewe?*' &c.
28. *te sune ne te dohter.* Cf. Meyer, p. 287, *sunum & dohtrum,* in OE.— Mätzner, i. 652: *dohtren & sunen,* Hali Meid. p. 41.—*sunen & dohtren,* ib. p. 19.—*to sunes & to dohtres,* OEH. ii. 19.—*sons & doghters,* Hamp. 5434.—*sonys & doutres,* Wycl. Sel. W. iii. 190.—*alle hise sunnen & alle hise dehtren,* Hali Meid. p. 19.

28 seq. *te broðer ne te swuster.* Cf. *Briþeren & sustren*; Hymns to the Virgin, p. 9.—Cf. Poema morale, v. 31 seq.,

Ne hopie wif to hire were, ne were to his wiue :
Beo for him selue euerich man, þe hwile he beo aliue.

32. Cf. 17/32 seq. and notes.

32 seq. *brene . . . chele.* Cf. Poema morale, v. 234 seq.,

Hi fareð from hete to þan chele, from chele to þere hete.
þanne hi beoð in þere hete, þe chele heom þincheð blisse :
þanne hi cumeð eft to chele, of hete hi habbeð misse, &c.

Cf. also above, 17/32 and 19/1, *for ðare michele hæte and unʒemæte brene, and . . . for ðe unmate chele.* A similar description is given in Sawles Warde, OEH. i. 251/19, *þer is remunge iþe brune, ant toðes hechelunge iþe snawi weattres; ferliche ha flutteð from þe heate in to þe chele, ne neauer nuten ha of þeos twa, hweðer ham þuncheð wurse, for eiðer is unþolelich.*

P. 65, l. 1–3. These lines show that the passage before was a description of purgatory (not of hell!), out of which tormented souls may be rescued, according to the Catholic faith, by masses, prayers, and alms.

3 seq. Cf. Poema morale, v. 33 seq.,

Wis is, þe hine selfne biþenchð, þe hwile he mot libbe :
For sone willeð hine forʒete þa fremede and þa sibbe.

3–5. Cf. the above-quoted passages of the Poema morale, v. 32 seq.

13. *hu ðu scalt fram ðan euele buʒen,* &c. Cf. 19/18 and note.

17. = 1 Cor. viii. 1. The Vulgate has *vero* before *aedificat.*

32. = 1 Cor. xiii. 3. Cf. above note to 39/16.

P. 67, l. 4. *se heiʒeste* is a biblical expression; Lat. *altissimus.*

Cf. Lev. xix. 18, *Diliges amicum tuum sicut teipsum.*—Matt. xix. 19, *Diliges proximum tuum sicut te ipsum.*—Ib. xxii. 39 = Rom. xiii. 9.—Mark xii. 31, *Diliges proximum tuum tamquam te ipsum.*

7 seq. Cf. Ælfred's version of Gregory's Pastoral Care (ed. Sweet), p. 353/7, *Swá mon ðonne sceal fulfremedlice Godes fiend hatigean, ðætte mon lufige ðæt ðæt hie béoð, & hatige ðæt ðæt hie dóð. Hé sceal weorðan his life tó nytte mid ðý ðæt hé næte his undéawas.*—OEH. i. 15, at the bottom, *þas ruperes and þas reueres and þas þeues þet nulleð nu nefre swike heore uueles, þu aʒest luuan heore saule for Cristes luue, and heore uuel þe heo doð þu aʒest to hetiene and wið-stewen ʒif þu miht,* &c.—Ib. 67/222, . . . *þin sunful efenling, luue him for godes þing, and þu aʒest to hatien wel his sunne.*—Ayenbite of Inwyt, p. 157/2, *Ich ssel alneway hatye þe zenne : and louie þe kende.* Orrm. also treats the same idea, 5058 seq. (Cf. note in vol. ii. p. 366, above.)

9 seq. *ðe writt* is an unknown source of the author's. Cf. Angl. vii. p. 283/25,

How merci passeþ strengþe & riʒt,
Mony a wyse seo we may ;
God ordeyned merci most of miht,
To beo above his werkes ay.

The same idea is later on in our text expressed by Truth, 115/29.

14 seq. = 1 Cor. iii. 18. The Vulgate has *in hoc saeculo* after *esse.*

15. Read *uos* instead of *nos.*

18 seq. Cf. 35/3 seq.

24 seq. Cf. Matth. xix. 16–24 ; Mark x. 17–25 ; Luke xviii. 18–25.

25. *an riche iungman.* See Matth. xix. 20, where he is called *adolescens*, and v. 22, *adolescens . . . habens multas possessiones.* The latter remark is also found in Mark x. 22. Luke calls him (xviii. 18) a *princeps*, and remarks, verse 23, *dives erat valde.*

26 seq. The Vulgate has, Matth. xix. 16, " *Magister bone ; quid boni faciam, ut*," &c.—Mark x. 17, " *Magister bone! quid faciam, ut vitam aeternam percipiam?*"—Luke xviii. 18, " *Magister bone! quid faciens vitam aeternam possidebo?*"

29. *Mandata nosti*=Luke xviii. 20.

30 seq. Cf. Matth. xix. 18, " *Non homicidium facies; Non adulterabis; Non facies furtum ; . . .*"—Mark x. 19, " *Ne adulteres; ne occidas; ne fureris ; . . .*" —Luke xviii. 20, " *Non occides! Non moechaberis! Non furtum facies!*"

31-33. Cf. Matth. xix. 20, " *Omnia haec custodivi a juventute mea ;*" . . . (=Luke xviii. 21).—Mark x. 20, " *Magister! haec omnia observavi a juventute mea.*"

33 seq. This answer of Christ is an addition and invention of our author's.

35 seq.=Matth. xix. 21.

P. 69, l. 1. *et cetera*=ib., " *et da pauperibus! .... et veni, sequere me!*"

2. *godes wrecchen.* Cf. *godes þearuen*, 57/31 and note.

3. *Ðies junge mann*, &c. Cf. Matth. xix. 22, *Cum audisset autem adolescens verbum, abiit tristis ; . . .*

7 seq. Cf. Matth. xix. 24, " *Facilius est camelum per foramen acus transire, quam divitem intrare in regnum coelorum*" (=Mark x. 25).

9 seq.=Luke vi. 24.

12-18 are evidently an allusion to the parable of the Sower. Cf. Matth. xiii. 3-23, Mark iv. 1-20, Luke viii. 4-15. Compare specially the following words of the biblical text, Matth. xiii. 22, " *Qui autem seminatus est in spinis, hic est, qui verbum audit, et sollicitudo saeculi istius, et fallacia divitiarum suffocat verbum, et sine fructu efficitur;*"=Mark iv. 18, " *Et alii sunt, qui in spinis seminantur ; hi sunt, qui verbum audiunt;* ib. 19, *et aerumnae saeculi, et deceptio divitiarum, et circa reliqua concupiscentiae introeuntes suffocant verbum, et sine fructu efficitur.*"=Luke viii. 14, " *Quod autem in spinas cecidit, hi sunt, qui audierunt, et a sollicitudinibus et divitiis et a voluptatibus vitae euntes suffocantur, et non referunt fructum.*"

19. *hundes and haueles.* For other examples of this phrase—or *havekes and hundes*—cf. Mätzner, sub *havek* (ii. 442 b), and *hund* (ii. 523). See also Engl. Stud. xiv. 186/135, *Houndes ladden & haukes beren*, and note.

Instead of *mai* we should expect *muȝen*. But *alle ðo þing* is, as a collective noun, construed with the sing. Cf. Mätzner, Engl. Gr.[3] ii. 150 seq.

22. Before *Weneð* the subject *ȝe* is to be supplied, as *he* before *Ðenþ*, 57/21. Cf. Mätzner, Engl. Gr.[3] ii. 30 seqq; Kaluza, Libeaus Desconus, pp. 175/903 and 198/1545.

24. *ðe is mid rihte Soð icleped*=Jesus Christ. Cf. 9/24, and note.

Cf. Matth. vi. 21, *Ubi enim est thesaurus tuus, ibi*, &c.

30. *witt and wisdom.* Cf. Fuhrmann, p. 17.

P. 71, l. 7.=Sirach xxxii. 24, *Fili, sine consilio nihil facias, et post factum non poenitebis.* This book is, however, not written by Solomon, but by Jesus Sirach ! Cf. the same blunder, p. 73/8.

19 seq.=Luke ix. 62, *Nemo mittens manum suam ad aratrum, et respiciens retro, aptus est r. D.*

25 seq. = Matth. xi. 28–30. For *honorati* read *onerati*. The text runs on, . . . *et ego reficiam vos.*—Ib. 29, *Tollite jugum meum super vos, et discite a me, . . . et invenietis requiem animabus vestris.*—Ib. 30, *Jugum enim meum suave est, et onus meum leve.*

32. *muȝen*, viz. don. Cf. *myght no more*, Zupitza, Guy, 411/6947.

34. *Christes marc* is the cross. Cf. Matth. xxiv. 30, *Et tunc parebit signum Filii hominis in coelo.*

P. 73, l. 3, = Matth. xix. 21. Cf. above, 67/35.

5. For the same idea, cf. above, 41/15 seq.

8. = Sirach ii. 1, *Fili! accedens ad servitutem Dei, sta in justitia et timore, et praepara animam tuam ad tentationem.*—Ib. 5, *Quoniam in igne probatur aurum et argentum, homines vero receptibiles in camino humiliationis.* In the side-note this passage again is wrongly ascribed to Solomon. Cf. above, note to 71/7.

12. *al swo is þe pott.* Cf. Sirach xxvii. 6, *Vasa figuli probat fornax, et homines justos tentatio tribulationis.*

13 seq. *bersteð & brekð.* Cf. Mätzner, i. 333 : *bursten & breken hire bondes*, St. Marher. p. 19. Cf. St. Juliana, p. 59.—Ib. p. 341 : *to bresten & to breken*, Leg. St. Kath. 2026.—*bursten & tobreken*, St. Juliana, p. 79. From Murray (sub *burst*) I take : *it brekes & brestes*, Pricke of Consc. 7014.— *brestethe & brekethe*, Higden, i. 319.

14. *hal & ȝesund.* Cf. Mätzner, ii. 399 : *all hal & sund*, Orm. 14818.—*bath hale & sound*, Holy Rood, 73/403.—*hole & sunde*, OEH. ii. 43.—*hol & sond*, R. of Gl. p. 163.—*al heil & sund*, Best. 363–6.—*al hol & sound*, St. Edm. King, 91.—*hole & sounde*, Gregorleg. 465, 590.—*hol & sounde*, Ferumbr. 519.—*heil & sund*, Best. 75.—Ib. iii. 99 : *Al ihal & al isund*, Laȝ. i. 35.—*hol & isunde*, OE. Misc. p. 42. Cf. Zupitza, Engl. Stud. xiii. 405/653 ; Kaluza, l. c. p. 144/232.

15 seq. *Þe apostele seið.* Cf. 1 Cor. x. 13, *Tentatio vos non apprehendat, nisi humana ; fidelis autem Deus est, qui non patietur vos tentari supra id, quod potestis ; sed faciet etiam cum tentatione proventum, ut possitis sustinere.*

18 seq. *swa full swa is bladdre of winde* was a frequent proverbial expression. Cf. *A bleddre ibollen ful of winde*, Ancr. R. p. 282.—*With a face so fat As a ful bleddere Blowen bretful of breth*, P. Pl. Creed, 441.—*Lyk a bladder ful of wynd*, Ch. C. T. 12367 (Mätzner, i. 292). Murray adds (p. 896/3), *as a blather full of wynde*, Myrr. Our Ladye, 17.—*Bladders blowen up with wynd*, Spenser, Col. Clout, 717.—Ib. sub 6, *A bladder of worldlie winde which swells in their hearts*, Pappe w. Hatchet (1844), 27.—*Them that are harebraines and bladders full of winde*, Tomson Calvin's Serm. Tim. 279/2.—*Thou bladder full puft vp with vanity*, R. C. Times' Whis. iii. 1115.

24 seq. Cf. 35/2 seq. and notes.

26. *mid hlutter herte.* Cf. Orm. 5707, *Iss clene & lutterr herrte.*

27. *We findeð on ȝewrite.* The Rule of St. Benet or Isidorus (De eccles. officiis) is probably meant. Cf. note to 35/2 seq.

P. 75, l. 2–4. Cf. 1 Cor. vii. 28, *Si autem acceperis uxorem, non peccasti, . . . tribulationem tamen carnis habebunt hujusmodi.* Cf. also 41/12 seq., 77/4 seq.

6. Cf. 71/7 seq.

8. See Matth. v. 25, *Esto consentiens adversario tuo cito, dum es in via cum eo, ne forte tradat te adversarius judici, et judex tradat te ministro, et in carcerem mittaris.*—Luke xii. 58, *Cum autem vadis cum adversario tuo ad*

principem, in via da operam liberari ab illo, ne forte trahat te ad judicem, et judex tradat te exactori, et exactor mittat te in carcerem.

12 seq. *Godes word, godes ræd is ðin unwine*, &c. Cf. Hieronymus, Expos. in Evang. Matth. (Migne, 30/563), *Esto consentiens adversario tuo, id est, Evangelium: dum es in via cum eo, id est, in ista vita; ... Ne forte, etc., id est, ne lex Evangelii tradat te Christo judici: quia non consensisti Evangelio, ministro, id est, angelo, qui animas in poenam mittit in carcerem, id est, in infernum.*

19. Cf. 9/29, and note.

20 seq. *forðan ðe ðu art godd unhersum al swa he.* Cf. 7/16 seq.

22. = Ps. lxi. 11 (lxii. 10).

25. On *hucche* cf. Skeat, Notes to Piers Plowman, p. 81.

26 seq. See Matth. vi. 19 seq., *Nolite thesaurizare vobis thesauros in terra,* ... ib. 20, *thesaurizate autem vobis thesauros in coelo.* (Cf. Luke xii. 33.)

29 seq. = Luke xiv. 12.

31 seq. = Ib., *Neque fratres tuos, neque cognatos, neque vicinos divites; ne forte te et ipsi reinvitent, et fiat tibi retributio;* ib. 13, *Sed cum facis convivium, voca pauperes, debiles, claudos, et caecos;* ib. 14, *Et beatus eris, quia non habent retribuere tibi; retribuetur enim tibi in resurrectione justorum.*

P. 77, l. 2. on *godes swiðre.* Cf. Matth. xxv. 33, *Et statuet oves quidem a dextris suis,* &c.; ib. 34, *Tunc dicet Rex his, qui a dextris ejus erunt: "Venite, benedicti Patris mei! possidete paratum vobis regnum a constitutione mundi.*

3. Cf. 75/19 seq.

4 seq. *Whi seggeð men*, &c. Cf. 41/13, 73/4 seq.

8. *wille werchen.* See Fuhrmann, p. 67.

9 seq. = Luke vi. 30.

11. *swa ðu woldest.* Cf. ib. 31, *Et prout vultis, ut faciant vobis homines, et vos facite illis similiter.*

12. Cf. ib. 33, *Et si benefeceritis his, qui vobis benefaciunt, quae vobis est gratia? Si quidem et peccatores hoc faciunt;* ib. 34, *Et si mutuum dederitis his, a quibus speratis recipere, quae gratia est vobis? Nam et peccatores peccatoribus foenerantur, ut recipiant aequalia.*

14 seq. Cf. ib. 32, *Et si diligitis eos, qui vos diligunt, quae vobis est gratia? Nam et peccatores diligentes se diligunt,* = Matth. v. 46, *Si enim dil. e. q. v. d., quam mercedem habebitis? Nonne et publicani hoc faciunt?*

16. *Ne don swa ðe heðene?* = Matth. v. 47, *Nonne et Ethnici hoc faciunt?*

16–18. *Ac luue*, &c. Cf. Luke vi. 35, *Verumtamen diligite inimicos vestros;* (= ib. 27, and Matth. v. 44) ... *nihil inde sperantes; et erit merces vestra multa, et eritis filii Altissimi,* &c.

17 seq. *and lat him wreke.* Cf. Deut. xxxii. 35, *Mea est ultio, et ego retribuam in tempore.*—Sirach xxviii. 1, *Qui vindicari vult, a Domino inveniet vindictam.*—Rom. xii. 19, *Scriptum est enim: "Mihi vindicta(m); ego retribuam, dicit Dominus."*—Heb. x. 30, *Scimus enim, qui dixit: "Mihi vindicta, et ego retribuam."*

18 seq. *ðe is riht deme*, &c. Cf. the Apostolic Creed, *Unde venturus est judicare vivos et mortuos.*

19 seq. Cf. Matth. v. 42, *Qui petit a te, da ei! et volenti mutuari a te, ne avertaris!*

21 seq. Cf. 11/29 seq. and note, besides Exod. xxii. 25, *Si pecuniam mutuam dederis populo meo pauperi, qui habitat tecum; non urgebis eum*

quasi exactor, nec usuris opprimes.—Lev. xxv. 35, *Si attenuatus fuerit frater tuus,* ...; ib. 36, *ne accipias usuras ab eo, nec amplius, quam dedisti* ...; ib. 37, *Pecuniam tuam non dabis ei ad usuram,* &c.—Deut. xxiii. 19, *Non foenerabis fratri tuo ad usuram pecuniam* ...; ib. 20, ... *Fratri autem tuo absque usura id, quo indiget, commendabis.* Cf. also Ps. xiv. 5, liv. 12, lxxi. 14; Prov. xxviii. 8; Ezek. xviii. 8, 13, 17, xxii. 12. Therefore, usury and taking interests was forbidden as a sin by the Canon law.

34. = Ps. xiv. 1 (xv. 1), which continues, *aut quis requiescet in monte sancto tuo?*

P. 79, l. 3. seq. = Ib. 4, which goes on, *et non decipit.*

5 seq. = Ib. 5, *Qui pecuniam suam non dedit ad usuram, et munera super innocentem non accepit. Qui facit haec, non movebitur in aeternum.*

11. *wise & ȝeape.* Cf. Laȝ. i. 117, *mid ȝeapscipe & mid wisdome.*—OEH. i. 269, *Wit & wisdom & ȝapschipe of werlde.*

On *paneȝes,* "money" (= dan. *penge*), cf. Sweet, Cura Pastor. p. 489/327.

13. *be londe & be watere.* Cf. *water & lond,* Gen. and Ex. 103.

19 seq. = Is. v. 21.

24 seq. = Ib. 23, *Qui justificatis impium pro muneribus, et justitiam justi aufertis ab eo.*

28. *auhte men & gode menn.* Cf. *As gode men & aȝte,* Rob. of Gl. v. 9420.

29. = Is. v. 20. The Vulgate has, however, the opposite order.

32. *Mammona iniquitatis.* See Luke xvi. 9.

P. 81, l. 2. = Luke vi. 25, *Vae vobis, qui ridetis nunc! quia lugebitis et flebitis!*

4. *and for ȝeure michele wele,* &c. Cf. ib. 24, *Vae vobis divitibus! quia habetis consolationem vestram.*

4-6 is evidently an address to deceitful advocates.

7 seq. Cf. 41/12 seq. and 77/4 seq.

19 seq. *ðe non god ne cunnen,* &c. Cf. 49/31, and note. It means, "that know not what to do."

23 seq. See 2 Sam. xi. Bersabee is a mistake for Betsabee.

25. *Miserere* = Ps. l. (li.).

27 seq. Cf. ib. 3 (li. 1), *Miserere mei, Deus, secundum magnam misericordiam tuam. Et secundum multitudinem miserationum tuarum, dele iniquitatem meam.*

P. 83, l. 1 seq. Cf. ib. 9 (li. 7), *Asperges me hyssopo, et mundabor.*

2. *mid tare ysope of ðare holi rode,* would be an enormous anachronism for King David, but the author here puts in ideas of his own.

2 seq. *of ðan holie watere ðe ȝiede ut of ðe riht side of ðine hali temple.* Cf. Ezek. xlvii. 1, *Et convertit me ad portam domus, et ecce! aquae egrediebantur subter limen domus ad Orientem;* ... *aquae autem descendebant in latus templi dextrum ad Meridiem altaris.* Ib. 2, *Et eduxit me per viam portae Aquilonis, et convertit me ad viam foras portam exteriorem, viam quae respiciebat ad Orientem; et ecce aquae redundantes a latere dextro.*—On the wonderful nature and effects of this water cf. ib. 8-12. For the allegorical explanation of this stream cf. Hieronymus, Comment. in Ezech. lib. xiv. c. 47 (Migne, 25/488), *Ex quo perspicuum fit, sacras esse aquas, et Salvatoris nostri significare doctrinam, juxta illud quod scriptum est,* &c. ...; (ib. 490), *et transduxit me per aquam usque ad talos, quos Aquila et Symmachus et Theodotio ἀστραγάλους interpretati sunt, pro quibus LXX transtulerunt: et transivit*

Al. *sed transibit*] *in aquam, aquam remissionis: quod intelligere possumus prima hominum significare peccata, quae ingredientibus nobis aquas Domini dimittuntur, et baptismi ostendunt gratiam salutarem et initia sunt profectuum, tamen ipsa sublimia.... Post mille autem cubitos qui perveniunt usque ad talum, mensus est alios mille cubitos in aqua, et transduxit me usque ad genua. Post remissionem siquidem peccatorum, et iter profectuum, quando paululum de terrenis ad altiora conamur ascendere, flectimus Domino genua, &c.... Tertio mensus est mille alios cubitos, et transduxit, inquit, me per aquam usque ad renes. His enim gradibus ad sublimia pervenimus: quae tamen ipsa sublimia usque ad lumbos et renes perveniunt, ut omnis in nobis ignobilis libido truncetur, et possideamus sanctificationem corporis, sine qua nemo videt Deum.*

3 seq. Cf. Ps. l. 9 (li. 7), *Lavabis me, et super nivem dealbabor.*

5. = Ib. 12 (li. 10).

9. *and rihtne gost*, &c. = ib., *Et spiritum rectum innova in visceribus meis.*

12. = Ib. 13 (l. 11), *Ne projicias me a facie tua* (=*fram ðine ansiene*, l. 15). —*min leue lauerd*, cf. Fuhrmann, p. 41.

17 seq. = Ib., *Et spiritum sanctum tuum ne auferas a me.*

18. *Sari and sorhfull.* Cf. Laȝ. iii. 38, *sari & sorhful an heorte*; and see Hoffmann, p. 66, *sárig & sorhful*, Wulfst. 154/4.—*sárlic & sorhful*, id. 273/6. —*sorhful & sárigmód*, id. 133/13.

19. *Redde*, &c. = Ps. l. 14 (li. 12), *Redde mihi laetitiam salutaris tui.*

21. *glad and bliðe.* Examples of the same combination are (after Mätzner, i. p. 300; ii. p. 273): *Full glade & bliþe wurrþenn*, Orm. 159.—*Well gladde & bliþe sholldenn ben*, id. 792.—*With all min herte glad and blithe*, Gower, i. 181. And vice versâ: *Moyses was bliðe an[d] glad of ðis*, G. & Ex. 3671.—*be blythe and glad*, Cov. M. p. 24. The New Engl. Dict. adds (p. 924, A. 2): *His frendes was ful gladd and bliþe*, Cursor M. 11066.—Ib. 3: *bees all blythe and glad*, York Myst. xv. 86.—*the wilie Adder, blithe and glad*, Milton, P. L. ix. 625. Cf. finally: Schleich, Ywain & Gawain, *gl. & blithe*, 3674; *ful gl. & blith*, 1315, 1550, 2282; *al gl. & blyth*, 1374; *blith & gl.*, 1097.

22. *And faste*, &c. = Ps. l. 14 (li. 12), *Et spiritu principali confirma me.*

25 seq. = Ib. 15 (li. 13), *Docebo iniquos vias tuas.*

28 seq. = Ib., *Et impii ad te convertentur.*

30. *heriȝen & blescien.* Cf. *god heryinde, & þene king of heuene ever blessynde*, OE. Misc. p. 55/655 seq.

33. *ðane froure gost.* Cf. John xiv. 26, *Paracletus autem Spiritus sanctus*, &c.—Ib. xv. 26, *Cum autem venerit Paracletus, quem ego mittam vobis a Patre, spiritum veritatis*, &c.

P. 85, l. 1. Cf. p. 81/33 and 83/1.

2 seq. = Ps. l. 18 (li. 16), *Quoniam si voluisses sacrificium, dedissem utique; holocaustis non delectaberis.*

4. = Ps. xv. 2 (xvi. 2), *Dixi Domino: "Deus meus es tu, quoniam bonorum meorum non eges."*

9 seq. = Ps. l. 19 (li. 17).

11 seq. Cf. ib., *Cor contritum et humiliatum, Deus, non despicies.*

14–17. Cf. Matth. xxvi. 69–75; Mark xiv. 66–72; Luke xxii. 54–62; John xviii. 15–18, 25–27.

16. *He ȝiede ut*, &c. = Matth. xxvi. 75, *Et egressus foras flevit amare.*— Luke xxii. 62, *Et egr. foras Petrus fl. a.*

17 seq. Cf. the story of the "*peccatrix*" (= Mary Magdalene, after the traditional interpretation), Luke vii. 36–50, espec. 38, ...'*Lacrymis coepit rigare pedes ejus, et capillis capitis sui tergebat, et osculabatur pedes ejus, et unguento ungebat.*—Ib. 48, *Dixit autem ad illam: "Remittuntur tibi peccata tua!"* To the whole passage, ll. 11-19, cf. also OEH. i. 157/2, *swiche teres scedde* M. *Magdalene, þa heo wosch ure drihtenes fet, and heo werð hire solf waschen of hire fule sunnen.*—See also OEH. ii. 65/9, *ne brin*[g]ð *no synful man quemere loc, þene teares sheding for his sinnen. And wiste se*[i]*nte Peter and seinte Marie Magdaleine, þe mid wope wessen hem seluen of heued synnes.*

19-22. Cf. 1 Reg. (Sam.) i., espec. 2, *Annae autem non erant liberi.*—Ib. 5, *Dominus autem concluserat vulvam ejus.*—Ib. 6, *Affligebat quoque eam aemula ejus, et vehementer angebat, in tantum, ut exprobraret, quod Dominus conclusisset vulvam ejus*; ib. 7, *Sicque faciebat per singulos annos, ... et sic provocabat eam. Porro illa flebat,* .... Ib. 10, *Cum esset Anna amaro animo, oravit ad Dominum, flens largiter,* ... Ib. 19, ... *et recordatus est ejus Dominus.* Ib. 20, *Et factum est post circulum dierum, concepit Anna, et peperit filium, vocavitque nomen ejus Samuel.*

32 seq. = Ps. xxxi. 8 (xxxii. 8), which continues, *in via hac, qua gradieris.*

P. 87, l. 2 seq. = Ib. *firmabo super te oculos meos.*

5 seq. Cf. p. 99/26 seq.

9. = Ps. lxxxiv. 9 (lxxxv. 8).

20 seq. Cf. Is. xlix. 14, *Et dixit Sion: "Dereliquit me Dominus, et Dominus oblitus est mei."*

21 seq. = Ib. 15, *Numquid oblivisci potest mulier infantem suum, ut non misereatur filio uteri sui? et si illa oblita fuerit, ego tamen non obliviscar tui.*

30 seq. *Ðis forbet godd,* &c. Cf. Matth. vi. 25, *Ideo dico vobis, ne solliciti sitis animae vestrae quid manducetis, neque corpori vestro quid induamini.*—Ib. 31, *Nolite ergo solliciti esse, dicentes: "Quid manducabimus, aut quid bibemus, aut quo operiemur?"* (= Luke xii. 22-32).

31. *houhfull ne care-full.* Cf. notes to pp. 7/1, 11/27, 27/11, 41/24.

33. = Matth. vi. 33, *Quaerite ergo primum regnum Dei, et justitiam ejus,* &c. (= Luke xii. 31, *Verumtamen quaerite primum,* &c.).

P. 89, l. 2 seq. = Deut. viii. 3, ... *quod non in solo pane vivat homo, sed in omni verbo, quod egreditur de ore Dei.* (Quoted Matth. iv. 4 and Luke iv. 4.).

3. *he bread,* read *be bread.*

5 seq. = Rom. xiv. 17, *Non est enim regnum Dei esca,* &c.

17. = Ephes. iv. 26.

23. *fareð hom.* Cf. p. 23/32 and note.

30. *lief* ought to have been translated "believe." Cf. *leueð,* 119/32.

30. = Ps. xxxi. 9 (xxxii. 9), *Nolite fieri sicut equus et mulus, quibus non est intellectus.*

33. *al swo doð fliȝen to sare.* Cf. Ilias xix. 25, μυῖαι καδδῦσαι κατὰ χαλκοτύπους ὠτειλάς, and E. Voigt, Egberts von Lüttich Fecunda Ratis, Halle, 1889, p. 34/142 (*musca sitit morbum*), and note.

33 seq. *All ðare hwile,* &c. Cf. Job vii. 1, *Militia est vita hominis super terram.* Cf. also the Sentences of St. Bernhard, Anglia, iii. p. 62/41, *Ne havest þou here bote fiȝt, þe wiles þou art a liue.*

P. 91, l. 3. *Nim ðin sweord,* &c. Is an allusion to Ephes. vi. 17, ... *assumite et gladium spiritus, quod est verbum Dei.*

3–4 were spoken by Christ to Peter, Mark viii. 33, *Vade retro me, Satana!*

9 seq. = Prov. ix. 1, *Sapientia aedificavit sibi domum, excidit columnas septem.* A different allegorical exposition of these is given by St. Bernhard, Sermones de tempore: De adventu Domini, ser. iii (Migne, 183, 45/4 B), *Beatus, in quo Sapientia aedificat sibi domum, excidens columnas septem. Beata anima, quae sedes est Sapientiae. Quaenam est illa? Anima utique justi. Merito plane, quia justitia et judicium praeparatio sedis tuae (Ps. lxxxviii. 15)... Justitia virtus est, quod suum est unicuique tribuens. Tribue ergo tribus quae sua sunt. Redde superiori, redde inferiori, redde aequali cuique quod debes, et digne celebras adventum Christi, parans ei in justitia sedem suam. Redde, inquam, reverentiam praelato, et obedientiam; quarum altera cordis, altera corporis est. Nec enim sufficit exterius obtemperare majoribus nostris, nisi ex intimo cordis affectu sublimiter sentiamus de eis...*; Ib. 5, *Sic et fratribus nostris, inter quos vivimus, ipso jure fraternitatis et societatis humanae consilii sumus et auxilii debitores. Haec enim volumus ut et ipsi nobis impendant: consilium, quo erudiatur ignorantia nostra; auxilium, quo juvetur infirmitas nostra...*; Ib. 6, *Porro si cui forte praelatus es, huic sine dubio teneris debitor sollicitudinis amplioris. Exigit a te et ipse custodiam et disciplinam. Custodiam quidem ut possit cavere peccatum, disciplinam vero, ut quod minus cavit, minime maneat impunitum. Quod etsi nemini fratrum praeesse videris, habes tamen sub te, cui custodiam hanc et disciplinam oporteat exhiberi. Dico autem corpus tuum, quod sine dubio regendum accepit spiritus tuus. Debes ei custodiam, ut non regnet in eo peccatum, nec membra tua arma fiant iniquitati. Debes ei disciplinam, ut dignos faciat poenitentiae fructus, castigatus et subditus servituti. Longe tamen graviori et periculosiori debito tenentur astricti, qui pro multis animabus reddituri sunt rationem ... Quod si priora quoque quatuor non defuerint, dico autem erga praelatos reverentiam et obedientiam, consilium et auxilium erga fratres, quod ad justitiam pertinet non imparatam sedem inveniet Sapientia.*—Ib. 7, *Et fortassis hae videantur sex columnae, quas excidit in ipsa domo, quam aedificavit sibi: et septima quoque quaerenda est, si forte et eam nobis notam facere ipsa dignetur. Quid vero prohibet sicut sex in justitia, septimam quoque intelligi in judicio? Neque enim justitia sola, sed justitia, inquit, et judicium praeparatio sedis tuae (Ps. lxxxviii. 15).—Denique si praelatis, et aequalibus, et inferioribus reddimus quod oportet, nihilne accipiet Deus?*

11. *þat bieð ðo seuen hali mihtes ðe we hier teforen habbeð jespeken,* &c.; They are the so-called seven gifts of the Holy Spirit: *timor Domini*, p. 59; *pietas*, p. 63; *scientia*, p. 65; *consilium*, p. 71; *fortitudo*, p. 81; *intellectus*, p. 85; *sapientia*. Cf. Wulfstán's Hom. 50 seq. and 56 seq., where they are enumerated after Is. xi. 2, *Et requiescet super eum Spiritus Domini; spiritus sapientiae, et intellectus, spiritus consilii, et fortitudinis, spiritus scientiae, et pietatis;* ib. 3, *et replebit eum spiritus timoris Domini.*

13. *godes dradnesse,* &c. Cf. 59/19 seq. and note.

15 seq. = Gen. xxviii. 17 (the words of Jacob after his wonderful dream).

19. *He* is Christ, who is called *Sapientia Dei, Verbum Dei* (λόγος) in l. 18. Cf. above p. 25/14 and note.

19 seq. = John xiv. 23. It continues: *Sermonem meum servabit, et Pater meus diliget eum, et ad eum veniemus, et mansionem apud eum faciemus.*

P. 93, l. 5 seq. Cf. Gregorius in vii Psalmos poenit. Expos., Ps. xxxvii.

(Migne, 79/569 B), *Sicut jam dictum est, per ossa virtutes accipimus, quia sine eis nullum in anima robur habemus.*

11. = Ps. lxxii. 23 (lxxiii. 22).

12. *soð seggen.* See Fuhrmann, p. 52 seq.

14. = Ps. lxii. 2 (lxiii. 1). The Vulgate reads: . . . *quam multipliciter tibi caro mea.*

17. *his biliue, ðe ic . . . mid mine swote biȝatt,* is probably an allusion to Gen. iii. 19, *In sudore vultus tui vesceris pane (tuo).*

18 seq. The same request, see p. 47/14 seq.

22 seq. = 1 Cor. iii. 17, *Templum enim Dei sanctum est, quod estis vos.*

24 seq. is not "*ðar after,*" but the beginning of this verse.

28 seq. = 1 Cor. iii. 11.

31 seq. = Matth. xvi. 16.

P. 95, l. 2–14. Cf. note to p. 91/9.

9. *beloked* ought to have been translated "looks to."

10. *wiðinnen and wiðuten.* See *wiþþinnen and wiþþutenn,* Orm. 1603, 12156, and cf. Fuhrmann, p. 36.

ðe is alre kiningene kyng, is the biblical *rex regum.* Cf. 1 Tim. vi. 15; Apoc. xvii. 14, xix. 16. It occurs again on p. 141/26. For more examples see Mätzner, i. p. 416.

20. *spiraculum vite* is taken from Gen. ii. 7.

22. *al swo hie ðe is godes aȝen anlicnesse.* Cf. Gen. i. 27, *Et creavit Deus hominem ad imaginem suam,* etc.—Sap. ii. 23, *Quoniam Deus creavit hominem inexterminabilem, et ad imaginem similitudinis suae fecit illum.*—Sirach xvii. 1, *Deus creavit de terra hominem, et secundum imaginem suam fecit illum.*

24. *on hungre & on ðurste.* Cf. OE. *hunger & þurst,* Gen. 802; Guth. 246; Cri. 1661.—ME. (Mätzner, ii. p. 525): *hunger & þurst,* OEH. i. 33.—*þ. & h.,* ib. 79.—*chele & h., þ. & stench,* ib. ii. 173.—*All hiss hunngerr & hiss þrisst,* Orm. 5688.—*ne honger ne þorst,* Ayenb. p. 75.—*Of hard hongur & þirst,* Alex. & Dind. 1028.—*hounger & þurst,* Harr. of Hell, 50 (Digby MS.).—I add from Orm., *Wiþþ chele & þrisst & hunngerr,* 1615.—*Wiþþ pine off þ. & h.,* 3735.—*Wiþþ swinnc, wiþ h., & wiþþ þ.,* 5524.—*þiss h. & tiss þ.,* 5682.—*I chele, i þ., inn h.,* 18179.

26. *þat he wot ðe wot alle þing.* Cf. p. 75/2, *He it wot, ðe all wot,* and 143/4.

30. *non swo god leiȝe se teares.* Cf. Anselmus, Medit. in Ps. Miserere (Migne, 158/826), *lava lacrymarum lixivio calido et amaro per singulas noctes conscientiae meae stratum.*

31 seq. Contains an allusion to the parable of the royal marriage feast, Matth. xxii. 1–14.—*ðat faire scrud of charite* is the *vestis nuptialis,* verse 11 seq. Cf. Godefridi Abbatis Hom. domin. aestivales, hom. lxxxix (Migne, 174/615), *Sancti Patres et doctores per vestem nuptialem intelligendam esse dixerunt veram et perfectam charitatem, quod et nos credimus et intelligimus.*

P. 97, l. 7. *on his fader swiðer hand.* Cf. the Apostolic Creed, *Sedet ad dextram Dei Patris omnipotentis.*

18. *wat wel.* Cf. Fuhrmann, p. 56.

19 seq. = Ps. lxxv. 3 (lxxvi. 2).

21 seq. = Gal. v. 17.

25 seq. = Ib. *haec enim sibi invicem adversantur, ut non q.,* etc.

P. 99, l. 3. *to healden and to habben.* Cf. Fuhrmann, p. 28.

6 seq. are an allusion to the song of the angels, Luke ii. 14, ... *et in terra pax hominibus bonae vol.*
10. seq. = Ps. cxviii. 165 (cxix. 165).
14 seq. See Matth. x. 5 seqq., Luke x. 1-16.
16 seq. = Matth. x. 12, *Intrantes autem in domum, salutate eam, dicentes:* "*P. h. d.!*" and Luke x. 5, *In quamcunque domum intraveritis, primum dicite: "P. h. d."*
18-20. Cf. ib. 6, *Et si ibi fuerit filius pacis, requiescet super illum pax vestra; sin autem, ad vos revertetur.*
23 seq. Cf. Hugo of St. Victor, De Anima, l. iv. c. 13 (Migne, 177/185 B), *Contra quem* [viz. *diabolum*] *et ejus satellites pater idem, ... domum suam forti custodia muniens, Prudentiam in primo aditu constituat, quae discernat quid sit admittendum, quid vitandum, quid excludendum.* See above, note to p. 17/12, on this allegory. (The father is the soul, the house is the consciensce.)

P. 101, l. 7 seq. = Matth. xii. 34; Luke vi. 45.
17 seq. = Matth. x. 16.
19. is taken from the Physiologus. Cf. Lauchert, Geschichte des Phys., Strassburg, 1889, and Reinsch, Le Bestiaire, Leipzig, 1890. The Greek text (Lauchert, p. 243/34 seq.) says :—Τετάρτη φύσις τοῦ ὄφεως. ὅταν ἐπέλθῃ αὐτῷ ἄνθρωπος, θέλων αὐτὸν ἀποκτεῖναι, τὸ σῶμα αὐτοῦ ὅλον εἰς θάνατον παραδίδωσι, τὴν κεφαλὴν μόνην φυλάσσων. But the following moral application is quite different from that of our author. The Latin translation (in Cahier et Martin, Mélanges d'Archéologie, iv, Paris, 1856, p. 68 seq.) runs, *De IV. natura serpentis. Quando venerit homo et voluerit occidere eum, totum corpus tradit, caput autem custodit.* Cf. also OEH. ii. 195/17 seq., *Est equidem genus serpentum quod, cum timet periculum, occultat caput sub corpore, et corpus obicit periculo.*
33. = Ps. xvi. 8 (xvii. 8).

P. 103, l. 1 seq. *scild me fram alle ðes kennes eueles ðe cumeð fro ðe dieule* is a variation of the text, ib. 9, *a facie impiorum, qui me afflixerunt.*
6. *bien* is to be supplied as on p. 117/6, 139/4, 147/6.
Supply *poliȝe* after *harm.*
12. *Syon, þat is tokned "Sceawinge."* This interpretation of ציון is given by Hieronymus, Liber de Nominibus Hebraicis (Migne, 23/863), *Sion, specula, vel speculator, sive scopulus.*—Id. De Situ et Nomin. Loc. Hebraic. (l. c. p. 970), *Sion, mons urbis Jerusalem.*—Since Austin it is generally interpreted "*Speculatio*" (cf. e. g. Ælfric, Hom. i. p. 210, *Sión is án dún, and héo is gecweden "Scéawung-stów"*), and mystically used of the soul or the Church; but in none of the Fathers I have found the same application as in our author.
14 seq. A similar idea occurs in Boetius, Consolatio philosophiae, lib. v (ed. R. Peiper, Lipsiae, 1871, p. 141/67), *Unde non praevidentia sed providentia potius dicitur, quod porro a rebus infimis constituta quasi ab excelso rerum cacumine cuncta prospiciat.*
23. *ðo werewede gostes ðe waitið ðo soules hier buuen on ðe wolkne.* Cf. Wulfstán's Hom. xlviii. p. 248/23, *ne cépð nán hungrig man néfre his gereordes ná swiðor, þonne þá sceoccan dóð þére sáwle. ǽrest stæpð sé módiga déofol tó mid his gefilce and wyle wið þinre sáwle campian and þé upgebrédan ǽlc þéra þinga, þe þú wið god ágylte ... eall hyt býð þǽr cúð, and býð mycel gewinn betwéox déoflum and englum. gif þǽra misdǽda béoð*

má, þonne þǽra óðra, þonne willað þá déoflu habban þá geswenctan sáwle; gif
þǽr béoð gemette má þǽra gódra weorca, þonne þǽra óðra, þonne underfóð þá
englas þá éadigan sáwle mid myclum lofsange and hig gebringað tó ére blisse.
symle þú scealt, lá geornfulla godes cempa, understandan, þæt þú hæfst wið
strangne gemǽne. eall þis lyft ys full hellicra déofla, þá geondscríðað ealne
middangeard, &c. The same idea is also found in the beginning of the Old
High German poem Muspilli (after Braune, Ahd. Leseb.³ p. 78) :—

uuanta sár só sih diu sêla in den sind arhevit,
enti si den lihhamun likkan lázzit,
só quimit ein heri fona himilzungalon,
5 daz andar fona pehhe : dâr pâgant siu umpi.

. . . .

uuanta ipu sia daz Satanazses kisindi kiuuinnit,
daz leitit sia sár dâr iru leid uuirdit,
10 in fûir enti in finstrî, daz ist rehto virinlîh ding.

Cf. also Skeat, Notes to Piers Plowman, p. 36/127.

24. *on ðe wolkne*, would best be translated by "*in the welkin.*"
25. *ne* should probably be corrected into *ðanne*. Cf. foot-note 11.
26. *Quia nullum malum inpunitum.* Cf. Innocentii III, papae, De Contemptu mundi, sive de miseria conditionis humanae, lib. iii, c. 15 (Migne, 217/745), *Ipse est judex justus, ... qui ... nullum malum praeterit impunitum*, &c.
28. This is the beginning of an antiphona, used, "*In festo unius virginis non martyris, in laudibus.*" See Breviarium ad usum insignis ecclesiae Eboracensis, vol. ii. p. 66 seq. (Surtees Society, vol. lxxv, 1883). It runs on, *quam tibi dominus preparavit in eternum. Hec est virgo sapiens quam dominus vigilantem invenit.*

P. 105, l. 6. = Ps. lxxxviii. 15 (lxxxix. 14). The Vulgate has *tuae* instead of *ejus.* But cf. xcvi. 2 (xcvii. 2), *justitia et judicium correctio sedis ejus.*

7 seq. *Anima justi,* &c. This sentence is frequently quoted as a biblical one by the Fathers (e.g. St. Austin, Gregory, Paschasius Radbertus, Bernhard, &c.), and seems to be an early (Itala?) translation of Prov. xii. 23, where the LXX have : 'Ανὴρ συνετὸς θρόνος αἰσθήσεως.

12 seq. = Ps. cxlii. 2 (cxliii. 2).
16. The "bright angel" is Lucifer. Cf. above, note to p. 5/8.
17. *hie brohte Criste to ðe deaðe.* Cf. Zupitza, Engl. Stud. xiii. p. 390/442.
18. *Morte morieris* = Gen. ii. 17.
18 seq. *Ne scall ðar non atbersten,* &c. Cf. note to p. 7/19.
20 seq. *wandian* means "*vereri, negligere,* to be afraid of, to avoid."
22. = 1 Cor. xi. 31, *Quod si nosmetipsos dijudicaremus, non utique judicaremur.*
30. *Mihi vindictam.* Cf. note to p. 77/17.
33. *Ne dieuel ne mann.* Cf. OE. *déofla & monna,* Cri. 1628.

P. 107, l. 5 seq. Cf. the book De Anima, l. c. (see note to p. 99/23), *Secus hanc* [viz. *Prudentiam*], *Fortitudo locetur, ut hostes, quos Prudentia venire nuntiaverit, repellat.*

7. Cf. Ps. lx. 4 (lxi. 3), *Deduxisti me, quia factus es spes mea: turris fortitudinis a facie inimici.*

13. The semicolon after *þing* is wrong, for *oðer* means here "either." In the translation read accordingly : "overdone thing on either side."

18 seq. Cf. Pricke of Consc. 7481, *Bot als a bathe of water, nouther hate ne cald.*—For the same combination cf. OE. *hát & ceald,* Dan. 377; Dóm. 106; Sat. 132; and Mätzner, i. p. 388: *ne to chald ne to hot,* Ayenb. p. 153.—*oðer allunge cold, oðer hot mid alle,* Ancr. R. p. 400.—*ne wel chald be poer, ne wel hot,* Ayenb. p. 170. *& chald & hot,* ib. p. 139.—*þe hattore loue, þe caldore care,* Holy Rood, p. 143.—*Wiþþ hat & kald,* Orm. 3733.—*hang in colde & in hote,* Langt. p. 50.—Id. ii. 437 : *Hot & cold,* Harr. of Hell, 50.— *Of cold of hot,* Gower i. 36.—*Neiþer in hoot ne coolde,* Hymns to the Virgin, p 46.

P. 109, l. 1 seq. Cf. above note to p. 7/19.

4. *ealde & junge.* Cf. R. Meyer, p. 287; Breul, Sir Gowther, p. 192/758; Kaluza, Libeaus Desconus, p. 177/952. Brandl, Thomas of Erceldoune, gives other specimens of coupled contrasts on p. 137/423.

5. On *hwaðer ... ðe ... ðe* cf. Mätzner, Engl. Gr.³ iii. p. 388 seq.

6. *ðe heui ðe liht.* Cf. Orm. 4500, ... *itt iss nohht lihht To betenn hefiȝ sinne.*

7. Cf. Philip. ii. 8, ... *factus obediens usque ad mortem, mortem autem crucis.*

19 seq. *hie falleð mid ða blinde in to ðan pette,* &c. Cf. Matth. xv. 14, *Sinite illos ! caeci sunt, et duces caecorum. Caecus autem, si caeco ducatum praestet, ambo in foveam cadunt.*—Luke vi. 39, *Dicebat autem illis et similitudinem : " Numquid potest caecus caecum ducere ? Nonne ambo in foveam cadunt ?"*

20 seq. = Is. lvi. 10, *Speculatores ejus caeci omnes, nescierunt universi; canes muti non valentes latrare, videntes vana, dormientes, et amantes somnia.*— Earlier, Hieronymus, Comment. in Isaiam, lib. xv. c. 56 (Migne, 24/563 seq.), combines this passage with those words of Christ.

22 seq. For *ðe luue of godd,* &c. I do not understand this sentence, nor am I able to find out its connection with the preceding one.

24 seq. Cf. Gen. xv. 6, *Credidit Abram Deo, et reputatum est illi ad justitiam.*—Ib. xii. 3, ... *Atque in te benedicentur universae cognationes terrae.*—Ib. xxii. 18, *Et benedicentur in semine tuo omnes gentes terrae, quia obedisti voci meae.*

27. = Gen. xii. 1, *Dixit autem Dominus ad Abram : " Egredere de terra tua, et de cognatione tua, et de domo patris tui ; et veni in terram, quam monstrabo tibi."*

32 seq. Cf. the same allegorical application by Ambrosius, De Abraham, lib. i. c. ii. 4 (Migne, 14/443), *" Exi de cognatione tua:" consideremus ne forte hoc sit exire de terra sua, de hujus terrae, hoc est, de corporis nostri quadam commoratione egredi ; ... et de illecebris et delectationibus corporalibus quas velut cognatas animae nostrae dixit, quam compati necesse est corpori, donec ejus colligata vinculo adhaeret. Ergo exire de conversatione terrena, et saecularibus oblectamentis et superioris vitae moribus atque actibus debemus ; ut non solum loca, sed etiam nosmetipsos mutemus. Si cupimus adhaerere Christo, deseramus corruptibilia. Sunt autem corruptibilia in nobis caro, delectatio, vox obnoxia passionibus corporalibus,* &c.—Beda, Hexaëmeron, lib. iii (Migne, 91/137), *Nam et hoc quod ille jussus exiit de terra et cognatione et de domo patris sui, universis promissionis ipsius filiis, in quibus et nos sumus, constat imitandum. Egredimur quippe de terra nostra, cum carnis voluptates abdicamus ; de cognatione nostra, cum vitiis omnibus cum quibus*

nati sumus, in quantum hominibus possibile est, nos exuere studemus ; de domo patris nostri, cum ipsum mundum relinquere cum principe suo diabolo vitae coelestis amore contendimus.—Idem, in Pentateuchum Comment. Genesis, c. xii (l. c. 230), *Ad illius quoque exemplum nobis exeundum est de terra nostra, id est, de facultatibus hujus mundi. Et de cognatione nostra, de conversatione et moribus, vitiisque prioribus, quae nobis a nativitate velut consanguinitate conjuncta sunt. Et de domo patris nostri, id est, de omni memoria mundi hujus velut gentilitate, ut renuntiantes possinus dilatari in populum Dei, et terram coelestis repromissionis cum advenerit tempus, introduci.*—The same Isidorus, quoted by Walafrid Strabo, Glossa ord. (Migne, 113/116), Gen. c. xii.—Cf. finally Alcuini Interrogationes Sigeuulfi in Genesin (Anglia, vii. p. 41), [*CLIV.*] *Quid in tribus illis egressionibus intelligendum est, in quibus praecipitur a Domino Abrahae ut egrediatur de terra sua, et de cognatione sua, et de domo patris sui ? R*[*esponsio*]. *Nihil aliud nisi nobis egrediendum esse de terreno homine, et de cognitione vitiorum nostrorum, et de domo patris, id est, mundo, qui diaboli domus dicitur, ut in Psalmo : Obliviscere populum tuum, et domum patris tui* [Ps. xliv. 11].

34. *iboren & ec ifedd.* Cf. Mätzner, iii. p. 24 : *boren & yfed*, Lyr. P. p. 110. P. 111, l. 4 seq. = John xii. 31.

9. *ðat lond of ðare heuenliche Ierusalem.* Cf. Gal. iv. 26, *Illa autem, quae sursum est Jerusalem, libera est, quae est mater nostra.*—Heb. xii. 22, *Sed accessistis ad Sion montem, et civitatem Dei viventis, Jerusalem coelestem,* . . .—Apoc. iii. 12, . . . *Et nomen civitatis Dei mei novae Jerusalem, quae descendit de coelo a Deo meo,* . . .—Ib. xxi. 2, *Et ego Ioannes vidi sanctam civitatem Jerusalem novam, descendentem de coelo a Deo,* . . .

9 seq. Cf. Gen. xxii. 1, *Quae postquam gesta sunt, tentavit Deus Abraham, et dixit ad eum :* " *Abraham, Abraham !* " *At ille respondit :* " *Adsum.*"— Ib. 2, *Ait illi :* " *Tolle filium tuum unigenitum, quem diligis, Isaac, et vade in terram visionis ; atque ibi offeres eum in holocaustum super unum montium, quem monstravero tibi.*"

13. *be his rihte spuse*, viz. Sara.

13 seq. *ðat was bijeten on his michele ielde.* Cf. Gen. xxi. 5, *Cum centum esset annorum ; hac quippe aetate patris, natus est Isaac.*

14. *Isaac, þat is, blisse.* Cf. Beda's Hexaëmeron, lib. iv (Migne, 91/185), *Isaac interpretatur Risus sive Gaudium.*

26 seq. See John xi. 1 seq.

27 seq. That Lazarus was raised from two deaths is also said in the Blickling Homilies, p. 77/8 seq., *& þá unlǽdan noldan geþencean þæt Drihten hine mihte eft áweccean, swá hé hine ǽr of sáwle déaþe áwehte þurh þone mægenþrym.*

28 seq. See John viii. 3-11.

31 seq. See Matth. xxvi. 58, 69-75; Mark xiv. 54, 66-72; Luke xxii. 54-62; John xviii. 15-18, 25-27. Especially Luke xxii. 61, *Et conversus Dominus respexit Petrum* . . . ; ib. 62, *Et egressus foras Petrus flevit amare.*

33 seq. See Luke xxiii. 39-43.

P. 113, l. 1. Cf. ib. 43, *Et dixit illi Jesus :* " *Amen, dico tibi, hodie mecum eris in paradiso !* "

4. = Luke vi. 36, *Estote ergo misericordes, sicut et Pater vester misericors est*

5 seq. = Matth. v. 7. *Consequentur* is the wanting word.

8. seq. = Ps. lxxxiv. 11 (lxxxv. 10).

9. *Soð, þat is, godd.* Cf. 1 John v. 6, . . . *Et spiritus est, qui testificatur, quoniam Christus est veritas.*

12. The following allegory of the four Virtues, disputing before God about man's redemption, was a favourite subject of medieval literature. Cf. Zeitschrift für deutsches Alterthum, xvii. 43 seq., xxi. 414, xxiii. 184, xxiv. 389, xxv. 128; Herrig's Archiv für das Studium der neueren Sprachen, xxxiii. Jahrgang, 62. Band, p. 376-379; E. Schröder, Das Anegenge (Quellen u. Forschungen, xliv.), Strassburg, 1881, p. 55 seq.; C. Raab, Über vier allegor. Motive in der lat. u. deutschen Lit. des Mittelalters, Leoben, 1885 (Programm); Speculum vitae humanae, ed. minor, Halle, 1889 (Braune's Neudrucke, nr. 79 und 80), p. xxxi seq.; Skeat, Notes to Piers Plowman, p. 405/120.— In our text the tale occurs for the first time in ME. literature; later on we find it in :—

(1) The Romance of Chasteau d'Amour, a metrical version of Robert Grosseteste's French poem by "a munk of Sallay;" edited from the Egerton MS. 927 by M. Cooke for the Caxton Soc. (No. 15, R. Grossetete Carmina Anglo-Normannica. R. G.'s Chasteau d'Amour, &c.), London 1852, p. 133 seq. The allegory is on p. 138/148 seq.

(2) Castel off Loue, another version of the same, ed. from the Vernon and the Add. MS. 22283 of the Brit. Mus. by R. Fr. Weymouth for the Philol. Soc., London and Berlin, 1864 (see our story p. 13/275 seq.), and in the Minor Poems of the Vernon MS. ed. by Horstmann, for the E.E.T.S. On these two versions see Haase, " Die altengl. Bearbeitungen von Grosseteste's ' Chasteau d'Amour' verglichen mit der Quelle," in Anglia, xii. p. 311 seq., espec. p. 325 seq.

(3) The Cursor Mundi, ed. Morris, part ii. p. 549/9517 seq. (= pt. v. p. 1664). —Cf. Haenisch, Inquiry into the sources of the "Cursor Mundi," Dissert. Breslau, 1884, p. 23 seq. [now in Part vii of the C. M.].

(4) Will. Langland's Vision of Piers the Plowman, ed. Skeat, vol. ii, B-text, passus xviii. p. 328 seq. verse 112-227, and p. 341 seq. verses 406-424; vol. iii, C-text, pass. xxi. p. 373 seq. verses 117-239, and p. 393 seq. verses 453-471.

(5) De Principio Creationis Mundi, a poem of 440 short rhyme-pairs, edited from the Ash. MS. 61 by Horstmann, Altengl. Legenden, Neue Folge, Heilbronn, 1881, p. 349 seq. The allegory begins with verse 223.

(6) In Lydgate's Life of our Lady, late published in " English Religious Literature," No. 2, London 1871.

(7) The eleventh play, "The Salutation and Conception" of the Coventry Mysteries, ed. Halliwell, " Ludus Coventriae," London, 1841, p. 105 seq.

(8) The Morality of the Castel of Perseveraunse. Cf. ten Brink, Geschichte der engl. Litter. ii. 311 seq.; Pollard, English Miracle Plays, &c. Oxford, 1890, pp. xlviii, 64, and 197.

(9) Walter Kennedy's Poem "The passion of Christ," ed. by D. Laing in The Poems of Will. Dunbar, vol. ii. Edinb. 1834, p. 97 seq. The story is told in str. 5-7, p. 101 (cf. note p. 450).

(10) A prose translation of the Speculum Vitae Christi, ed. by Will. Hone, Ancient Mysteries, London, 1823, p. 73 seq. as "Council of the Trinity" from a vellum MS. in his possession.

18. See Gen. ii. 17, *De ligno autem scientiae boni et mali ne comedas. In quocumque enim die comederis ex eo, morte morieris.*

22. = Gen. i. 26, where *nostram* is added.

34. Cf. p. 7/20 and note.

P. 115, l. 5. *ðin handiwerc.* Cf. note to p. 13/7.

8. *welle of alle godnesse.* Cf. OEH. ii. 199/5, *ure drihten . . þe is alre lemene fader and welle of alle mihtin.*

29. Cf. above, p. 67/9.

31 seq. Cf. above, note to p. 109/25.

33. = Ps. cxxxi. 11 (cxxxii. 11).

P. 117, l. 2. = Ps. ii. 7, which continues *es tu, ego hodie genui te.*

5. Cf. note to p. 25/14, aud Ælfric's Hom. ii. 6, . . . *and his Wisdóm, þæt is, his Sunu, wæs æfre of him ácenned, búton ǽlcere méder. þeos ácennednys, þe wé nú tó-dæg wurðiað, wæs of eorðlicere méder, búton ǽlcum eorðlicum fæder.*

8. = Ps. ii. 8, *Postula a me, et dabo tibi gentes haereditatem tuam, et possessionem tuam terminos terrae;* ib. 9, *Reges eos in virga ferrea,* &c.

12 seq. are taken from Ps. xxxix. 7–9 (xl. 6–8) and Heb. x. 5–10, where the passage is applied to Christ. The Vulgate has (Ps. xxxix.), 7, *Sacrificium et oblationem noluisti; aures autem perfecisti mihi. Holocaustum et pro peccato non postulasti;* ib. 8, *Tunc dixi: "Ecce venio! In capite libri scriptum est de me;* ib. 9, *Ut facerem voluntatem tuam; Deus meus, volui, et legem tuam in medio cordis mei.*—Heb. x. 5, *Ideo ingrediens mundum dicit: "Hostiam et oblationem noluisti; corpus autem aptasti mihi;"* ib. 6, *Holocautomata pro peccato non tibi placuerunt;* ib. 7, *tunc dixi: "Ecce venio;" in capite libri scriptum est de me,"ut faciam, Deus! voluntatem tuam;"* ib. 8, *Superius dicens: "Quia hostias, et oblationes, et holocautomata pro peccato noluisti, nec placita sunt tibi," quae secundum legem offeruntur;* ib. 9, *Tunc dixi: "Ecce! venio, ut faciam, Deus! voluntatem tuam." Aufert primum, ut sequens statuat;* ib. 10, *In qua voluntate sanctificati sumus per oblationem corporis Jesu Christi semel.*

21. *te bien hersum godd anon to ðe deaðe.* Cf. note to p. 109/7.

22. = Ps. lxxxiv. 11 (lxxxv. 10).

24. = Ib. 12 (11).

26. = Gen. iii. 17.

28. = Ps. lxxxiv. 2 (lxxxv. 1).

28 seq. = Luke i. 28, *Et ingressus Angelus ad eam dixit: "Ave, gratia plena! Dominus tecum! Benedicta tu in mulieribus!"* This is confused with the words of Elizabeth, ib. 42, *"Benedicta tu inter mulieres, et benedictus fructus ventris tui!"* as we find it still in the *Ave Maria* of the Roman Church.

34. *he ðe was wisdom him self.* Cf. note to p. 25/14.

34 seq. This parallel between Eve and St. Mary is very frequent in the Fathers. Cf. Skeat, Notes to Piers Plowman, p. 151/250; Schröder, Das Anegenge, Strassburg, 1881 (QF. xliv), p. 64; Breul, Engl. St. xiv. 406/10.

P. 119, l. 1 seq. The forbidden tree of paradise and the holy cross are contrasted earlier in the Evangelium Nicodemi, pars ii (Descensus Christi ad inferos), c. vii (Tischendorf[2], p. 401), where Inferus says to Satan: "*Illas tuas divitias quas acquisieras per lignum praevaricationis et paradisi amissionem, nunc per lignum crucis perdidisti,* &c. They are also compared in OEH. i. 129/9: *ac him þuhte bicumelic þet we, þe weren þurh þe treo forgult in to helle, weren eft þurh þet treo of þere rode alesede.*

6. *ðane calde dieuel.* Further examples of this and similar expressions are

given by Mätzner, i. p. 60/5 and 608 (*He . . . schrencte þen alde deouel*, Leg. St. Kath. 1189).

he was hersum. Cf. note to p. 109/7.

9. *mid his eiȝene iseih*. Cf. Zupitza, Engl. Stud. xiii. p. 392/458, and in our text 125/9 and 16.—On this contrast between Adam and Christ, cf. Schröder, l. c.

21. *On ða watere*, &c. Cf. Ælfric, Hom. ii. 260/14: *þæt wæter witodlice wæs ǽre fulluht, on ðám béoð áðwogene ðéoda menigu fram fyrmlicere synne ðæs frumsceapenan mannes*.—OEH. i. 283/31: *þe water þat te world wesch of sake and of sunne*.—The Pearl, 652:—

> *þe water is baptem, þe soþe to telle,*
> *þat folȝed þe glayue so grymly grounde,*
> *þat waschez away þe gyltez felle,*
> *þat Adam wythinne deth vus drounde.*

For further parallels cf. Elard Hugo Meyer, Völuspa, Berlin, 1889, p. 121 seq.

26. *he ðe was soð lif*. Cf. John xiv. 6, *Dicit ei Jesus: " Ego sum via, et veritas, et vita*," &c.

29 seq. = Matth. xvii. 5.

P. 121, l. 1 seq. Cf. John xiv. 3, "*Et si abiero, et praeparavero vobis locum, iterum venio, et accipiam vos ad me ipsum, ut, ubi sum ego, et vos sitis.*"

6. *flū* was to be expanded as *flum*, see Mätzner, ii. p. 144, who gives numerous examples of the phrase *flum Jordan*. Cf. also Zupitza, Notes to Guy, p. 428/8712.

6 seq. = Matth. iv. 17, *Exinde coepit Jesus praedicare, et dicere: " Poen.*," &c.

12. I have not succeeded in finding this passage, but cf. Ambrosius, Sermo xxv (Migne, 17/677), *Poenitentia est et mala praeterita plangere, et plangenda iterum non committere*.—Gregorius, Homil. in Evangelia, lib. ii. hom. xxxiv (Migne, 76/1256), *Poenitentiam quippe agere est et perpetrata mala plangere, et plangenda non perpetrare*. Both are quoted by Vincentius Bellovacensis in his Speculum Morale, lib. iii, pars x, distinctio 1 (edition of the Benedictines, Duaci 1624, tom. iii, p. 1405).

15 is found in the Pseudo-Augustinean Book, De vera et falsa poenitentia, c. xix (Migne, 40/1128), *Poenitere enim est, poenam tenere: ut semper puniat in se ulciscendo, quod commisit peccando*.

17–23 is again a quotation from an unknown source.

25. *ðe* is construed ἀπὸ κοινοῦ as object to *nacoureð* and subject to *is forð ȝegan*.

30 seq. The author here gives a popular etymology of *andetnesse*, which must be attributed to, and is easily explained by, his dialect. In Old English, of course, *andetnes, and(h)ettan* (on which cf. Paul-Braune's Beiträge, vii. 121 seq.) had nothing to do with *undyttan*.

P. 123, l. 1. Is. xliii. 26, where the Vulgate reads, *narra, si quid habes, ut justificeris*, but the LXX, λέγε σὺ τὰς ἀνομίας σου πρῶτος, ἵνα δικαιωθῇς.

4 seq. are taken again from the Pseudo-Augustinean Book, De vera et falsa poenitentia (cf. above note to 121/15), c. x (Migne, 40/1122), *Sed qui per vos peccastis, per vos erubescatis. Erubescentia enim ipsa partem habet remissionis*, &c.

196   VICES AND VIRTUES.

7 seq. Cf. ib., *Fit enim per confessionem veniale, quod criminale erat in operatione.*

10 seq. = Ps. cv. 1 (cvi. 1), cvi. 1 (cvii. 1), cxvii. 1 (cxviii. 1), cxxxv. 1 (cxxxvi. 1). It ends: *quoniam in saeculum misericordia ejus.*

14 seq. *We findeð on ðe hali write,* &c. The same book is meant as above sub 4, c. x, *Tanta itaque vis confessionis est, ut si deest sacerdos, confiteatur proximo. Saepe enim contingit, quod poenitens non potest confiteri coram sacerdote, quem desideranti nec locus nec tempus offert. Et si ille cui confitebitur potestatem solvendi non habet, fit tamen dignus venia, ex desiderio sacerdotis, qui socio confitetur turpitudinem criminis.... Unde patet Deum ad cor respicere, dum ex necessitate prohibentur ad sacerdotes pervenire. Saepe quidem eos quaerunt sani et laeti: sed dum quaerunt et antequam perveniant ad eos, moriuntur.*

21 seq. Cf. Sirach v. 5, *De propitiato peccato noli esse sine metu, neque adjicias peccatum super peccatum.* Ib. 6, *Et ne dicas:* " *Miseratio Domini magna est, multitudinis peccatorum meorum miserebitur.*"

27. *ne beneðen . . . , ne abuuen.* Cf. OE. *ufan & neoðone,* Gen. 375; Met. 20/141.—Mätzner, i. p. 9 has: *Her bineðen & ȝund abuuen,* Gen. & Ex. 9.— *What above, what bynethe,* Pop. Sc. 87.—*Bathe fra aboven & fra byneþe,* Hamp. 611.—Id. 255: *buuen ba & bineoðen,* St. Marher. p. 4.—*Brod ase scheld buuen . . . & neruh bineoðen,* Ancr. R. p. 390.—*buuen, & eft seoððen bineoþen,* Laȝ. iii. 15.—*bothe aboven & benethen,* Maund. p. 158.—*His hore bineðe & him abuuen,* Gen. & Ex. 4081.—*Ofte heo weren buuenne, & ofte binoðen,* Laȝ. i. 160.—*He is buuen us & binoþen,* OEH. 165.—Ib. 362: *buuen ba & bineoðen,* St. Marher. p. 4.—*He is buuen us & bineþen,* Mor. Ode, st. 44.

28. *wat wel.* Cf. Fuhrmann, p. 56.

32 seq. = Is. lii. 11.

P. 125, l. 1 seq. = Ps. cxviii. 11 (cxix. 11).

4 seq. Cf. Luke ii. 19, *Maria autem conservabat omnia verba haec, conferens in corde suo.*

7. = Matth. v. 8.

9 seq. Cf. Augustinus, De Sermone Domini in monte sec. Matthaeum, lib. ii. c. ii. 8 (Migne, 34/1232), *Quam ergo stulti sunt qui Deum istis exterioribus oculis quaerunt, cum corde videatur, sicut alibi scriptum est,* " *Et in simplicitate cordis quaerite illum*" *(Sap. i. 1). Hoc est enim mundum cor, quod est simplex cor: et quemadmodum lumen hoc videri non potest, nisi oculis mundis; ita nec Deus videtur, nisi mundum sit illud quo videri potest.*

14 seq. Cf. Liber de Spiritu et Anima, c. xxxviii (Migne, 40/809), *Ratio est quaedam vis animae, quae omnia discernit et judicat; . . . Intellectus est rerum vere existentium perceptio.*

23. *sunne & mone.* Cf. Meyer, p. 287.

28 seq. = Ps. ii. 12, *Apprehendite disciplinam, ne quando irascatur Dominus, et pereatis de via justa.*

P. 127, l. 3. *ða ane rihte weiȝ þe gað to heuene.* Cf. 2 Pet. ii. 15, *Derelinquentes rectam viam erraverunt.*

6 seq. = Is. vi. 10, *Excaeca cor populi hujus, et aures ejus aggrava, et oculos ejus claude; ne forte videat oculis suis, et auribus suis audiat, et corde suo intelligat, et convertatur, et sanem eum,*

10. *þat ðe blinde latt ðane blinde.* Cf. note to p. 109/19, and Matth. xxiii. 16, *Vae vobis, duces caeci!* Ib. 24, *Duces caeci,* &c. Rom. ii. 19, *con-*

filiis te ipsum esse ducem caecorum, &c. Ib. 21, *Qui ergo alium doces, te ipsum non doces ; qui praedicas non furandum furaris*, &c.

11 seq. *and ec he him lareð*, &c. Cf. Wulfstán's Hom. 55/23, *cwepað éac tó worde þá, ðe syndan stunte, þæt mycel forhæfednes lýtel behealde, ac þæt mete wǽre mannum gescapen tó ðám ánum, þæt men his scoldan brúcan, and wimman éac tó hǽmede þám, ðe þæs lyste*.

12. *ne for wifmanne, ðe godd haueð ȝescapen manne to ȝemoane*. Cf. Gen. ii. 18, *Dixit quoque Dominus Deus : " Non est bonum, esse hominem solum ; faciamus ei adjutorium simile sibi."* For the alliteration cf. Mätzner, ii. p. 353 : *Monnes imone*, OE. Misc. p. 100.—*wythoute mannes ymone*, Shoreh. p. 118.—*of monnes imeane*, Hali Meid. p. 25.

17 seq. = Ps. xii. 4 (xiii. 3), *Illumina oculos meos, ne unquam obdormiam in morte*; ib. 5, *ne quando dicat inimicus meus : " Praevalui adversus eum!" Qui tribulant me, exultabunt, si motus fuero.*

20. *ðe heiȝere hand.* See Mätzner, ii. pp. 418/2 b and 459/6.

20 seq. = Ps. cxviii. 66 (cxix. 66), which ends, *quia mandatis tuis credidi.*

28 seq. = Matth. v. 39, *"Ego autem dico vobis, non resistere malo ; sed si quis te percusserit in dexteram maxillam tuam, praebe illi et alteram.* Ib. 40, *Et ei, qui vult tecum judicio contendere, et tunicam tuam tollere, dimitte ei et pallium !* Ib. 41, *Et quicunque te angariaverit mille passus, vade cum illo et alia duo!"*—Luke vi. 29, *" Et qui te p^ercutit in maxillam (unam), praebe (illi) et alteram. Et ab eo, qui aufert tibi vestimentum, etiam tunicam noli prohibere."*

32 seq. *wisdom hit sade*, viz. Christ. Cf. note to p. 25/14.

P. 129, l. 1. *wið-uten senne one*. Cf. 51/11, and note.

2 seq. = Prov. xvi. 32, which goes on, *et qui dominatur animo suo, expugnatore urbium.*

7. *on ðe smec-huse of ðine likame*. Cf. (?) Sap. ii. 2, *Quoniam fumus flatus est in naribus nostris ; et sermo scintilla ad commovendum cor nostrum;* Ib. 3, *qua extincta, cinis erit corpus nostrum, et spiritus diffundetur tamquam mollis aër*, &c.

14. *maidenhad, ðe folȝið ðe hali lombe*. Cf. Apoc. xiv. 4, *Hi sunt, qui cum mulieribus non sunt coinquinati; virgines enim sunt. Hi sequuntur Agnum quocunque ierit.*

16 seq. *Hie behet maidenhad to healden.* Cf. note to p. 55/5.

17. *and hie wel it ȝelaste.* According to the traditional doctrine of the Fathers, St. Mary remained a virgin after she was married to Joseph.

19 seq. Cf. Matth. xix. 11, *Qui dixit illis : " Non omnes capiunt verbum istud, sed quibus datum est.* Ib. 12, *... et sunt eunuchi, qui se ipsos castraverunt propter regnum coelorum. Qui potest capere, capiat !"*—1 Cor. vii. 1, *De quibus autem scripsistis mihi : Bonum est homini mulierem non tangere.* Ib. 7, *Volo enim omnes vos esse, sicut me ipsum ; sed unusquisque proprium donum habet ex Deo ...*.—Ib. 8, *Dico autem non nuptis, et viduis : bonum est illis, si sic permaneant, sicut et ego.* Ib. 25, *De virginibus autem praeceptum Domini non habeo ; consilium autem do, tanquam misericordiam consecutus a Domino, ut sim fidelis.* Ib. 38, *Igitur et qui matrimonio jungit virginem suam, bene facit : et qui non jungit, melius facit.*

24. = Matth. xix. 12.

30. = Hebr. xii. 14, *Pacem sequimini cum omnibus, et sanctimoniam, sine qua nemo videbit Deum.*

P. 131, l. 9 seq. I have not found these sayings in St. Austin's works, but cf. Enarrat. in Ps. lxxv. 16, verse 12 (Migne, 36/968), *Quid si enim sit corpore integra, et mente corrupta?* with l. 12 seq., and the same Father's words as quoted in Defensor's Liber Scintillarum (Migne, 88/632), *Nihil prodest virginitas corporis ubi operatur corruptio mentis.*—Ib. Hieronymus, *Nihil prodest carnem habere virginem, si mente quis nupserit.*

17. As Kölbing has shown (Sir Tristrem, p. 137, note 828), *forliggen* is also used of legitimate matrimonial intercourse. The same is certainly meant here, and so we have to translate, " after the copulation."

22 seq. = 2 Cor. xi. 2.
25 seq. Cf. note to p. 27/5.
28 seq. = Rom. viii. 35.

P. 133, l. 7 seq. The children of Bethlehem are meant. Cf. Matth. ii. 16. Their festival is the 28th of December, called "Innocents' Day." In the Roman Church, they are canonized as saints.

14. = Prov. xi. 21, where the Vulgate reads *in manu*.

15 seq. Cf. Beda, Super Parabolas Salomonis allegorica Expositio, lib. ii. c. xi (Migne, 91/972), *Qui manum jungit in manu, nil utique operatur. Sed manus in manu, non erit innocens malus, quia etsi ab impia actione manus ad horam subtrahit, cordis tamen innocentiam malus habere non valet. Unde et praemittitur : " Abominale Domino cor pravum."*

21. *bien abuten* means "are intent upon," cf. Mätzner, i. p. 11/3. Cf. also the New English Dictionary, i. p. 29/11, " To be about (*for*) to do, to ·be engaged in, to be busied in preparation for, to be scheming, preparing, or intending.

24 seq. Here we find for the first time in English literature a specimen of those rules of behaviour, which later on became a much cultivated and relished branch of popular writing. Cf. The Babees Book, ed. Furnivall (E.E.T.S. 32), especially p. 13, "Urbanitas," 17 :—

Foot and hond þou kepe fulle stylle
Fro clawyng or tryppyng, hit ys skylle.

(Cf. l. 31 seq.); and R. Weste's Booke of Demeanor, p. 296/149 :—

And in thy sitting use a meane, as may become thee well,
Not straddling, no nor tottering, and dangling like a bell.

29 seq. *þanne hie wið gode scall speken on hire benes.* Cf. note to p. 141/19.

31. *baðe his handen & hise fett.* Cf. Mätzner, ii. p. 193 seq.: *bi hondes oðer bi fot*, La3. i. 434.—*binden ham swa þe fet & te honden*, Leg. St. Kath. 1866.—*band itt fet & hande*, Orm. 14672.—*mid foten & mid honden*, OEH. ii. 179.— Id. p. 417: *fote & hand*, Ywain & Gaw. 2086.—*Boþe here feet & here handes*, Ass. B. Marie, 713.—*his fet and his hondan*, OEH. i. 23.—*bunden by hend & fete*, Hamp. 3214.

P. 135, l. 1. *pleiȝende mid . . . strawe*. Cf. Cant. Tales, The Maunciple's prologue, 44 seq.:—

"*I trowe that ye dronken han wyn ape,
And that is whan men pleyen with a straw.*"

13 seq. = 1 Pet. ii. 11, *Charissimi! obsecro vos tamquam advenas et peregrinos abstinere vos a carnalibus desideriis, quae militant adversus animam.*

16 seq. = 2 Thess. iv. 3 seq., which ends, *in sanctificatione et honore*. *ȝiet he* is a slip, as the apostle above (13) is *St. Peter*, but here *St. Paul*.

22 seq. Cf. ib. 8, *Itaque, qui haec spernit, non hominem spernit, sed Deum; qui etiam dedit Spiritum suum sanctum in nobis.*

P. 137, l. 3 seq. See Jonah iii.

4. *Niniue, ðare muchele burʒh ðe ʒelaste ðrie daiʒes fare,*=l. c. 3, *et Ninive erat civitas magna itinere trium dierum.*

8 seq. See Matth. iv. 1, *Tunc Jesus ductus est in desertum a Spiritu, ut tentaretur a diabolo.* Ib. 2, *Et cum jejunasset quadraginta diebus, et quadraginta noctibus, postea esuriit.*—Luke iv. 1, . . . *et agebatur a Spiritu in desertum;* ib. 2, *diebus quadraginta, et tentabatur a diabolo. Et nihil manducavit in diebus illis,* &c.

13 seq. See Exod. xxiv. 18, *Ingressusque Moyses medium nebulae, ascendit in montem; et fuit ibi quadraginta diebus, et quadraginta noctibus.*—Ib. xxxiv. 28, *Fuit ergo ibi cum Domino quadraginta dies et quadraginta noctes; panem non comedit, et aquam non bibit, et scripsit in tabulis verba foederis decem.* Cf. also Deut. ix. 9-18.

14 seq. Cf. 3 (1) Reg. xix. 8, *Qui cum surrexisset, comedit et bibit, et ambulavit in fortitudine cibi illius quadraginta diebus et quadraginta noctibus, usque ad montem Dei Horeb.* The fasting of Christ, Moses, and Elijah is also mentioned, for the same reasons, in Wulfstán's Hom. lv. 285/15 seq. and in Ælfric's Hom. ii. 100.

25. *all þat none.* On *noon* cf. Skeat, Notes to Piers Plowman, p. 165.

26 seq. To drink during fasting is also forbidden in Wulfstán's Hom. xvii. 102/24 seq., . . . *healde his fæsten swýðe rihtlíce, þæt is, þæt ǽfre ǽnig cristen man ǽnige dæge ǽr nóntíde náðor ne ábyrige ne ǽtes ne wǽtes, búton hit for unhǽle sý* . . . Ib. 103/8, *and beorge húru manna gehwylc wið oferdruncen him georne, forðám Críst hit forbéad sylf on his godspelle; and witodlice, þeah hwá on dæg gefæste ful lange, gyf hé syððan hine sylfne gedweleð mid gedrynce and mid oferfylle ealles tó swýðe, eal him bið þæt fæsten ídel geworden.*

30 seq.=Philip. iii. 18 seq. The whole passage runs, *Multi enim ambulant, quos saepe dicebam vobis (nunc autem et flens dico) inimicos crucis Christi;* ib. 19, *quorum finis interitus, quorum Deus venter est, et gloria in confusione ipsorum, qui terrena sapiunt.*

33. *icwemen, & him betst hersumen.* Cf. OEH. i. 221/8, *hu hi mugon god hihersamian & him ʒecwemen.*

P. 139, l. 1.=1 Cor. vi. 10, *neque ebriosi,* . . . *regnum Dei possidebunt.*

4. The same counsel has already been given by St. Austin. Cf. Blickl. Hom. p. 99/12, "*Ic éow hálsige,*" *cwæþ Águstínus,* "*þæt gé gongan tó byrgenne weligra manna, þonne magon gé geséon sweotole bysene,* &c.

5 seq. Such detailed descriptions of a rotting corpse were a favourite theme of medieval moralists and preachers.

7. *ðe faire fiere.* Mätzner gives (ii. 234): *and maked hir a ful fair fer,* Seuyn Sag. 2603, cf. 2635.

16 seq.=1 Pet. v. 8. The end is, *quia adversarius vester diabolus tanquam leo rugiens circuit, quaerens, quem devoret.*

20 seq. I do not know whence this definition is taken.

28.=2 Cor. ix. 7. The Vulg. has, *hilarem enim datorem,* &c.

30 seq. *Chierche-þinges,* . . . *ne awh me nauhwer to ʒiuene,* &c. Cf. Ayenbite of Inwyt, p. 41, *Of þise zennes ne byeþ naʒt kuytte þo þet þe guodes of holy cherche, þe patremoyne of Jesu Crist, despendeþ ine kueade us.*

P. 141, l. 12 seq.=1 John iii. 21, *Charissimi! si cor nostrum non reprehenderit nos, fiduciam habemus ad Deum;* ib. 22, *et quidquid petierimus, accipiemus ab eo.*

14 seq. *ðe godd hateð & ðe luuieð* ought to have been translated: "which hates God and loves thee."

19 seq. *Ðanne we on boke radeð*, &c. Cf. Sermo 302 of the Sermones suppositi S. Augustini (Migne, 39/2324), *Nam cum oramus, ipsi cum Deo loquimur; cum vero legimus, Deus nobiscum loquitur*. A part of this sermon forms ch. v, "De lectionis studio" of Alcuin's Liber de virtutibus et vitiis, where the same sentence occurs (Migne, 101/116). Again, it is quoted as a saying of Isidor in Defensor's Liber Scintillarum, c. 80, "De lectione" (Migne, 88/715).

21 seq. This comparison of prayer with speaking before the king in open court may be an extension from ch. xx of St. Benet's Rule, *Si cum hominibus potentibus volumus aliqua suggerere, non praesumimus nisi cum humilitate et reverentia, quanto magis Domino Deo universorum omni humilitate et puritatis devotione supplicandum est!*

at te kinge . . . into his halle. Cf. King Horn, ed. Wissmann, verse 472, *Bifore þe king in halle.*—Havelock, 157, *Bifore þe king into þe halle*.

26. *ðe is alre kinge king.* Cf. above, p. 95/10, and note.

30. = Matth. xxvi. 39. The Vulgate leaves out *vis*.

P. 143, l. 1. = Matth. vi. 6; which continues, *et clauso ostio, ora patrem tuum in abscondito; et pater tuus, qui videt in abscondito, reddet tibi*.

2. *ȝebidden ðe* is an old construction with the reflex. dat., cf. Mätzner, i. p. 227/5.

4. *he þe wat . . . alle þing*. Cf. p. 95/26, and note.

5. This interpretation goes back to Hieronymus, Comment. in Ev. Matthaei, lib. i. c. vi (Migne, 26/43), *Sed mihi videtur hoc magis esse praeceptum, ut inclusa pectoris cogitatione, labiisque compressis oremus Dominum*, &c.—Beda, in Matth. Ev. Expos. lib. i. c. vi (Migne, 92/32), *Id est, revertere in mundam cordis conscientiam de visibilibus ad orandum invisibilem Dominum, et claude ostium carnalium et phantasmatum; . . . ut intimo corde ad Patrem spiritalis dirigatur oratio*.

10. = Matth. xiv. 23. The Vulg. leaves out *Jesus*.

14. Cf. p. 137/10.

16. *hure and hure* ought to have been translated "at least." For the duplication see Mätzner, ii. p. 529.

22. = Ps. cxl. 2 (cxli. 2), *Dirigatur oratio mea sicut incensum in conspectu tuo*.

26. = James v. 16.

28 seq. Cf. ib. 17, *Elias homo erat similis nobis passibilis, et oratione oravit, ut non plueret super terram, et non pluit annos tres et menses sex*. Ib. 18, *Et rursum oravit; et coelum dedit pluviam, et terra dedit fructum suum*. See 3 (1) Reg. xvii. seq.

P. 145, l. 3 seq. = Prov. xxviii. 9, *Qui declinat aures suas*, &c.

7. = Is. lviii. 9, *Tunc invocabis, et Dominus exaudiet; clamabis, et dicet: "Ecce adsum!"*

12. = Luke xviii. 13.

24. See Luke xxii. 61, 62. (Cf. also note above to p. 111/31.)

26. See Luke xxiii. 33, 39–43. (Cf. also note to p. 113/1.) The Scripture does not tell us that it was the "thief" on Christ's right hand who was pardoned, but this has been the traditional assumption after the apocryphal "Gesta Pilati" (cf. note to 17/30). They tell us (Tischendorf[2], cap. x. p. 361 seq.),

Similiter et duos latrones suspenderunt cum eo, Dismam a dextris et Gestam a sinistris.... Unus autem de suspensis latronibus nomine Gestas dixit ei: "*Si tu es Christus, libera te ipsum et nos.*" *Respondens autem* [D^a : *latro qui a dextra eius suspensus erat nomine*] *Dismas conturbavit eum.... Et dicebat ad Jesum:* "*Memento mei, domine, in regno tuo.*" *Dixit autem illi Jesus:* "*Amen dico tibi quia hodie mecum eris in paradiso.*"

27 seq. Cf. above note to p. 85/17.

33. *fordruʒede hierte*. Cf. p. 83/1.

P. 147, l. 3 seq. Cf. with this chapter OEH. i. 155 seq. and ii. 145.

6 seq. = Ps. xli. 4 (xlii. 3).

9. = Ps. vi. 7 (6).

10 seqq. Cf. Gregorius, in vii Psalmos Poenitent. Expos., Ps. vi. (Migne, 79/556), *Per lectum, conscientiam accipimus; quia sicut in lecto jacentes quiescimus, ita in ea vel legi Dei, vel legi peccati consentimus. Et sicut laboribus pressi in lecto quiescentes reficimur, ita dum mundi hujus adversitatibus premimur, in bona conscientia interius delectamur,... Lectum ergo per singulas noctes lavat, qui conscientiam a cogitationibus tenebrosis, lacrymis compunctionis emundat.... Rigat ergo lacrymis stratum suum, quia continuo luctu et dolore carnis maculas diluit, et cordis duritiam imbre compunctionis emollit,* &c.—St. Bernhard, In festo omnium sanctorum sermo iii (Migne, 183/467 C), *Hoc est suavissimum animae stratum, quod nullis jam lavet aut riget lacrymis,... Hoc plane stratum animae, quod minime jam versatur in infirmitate ejus;... Haec est, inquam, animae suavissima et saluberrima requies, conscientia munda, quieta, secura.*—Ayenbite of Inwyt, p. 171,... *and ofte mid his teares his bed wesse, þet is, his inwyt.* Cf. also notes to pp. 143/5 and 95/30.

15 seq. See 2 Kings xx. 1-6; Is. xxxviii. 1-5.

16. = Ib. xxxviii. 1.

19. *swiðe lef to libben.* Cf. Patience, 156, *þe lyf is ay swete.*—York Plays, p. 65/279, *lyff is full swete.*—Sprüche des h. Bernhard (Angl. iii. p. 65), 165, *His lif þat wes so lef.*—Every German will at once be reminded of Marquis Posa's words in Schiller's Don Carlos, iv. 21, *O Gott! das Leben ist doch schön.* Cf. also Goethe's Egmont, v, *Süsses Leben, schöne, freundliche Gewohnheit des Daseins....*

19 seq. Cf. Is. xxxviii. 2, *Et convertit Ezechias faciem suam ad parietem, et oravit ad Dominum;* ib. 3, *et dixit:* "*Obsecro, Domine! memento quaeso, quomodo ambulaverim coram te in veritate, et in corde perfecto, et quod bonum est in oculis tuis, fecerim.*" *Et flevit Ez. fletu magno.*

24 seq. See 2 Kings xx. 4, *Et antequam egrederetur Isaias mediam partem atrii, factus est sermo Domini ad eum, dicens:* ib. 5, "*Revertere, et dic Ezechiae duci populi mei...*"

25 seq. = Is. xxxviii. 5, "*Audivi orationem tuam, et vidi lacrymas tuas; ecce! ego adjiciam super dies tuos quindecim annos.*"

31. = Ps. lxxix. 6 (lxxx. 5).

P. 149, l. 1 seq. = Ib.

9 seq. See Vitae Patrum, lib. iv. c. 42 (Migne, 73/841),... *Universorum sententia definitum est, discretionem esse quae fixo gradu intrepidum monachum perducat ad Deum, et praedictas virtutes jugiter conservet illaesas. Omnium namque virtutum genitrix et custos atque moderatrix discretio est.*

12 seq. Cf. ib. 840 B, *Quodam autem tempore convenerunt plurimi*

seniorum ad beatum Antonium, commorantem in Thebaidae partibus, perfectionis inquisitione et collationis gratia. Cumque a vespertinis horis usque ad lucem fuisset protracta collatio, quaestio discretionis maximum noctis spatium consumpsit. Nam diutissime inter eos quaerebatur, quaenam virtus vel observatio monachum a diaboli laqueis custodire posset illaesum, vel certe ad Deum recto tramite firmoque gressu perduceret. Cumque pro captu mentis suae unusquisque sententiam proferret in medium; et alii quidem hoc in jejuniorum vigiliarumque studio collocarent, alii in nuditate et contemptu rerum, alii remotiorem vitam et eremi secretam censerent; et nonnulli in primis sectanda charitatis, id est, humanitatis officia definirent (quia ipsa pie erga fratres et peregrinos studio susceptionis impenduntur); cumque in hunc modum pia contentione decertarent, essetque jam noctis maximum tempus consumptum, respondens demum beatus Antonius universis, dixit: "Omnia quidem haec quae dixistis, necessaria sunt et utilia sitientibus Deum: sed his principalem tribuere gratiam, nequaquam nos innumerabiles multorum fratrum casus et experimenta permittunt. Nam saepe vidimis fratres has observationes tenentes, repentino casu deceptos, eo quod in bono quod coeperant, discretionem minime tenuerunt. Nec etiam alia causa lapsus eorum deprehenditur, nisi quod minus a senioribus instituti, nequaquam potuerunt rationem discretionis hujus adipisci, quae viam regiam docet monachum semper incedere, et nec excessu continentiae modum transire permittit, nec deflectere ad vitia concedit. In omnibus ergo quae agimus, discretio anteponenda est. Manifestissime enim declaratur nullam sine discretionis gratia perfecte posse vel perfici vel stare virtutem.

13. *togedere igadered.* Cf. Mätzner, ii. p. 240: *Gadred folk togider*, Langt. p. 21.—*gedere togidere*, Wycl. Ex. xxiii. 10.—*gederen togederes*, Leg. St. Kath. 988.—Ib. p. 343: *igedered togederes*, Ancr. R. p. 74.

17. *feden & screden.* Cf. Mätzner, ii. p. 85: *to feden & to shruden*, OEH. ii. 157.—*He hine lette ueden, he hine lette scruden*, La3. i. 381.—*fet & shrut*, OEH. ii. 107.—Ib. iii. p. 24: *He us haueð wel iued, he us haueð wel iscrud*, La3. ii. 143.

24 seq. *sume wel a-gunnen*, &c. Cf. Ælfric, Hom. i. p. 532, *Sume menn habbað gód anginn sume hwíle, ac hi geendiað on yfele.*

29 seq. Cf. Lev. xxii. 19, *Ut offeratur per vos, masculus immaculatus erit ex bobus, et ovibus, et ex capris;* ib. 20, *si maculam habuerit, non offeretis, neque erit acceptabile;* ib. 23, *Bovem et ovem, aure et cauda amputatis, voluntarie offerre potes, votum autem ex eis solvi non potest.* See also Deut. xv. 21, *Sin autem habuerit maculam, vel claudum fuerit, vel caecum, aut in aliqua parte deforme vel debile, non immolabitur Domino Deo tuo.*—Ib. xvii. 1, *Non immolabis Domino Deo tuo ovem, et bovem, in quo est macula, aut quidpiam vitii; quia abominatio est Domino Deo tuo.*

P. 151, l. 1 seq. Cf. Rab. Maurus, Allegoriae (Opp. vol. v. p. 762), *Cauda est perseverantia, ut in lege jubetur auferri in sacrificio, quod habeatur perseverantia in bono opere.*

3 seq. = Matth. x. 22.

8 seq. *he it wat þat wot alle þing.* Cf. p. 95/26, and note.

9. *for ðe to wissin, for ðe to warnin.* Cf. p. 21/27, and note.

21. *se ðe liueð & rixeð*, &c. is the translation of the Latin doxology, *qui vivit et regnat per omnia saecula saeculorum. Amen.*

23 seq. *ofte and 3elome.* For more examples of this phrase see Mätzner,

iii. p. 46; Lewin, Poema morale, p. 74, note to verse 47. I add, *ilome & ofte*, Owl & Night. 1545. It occurs already in OE. Cf. Meyer, p. 289, and Blickling Hom. 209/14, *oft & gelóme*.

25 is the beginning of the celebrated hymn which was formerly ascribed to Charlemagne, but is much older, as Mone has shown. He thinks the pope St. Gregory was its author (Lat. Hymnen des M. A. i. 242).

ADDITIONAL NOTES.

P. 13, l. 9. *Fremde & sibbe* occurs also in Altengl. Legenden, ed. Horstmann, Paderborn, 1875, p. 29/843, 60/1831 (Kindheit Jesu).

P. 21, l. 16. Cf. *before and ek behinde*, Kaluza, Libeaus Desconus, 134, and note.

P. 33, l. 5. Cf. l. c. *þat fier briȝt gan berne*, 628.—*was liȝt & brende briȝt*, 1869.—*brenninge faire & briȝt*, 1887 (cf. note).

14. Cf. *gold, selver, & lond*, Altengl. Leg. p. 130/603.—*gold & selver*, ib. p. 140/976.—*gold ne silver*, Cant. Tales, Pard. prol. 440, Chan. Yem. t. 1050 (Skeat's ed.).

P. 35, l. 4. Cf. *for child ne wif*, Altengl. Leg. p. 127/490.—*wif & childrin*, ib. p. 130/600 (Barl. & Jos.).

P. 43, l. 28 seq. and 45, 8 (world a sea). Cf. Roethe, Die Gedichte Reinmars von Zweter, Leipzig, 1887, p. 613, note to 170.

P. 45, l. 14 seq. *ure ropes. . . . ðe bieð ibroiden mid þrie strænges, of rihte ileaue and of faste hope te gode and of ðare soðe luue*. This allegory is founded on Eccl. iv. 12, *funiculus triplex difficile rumpitur*, as explained by Rupertus, abbas Tuitiensis, Comment. in Eccles. (Migne, 168/1239 A), *Numquid his abesse debet fides, spes, charitas?*—About 1490, Nic. Rutze, of Rostock, wrote a little book on the same subject in Low German, "Dat bôkeken van deme rêpe," ed. by K. Nerger, Rostock, 1886 (Gymnas. Progr. no. 594).

P. 67, l. 9 seq. Cf. Haeckel, Das Sprichwort bei Chaucer (Erlanger Beitr. viii), p. 47/159.

P. 83, l. 21. Add: *bliþe & glad*, Altengl. Leg., Kindheit Jesu, 1725, 1814.—*bl. & glade*, ib. 1791, 1795.—*glad & bliþe*, Lib. Desc. 1270; 1630, 1762, 2143, 2191, 2220k (p. 126).—*glad & blythe*, Cant. Tales, Squieres t. 338 (Skeat's ed.). —*gladde & blythe*, ib. Chan. Yem. t. 937.—*bliþe & glad*, Engl. Stud. vii. 117/396.

P. 129, l. 22 seq. *Hit is angelich lif of heuene*, &c. Cf. Augustinus, Sermo cxxxii, cap. iii, *Mementote in quocumque sexu sitis, sive mares, sive feminae, angelorum vitam ducere vos in terra. Angeli enim non nubunt, neque uxores ducunt* (Migne, 38/736).

P. 131, l. 12. Cf. Augustinus, Enarrat. in Ps. xc (verse 13), 9 (Migne 37/1168), *quam qui perdiderint, sine causa sunt virgines corpore. Corrupta enim corde quid servat in corpore?*

INDEX TO THE PRINCIPAL NOTES.

A star refers to the additional notes.

Abraham's emigration, allegorically explained, 109/32.
Adam 5000 years in hell, 7/20.
adnomination, 23/20, 31/11, 49/29, 51/3, 55/16, 59/2, 149/13.
Allegory of the four Virtues, 113/12.
andettan, 121/30.
ἀπὸ κοινοῦ, 61/14, 121/25.
appearance of the devil, 19/5.
are and forjiveneſſe, 15/33.
are and mildze, 21/10.
ark of Noah, the Church, 43/28.
arm "poor," 17/24.
auht as adverb, 39/4.

bad reasons for doing good, 5/28.
bare, 63/19.
barrenness cursed, 55/2.
becnawe bien "to confess," 7/6.
bed of conscience, 147/10.
*before & behind, 21/16.
behotes behaten, 31/11.
beneðen & abuven, 123/27.
beren ȝewitnesse, 41/5.
beseech & bid, 47/14.
beseech to, 21/6.
bezant, 17/5.
bien abuten, 133/21.
bien (to be supplied), 103/6.
bind with bond, 49/29.
bladder full of wind, 73/18.
blind in the sun, 49/22.
*blithe & glad, 83/21.
bones, mean virtues, 93/5.
book, an unknown source, 37/33.
breadth & length, 45/32.
breviary prayer, 19/25.
bringen out of, 51/19.
bringen to deaðe, 105/17.
*burn bright, 33/5.
burst & break, 73/13.
buy & sell, 11/26.

change of persons addressed, 21/12; of tenses, 5/1, 21/11.
Christ born without heavenly mother and earthly father, 25/14; he is our head, 27/5.

Church compared with the ark or a ship, 43/28.
church-things are not to be spent, 139/30.
*contrasts, 3/27, 11/16, 26, *13/9, 15/24, *21/16, 27/33, 29/1, 43/10, 49/25, 63/28, 95/10, 24, 107/18, 109/4, 123/27.
Cross compared with the trees of Life and of Knowledge, 51/26, 119/1.
cross means mortification, 33/28.

Daniel as example, 43/21.
day & night, 3/27.
days, superstition concerning, 27/22.
death, synonyms for, 17/24.
Devil as accuser, 9/29; deceived by Christ, 51/11, 17; devils expect souls in the air, 103/23; their appearance would madden a man, 19/5; old devil, 119/6.
die, synonyms for, 15/2.

eat & drink, 37/15.
ellipsis of are, 21/15.
erres "earnest," 19/28.
Eve & St. Mary, 117/34.
evil and good, 27/33.

fair fire, 139/7.
fall of angels, 5/8, 7/16.
faren of live, 15/2.
fasting, 137/14, 26.
father & mother, 35/3.
feden & screden, 149/17.
feed & foster, 43/12.
five thousand years elapsed before Christ came, 7/20; 5 talents, 17/6.
flies seek wounds, 89/33.
flum Jordan, 121/6.
foot "man," 29/8.
forliggen (of matrimonial copulation), 131/17.
forme fader (Adam), 7/18.
four Virtues dispute before God, 113/12.

get & loose, 11/26.

ȝielden, 21/28.
*glad & blithe, 83/21.
God knows everything, 21/3, 95/26, 143/4, 151/8; will avenge, 77/17; our shield, 39/11.
godes handiwerc, 13/7; wrecchen, 69/2; g. þearven, 57/31.
*gold & silver, 33/14.
golden bezants, 17/5.
good and evil, 27/33.
gospel our adversary, 75/12.
grace (in phrases), 21/23.
granum sinapis, 29/19.

hadede & leawede, 13/9.
hal & ȝesund, 73/14.
hali writ, an unknown source, 15/5, 41/14.
hám means paradise or Heaven, 23/32.
hands & feet, 133/31.
handsel, superstition, 29/10.
handwork of God, 13/7.
hard heart, 45/18.
harm & shame, 59/4.
hate sins, love sinners, 67/7.
hawks & hounds, 69/19.
heaven & earth, 49/25.
heiȝere hand, 127/20.
hell described, 17/32; its pains, 19/1.
Holy Spirit, love of Father and Son, 25/16, 37/2.
hom faren, 89/23.
hot & cold, 107/18.
house & home, 35/4.
hunger & thirst, 95/24.

icnawe bien "to confess," 21/28.
idle and empty, 23/22.
infinitive omitted, 17/29, 25/29, 71/32, 103/6.
Innocents, children of Bethlehem, 133/7.
invocations, 21/12.
is omitted, 57/13.

Job as example, 41/17, 43/21.
Jordan, river, 121/6.

King in hall, 141/21; King of Babylon = Satan, 9/26; King of kings, 95/10, 141/26.
kneel, 51/3.

lare liernin, 23/20.
laten of, 5/14.
laymen, how to be saved, 73/5.
Lazarus twice raised, 111/27.
lichame & saule, 11/16, 43/28.

life, synonyms for, 9/1; is a strife, 89/33; is sweet, 147/19; lif leden, 5/3.
light in hell when Christ appeared there, 17/30.
live, synonyms for, 9/1.
love sinners, hate sins, 67/7.
Lucifer's fall, 5/8, 105/16.

man "one," 5/2.
mannes ȝemane, 55/13, 127/12.
St. Mary always a virgin, 55/5; mother of mercy, 21/5; & Eve, 117/34.
Mary Magdalene, 85/17.
mea culpa, 15/25.
meeting of evil omens, 29/8.
*mercy the highest virtue, 67/9.
messengers of death, 17/12.
metes & drinkes, 43/10.
mid muðe seggen, 19/8.
might & strength, 39/7.
mine iliche, 13/25.
monks & hermits, their difference, 35/2; evil omens, 29/8.
moon, superstition concerning, 27/22.

ne, after negative expressions, 11/27, 27/11, 41/24; = "nor," 7/1, 87/31.
nielnesse, 45/17.
niht ne dai, 31/31.
Noah, as ship-wright, 43/23; with Daniel and Job, as examples, 43/21.
non god ne cunnen, 49/31, 81/19.
noon, 137/25.

ofte & ȝelome, 151/23.
oil, its qualities & their meaning, 33/3.
old & young, 109/4.
old devil, 119/6.
order of capital sins, 3/2.
own, emphasizing, 3/2.

pains of hell, 19/1; of purgatory, 63/32.
Parable of the five talents = the five senses, 17/6; of the sower, 69/12.
St. Peter as foundation of the Church, 27/3.
Physiologus (the serpent), 101/19.
pity oneself, 63/23.
play with a straw, 135/1.
poenitentia defined, 121/12, 15.
portae inferi are the cardinal sins, 27/9.
praying and reading, 133/29, 141/19.
prelates compared with ships, 45/10.

preterit after a present, 5/1, 21/11.
pronoun as subject omitted, 69/22; doubled, 23/3, 35/29, 57/7; repeats the subject, 3/12, 5/17.
providentia, 103/14.
purgatory, 65/1.

religion "order," 3/12, 5/33, 43/3.
rest & sleep, 51/10.
right, mid rihte, 9/24.
rimen ne tellen, 15/30.
*ropes of 3 strings, the three cardinal virtues, 45/14.
rules of behaviour, 133/24.

sari & sorhfull, 83/18.
Satan represented by the King of Babylon, 9/26.
scilden fram, 23/31.
sculen with infinitive omitted, 25/29.
*sea, means the world, 43/28, 45/8.
see & hear, 41/12; *see with eyes*, 119/9.
scek saints, of pilgrimages, 3/17, 5/27.
serpent, its nature, 101/19.
seven columns of Wisdom's house, 91/9; seven gifts of the Holy Spirit, 91/11.
ships, the Church, 43/28; prelates, 45/10.
shrift defined, 19/15.
sibbe & framde, 13/9.
simile of the mustard corn, 29/19.
singular of verb after plural of subject, 69/19; after *pára þe*, 43/7.
sonde, 17/12, 43/14, 55/16.
sons & daughters, 63/28.
soð seggen, 9/16, 93/12.
souls expected by devils in the air, 103/23.
speeches & deeds, 15/21.
subject, if a pronoun, omitted, 13/24, 69/22; repeated, 3/12, 5/17.
superstitions, 27/22, 29/8, 10.

tail, means perseverance, 151/1.
tears are a good lye, 95/30.
teforen & baften, 21/16.
tellen wel, 53/33.
temptations compared with winds and storms, 43/29.

tenebrae, exteriores et interiores, allegorically explained, 17/28.
terra viventium, land of the living, is Heaven, 41/11.
that doubled, 9/1.
thief on Christ's right hand saved, 145/26.
timor Domini, 63/2.
togedere igadered, 149/13.
trees of Life and of Knowledge compared with the Cross, 51/26, 119/1.

usury forbidden, 11/28, 77/21.

verb of motion omitted after auxiliaries, 17/29, 25/29.
vestis nuptialis, means charity, 95/31.
*virginity is nothing, if the heart is not pure, 131/9, 12.
*virgins live an angelic life on earth, 129/22.
virtues & vices represented as sisters, 3/22, 29/31.

warning against almsgiving, 45/23.
water from Christ's side, means baptism, 119/21; springing from the temple of Jerusalem, 83/2.
wedded wife, 41/16.
wepen & wanien, 19/18.
werdles wele, 31/19.
weres gemána, 55/13.
whole & sound, 73/14.
wife & children, 35/4.
winter "year," 7/20.
wise "manner," 9/8.
wissin & warnien, 21/27, 151/9.
within & without, 15/24, 95/10.
wittes bedæld, 41/9.
woe, exclamation of pity, 19/9.
women want to be called ladies, 53/33.
wrop & woninge, 17/32.
*world, synonyms for, 29/34; compared with the sea, *43/28, 45/8.
writ, an unknown source, 67/9, 73/27 (*jewrit*).
wrong measures & weights, 11/27.

Zion interpreted, 103/12.

INDEX TO PROPER NAMES.

Abraham, *nom. d.* 109/25, 29, 115/31; Abraam, 111/12; *d.* Abrahame, 109/27.
Adam, *nom. ac.* 7/18, 105/17, 115/22, 117/33, 119/5, 9; *d.* Adame, 7/27, 105/18, 113/13, 33, 117/27; *g.* Adames, 9/23, 51 24, 95/23, 115 9, 11, 117/8, 26, 32, 119/16.
Anna, *nom.* 85/19.
Augustinus, *nom.* 121/15, 123/3, 131/9.

Bersabee, *d.* 81/24.

Crist, *nom. d. ac.* 7/20, 32, 9/24, 15 8, 11, 25/9, 27/1, 3, 11, 29/15, 35/22, 37/5, 45/16, 49/10, 15, 51/17, 28, 67/25, 34, 69/6, 75/8, 30, 99/14, 105/21, 109/19, 111/4, 119/5, 10, 18, 121/5, 137/8, 141/28, 32, 151/3; *d. ac.* Criste, 9/32, 21/31, 27/20, 31/9, 33/19, 35/26, 41/10, 49/24, 57/9, 73/23, 95/2, 97/2, 105/17, 129/15 131/22, 25, 133/6, 7; *g.* Cristes, 17/31, 19/34, 49/4, 53/1, 57/5, 67/23, 71/22, 34, 73/7, 75/28, 101/32, 103/29, 107/10, 119/12, 14, 121/8, 131/26. (*Cf.* Jesu Crist.)
Daniel, *nom.* 43/19; *d. ac.* Daniele, 43/3, 16.
Davið, *nom. ac.* 19/23, 31/15, 20, 33/10, 59/21, 81/23; *d.* Daviðe, 115/32.
Eve, *g.* 53/33, 89/21; *ac.* 117/34.
Ezechie, *d.* 147/15.

Gabriel, *nom. ac.* 53/26, 55/16.
Gregorius, *nom.* 39/21.

Helyas, *nom.* 137/14, 143/31, 145/2.

Isaac, *nom. ac.* 111/14; Ysaac, 111/1.
Israele, *g.* 85/20.

Jacobus, *nom.* 143/27.
Jeronimus, *nom.* 121/12.
Jerusalem, *d.* 103/12, 111/9.
Jesu Crist, *nom. ac.* 93/31, 101/16, 17, 109/7, 117/31; jħu Crist, 51/5, 61/27, 113/3, 119/25; jħc x̅p̅c̅, 93/31; *d.* Jesu Criste, 21/7. (*Cf.* Crist.)
Job, *ac.* 41/17, 81/9.
Johannes, *nom.* 35/24, 37/11, 41/6, 141/12.
Josepe, *d.* 51/4.

Lazarum, *ac.* 111/27.

Maria, *nom.* 125/4; Marie, 55/24, 31, 53/27, 59/15, 111/26; *g.* 129/16; *d. ac.* 9/25, 21/5, 25/24, 53/26, 57/7, 117/35.
Marie Magdalene, *nom.* 85/17, 18; *d.* 145/27, 28.
Martha, *nom.* 111/26.
Moyses, *nom.* 137/13.

Ninive, *d.* 137/4.
Noe, *ac.* 43/21.

Paulus, *nom.* 39/15.
Petrus, *nom.* 85/15; Peter, 93/31, 145/23; *d.* Petre, 25/32, 111/31, 145/32.

Salamun, *nom.* 59/19; Salomon, 71/7; Salemon, 91/9; Salemun, 129/2; *g.* Salomones, 81/24.
Samuel, *ac.* 85/22.
Synay, *d.* 137/14.
Syon, *nom.* 103/12.

Urie, *d.* 81/24.

GLOSSARY.

(æ see under a, c under k, ʒ under g, ð and þ after t, y under i.)

A, Æ.

a, *int. oh,* 67/31 ; 147/20.
a, *prep. and* a-, *prefix, see* an.
a, *num. pron. see* an.
abach, *adv. backwards,* 71/23 ; 91/4.
abeggen, *v. to pay penalty, redeem,* 103/26 ; *part. pret.* aboht, 65/1.
abiden, *v. to abide,* 3 *sg. opt. pres.* abide, 69/5.
aboht, *see* abeggen.
abuten, *prep. adv. about, round,* 91/32 ; 101/19, 21 ; 103/18 ; 133/21 ; 137/19 ; 139/17, 19, 20 ; 143/12 ; onbuten, 125/13.
abuven, *adv. above,* 123/27.
ædinesse, *see* eadinesse.
affleien, *v. to put to flight,* 73/20.
aforewarde, *adv. first, before,* 105/3.
after, (1) *prep. after, according,* 13/26 ; 17/16, 31 ; 19/15 ; 21/17 ; 23/14, 28 ; 25/18 ; 27/25, 26 ; 33/24, 26 ; 63/1 ; 67/6 ; 71/8 ; 73/34 ; 75/19 ; 77/24 ; 79/2 ; 81/28, *etc.* ; (2) *adv. afterwards,* 97/24.
after ðan ðe (þe), *conj. after what, according to, accordingly,* 13/27 ; 41/14 ; 57/17 ; 59/17 ; 71/12, 85/10 ; 105/4 ; 149/18.
after ðat ðe, *conj. according to,* 81/27 ; 109/4 ; after ðat, 93/22.
agann, *see* anginnen.
aʒean, *prep. against, anent, towards,* 9/10 ; 13/19 ; 15/19 ; 27/8, 11 ; 61/1 ; 63/21 ; 89/35 ; 97/23 ; 99/26, 27 ; 107/2, 8 ; 133/16 ; 135/15 ; aʒen, 73/11.
aʒean, *adv. again, back,* 77/22 ; 83/20 ; 89/22, 23 ; 99/19 ; 113/14 ; 115/28 ; 147/25.
aʒeanes, *prep. see* onʒeanes.
aʒen, *adj. own,* 15/6, 15 ; 23/12, 14 ; 53/30, 32 ; 67/21 ; 95/22 ; 113/24 ; auʒen, 91/25 ; 129/6 ; awen, 35/5 ; 103/29 ; auwen, 53/28 ; aʒene, 7/1 ; 15/10 ; 23/17, 28 ; 41/21 ; 67/23 ; 85/9 ; 111/18, 20 ; 119/29 ; 135/5 ; aʒwene, 9/7 ; auʒene, 11/19 ; 23/18 ; 29/17 ; 61/26 ; 113/19 ; 117/18 ; awene, 3/2 ; 13/27 ; 19/28 ; 23/1 ; 25/21 ; 33/30 ; 37/28 ; 49/4 ; 75/20 ; 101/30 ; auene, 41/22 ; *g. sg.* aʒenes, 111/7.
aʒen, *v. to have, to own, to be obliged, pres. ind.* 1, 3 *sg.* ah, 143/6 ; auh, 45/3 ; 89/14 ; 109/10 ; awh, 15/16 ; 69/4 ; 105/5 ; 109/11 ; 189/31 ; 143/18, 24 ; aw, 35/23 ; owh, 73/27 ; 123/34 ; 3 *sg.* auhte, 61/33 ; auþ, 71/12 ; 2 *sg.* auʒhst, 141/25 ; aust, 33/24 ; 41/17 ; 75/20 ; 77/10, 13 ; n'aust, 65/24 ; *pl.* aʒen, 137/17 ; 143/14 ; aʒeð, 15/3 ; 109/1 ; aweð, 35/6 ; 61/30.
aʒen, *prep. see* aʒean.
aʒen-wille, *sb. self-will, sg. nom. d. ac.* 13/28 ; auʒen-wille, 13/30 ; aʒen-will, 15/3.
agrisen, *v. to shudder,* 3 *sg. ind. pres.* n'agrist, 139/10.
ah, *v. see* aʒen.
aingles, *see* ængel.
aiðer, *pron. either,* 81/7 ; oðer, 107/13.
aiðer, *conj.* + *and, as well—as, both—and,* 7/27 ; 13/22 ; 35/12 ; 41/21 ; 95/11 ; + ʒe, 13/9.
ac, *conj. but,* 5/2, 16, 26 ; 7/31 ; 9/16, 30 ; 11/11, 28 ; 13/20, 24 ; 15/10, 32 ; 17/11, 23, 32 ; 19/4 ; 21/19 ; *etc.* ; acc, 83/14.
aken, *v. to ache,* 3 *sg. ind. pres.* acþh, 91/28.
akenned, *part. pret. begotten,* 25/14.
acolen, *v. to cool,* 3 *sg. pret.* acolede, 81/27.
acovren, *v. to recover,* 3 *sg. ind. pres.* n'acovreð, 121/25.
acsien, *v. to ask,* 3 *sg. ind. pres.* acseð, 105/10.
acwellan, *v. to kill,* 9/19.
al, *adj. all, whole, every,* 9/13, 28 ;

GLOSSARY.

25/27; 27/13, 19, 21, 27; 31/18; 37/3; 39/2; 45/24; 65/1; 67/22; 71/22, 24; 75/13; 89/32; 97/28; 109/1; 113/29; 119/2; 129/7; all, 7/19; 9/23; 11/11; 23/24; 27/16, 17, 30; 29/14, 31, 32; 33/18, 33; 35/1, 30; 37/22; 39/17, 18; 41/3; 43/25; 45/26; 49/5, 6; 53/14; 55/15; 59/6, 13; 65/33; 67/2; 69/2, 4, 20, 21; 71/33; 75/2; 77/25; 87/31; 89/33; 95/4; 97/28; 99/28; 103/7; 105/14; 109/6, 26; 111/3; 113/10, 11, 14; 115/2, 26, 27, 32; 117/10, 11, 35; 125/15; 137/4, 25, 26; alle, 8/2, 11, 12, 18; 5/8, 11, 12, 18, 31; 7/21, 23, 24, 25, 27, 32; 9/2, 30, 31; 11/4, 29; 13/24; 15/5, 13, 29, 30 (3); 17/26; 19/9, 11, 24, 26, 31, 33; 21/3, 7, 12; 23/14, 16, 20, 25; 25/7, 20, 29; 27/4, 12; 29/16, 34; 31/6, 7, 11; 33/4-9, 12, 32-34; 35/4, 6, 11, 16; 39/3, 11, 12, 25; 41/19; 43/9, 15-17, 33; 45/4, 8; 49/18, 25, 26, 28, 30; 51/1-3, 8, 10, 15, 24, 32; 53/29; 55/22, 26, 29; 57/2, 4, 5, 18, 25, 33; 59/4, 14; 63/24, 30, 31; 65/1, 11; 67/19, 32; 69/16, 19, 32; 71/8, 27, 31; 75/6; 81/21, 22; 83/4, 32; 85/7, 18, 30; 87/3, 5, 34; 89/13, 15, 32; 91/1, 4; 95/2, 4, 6, 7, 26, 28; 97/14; 99/6, 26, 27; 101/13, 20, 26; 103/2, 10, 14, 17; 105/4, 10, 11, 27; 107/2, 6, 8, 9, 10, 12, 19, 21, 23, 28; 109/4, 34; 111/26, 30; 113/2, 28; 115/3, 8, 11, 12, 18; 117/19, 30; 119/21, 31, 32; 123/31; 125/14, 17, 29; 131/9, 18, 25; 133/24; 135/6, 12; 137/6, 9, 15, 17; 139/5; 141/8, 9, 23; 143/4, 11, 15, 18, 24, 25, 31; 145/3, 29; 149/9, 10, 20, 21, 30; 151/9, 22; ælle, 49/30; allen, 99/12; alles, 25/17; 31/27; 43/11, 18; 49/16; 75/1; 119/23; 127/33; 137/16; 141/5, 6; alre, 3/5; 47/28; 65/31; 85/26; 95/10; 111/18; 131/26; 141/26; 143/19; allre, 121/9.

al, *adv. all, quite, wholly,* 19/6; 61/26; 65/1; 67/1; 77/31; 89/35; 101/19; 145/26; all, 3/26; 31/23; 59/7; 65/1; 83/27; 95/9, 31; 101/21; 117/21, 33; 131/27; 145/1, 11, 13, 18.

alche, ælche, *see* elch.

alder, *sb. prince, nom. sg.* 111/5.

æld-mone, *sb. old moon, nom. sg.* 27/24.

alhwat, *conj. until,* 7/20; 51/12; 83/19; allhwat, 69/5; 115/13.

aliesen, *v. to save, redeem, release, deliver,* 63/27; 117/16, 22; *pres. opt.* 3 *sg.* aliese, 15/16; *pret.* 3 *sg.* aliesde, 119/26.

aliesend, *sb. redeemer, saviour, nom.* 119/26; *d.* aliesende, 101/33.

aliesendnesse, *sb. release,* 115/14.

all, *see* al.

all-ane, *adj. alone,* 63/30; all-hone, 123/18.

alles, *adv. quite, at all,* 23/27; 29/27; 137/25; 141/17.

ælle, *int. well, ay,* 91/23; 103/16 (?); 115/7.

almesse, *sb. alms, sg. d. ac.* 5/28; 37/31; 67/23; 127/2; *pl. ac.* ælmesses, 65/3; almesses, 139/31; almessen, 67/21.

almihti, *adj. almighty,* 15/32; 25/11; 37/3; 117/3; 145/17; all-mihti, 23/6; almihtin, 151/15 (*see* godalmihti).

alswa, *adv. conj. as, so, if, as if, also,* 7/16; 13/21; 15/7, 23; 19/17; 21/19, 22; 25/14, 16; 29/7; 37/2, 25, 33; 39/21; 41/30; 49/31; 53/4, 8, 13; 55/31; 57/5, 15, 23, 24; 63/5; 65/25, 26; 67/5; 73/34; 75/21; 77/20, 30; 81/20; 83/15; 85/7, 8; 91/1; 97/8; 101/18; 109/1, 2, 14, 15; 113/21 (2); 121/27; 125/13; 129/22; 131/14; 135/22; 137/27, 28, 29, 33; 139/19, 24, 25, 26; 141/31 (2); 143/13, 29; 145/5, 11, 14, 22 (2), 23; 147/18; 149/5 (2), 6; 151/22, 24; allswa, 57/3; alswo, 3/15; 5/21; 7/24, 26; 9/1; 15/3; 25/23; 27/29; 29/3; 37/11; 39/22, 24, 25; 45/19; 47/2, 9; 49/7, 26; 51/11; 53/30; 55/33; 57/14; 67/8, 20, 34; 73/12; 81/20; 89/33; 93/5, 6, 10, 12; 95/20, 22; 101/7, 30; 103/14; 105/34; 111/2, 14; 113/4; 117/34; 119/26; 121/17; allswo, 53/2; 91/23; also, 29/21; 67/9; 91/2; 95/19; 103/18; 107/18, 19; 111/26; alse, 19/6; 65/25; 77/31; 103/18; 113/26.

am, *see* bien.

amang, *prep. among,* 69/16; amanȝ, 77/2; among, 81/19.

amen, *int. amen,* 21/25; 125/25; 151/21, 24.

amidde, *prep. amidst,* 51/27.

amidewardo, *prep. amidst, in,* 47/27; 49/22; 51/25.

amti, *adj. empty,* 23/23.

GLOSSARY. 211

an, *prep. adv. on, at, in,* 19/6; 21/
14, 30; 25/12; 27/31; 29/6, 19;
41/8; 81/2, 7; 107/13; 117/2; a,
9/8; 11/11; 13/14; 25/27; 27/18;
37/33; 39/20; 99/29, 32; 101/26;
133/9 (2); 151/21; on, 8/2, 14, 18,
24, 27; 5/2, 3, 28; 9/2, 9; 13/6, 14;
15/5, 8, 21; 17/13, 19, 23; 19/7,
9, 12; 21/12, 14, 16 *etc.*; o, 119/8.
an, (1) *num. one,* 3/8; 25/6, 11, 18;
27/6; 99/25; 115/31; 131/28;
149/27; on, 3/28; 63/14; 77/6;
93/3; 99/22; 109/25; 123/6; 133/
18; 145/19; ane, 5/18; 127/3; 131/
24; 135/24; one, 41/25; 49/27;
53/19, 22; 59/8; 95/18; 107/21;
149/7; ones, 39/33; onen, 125/17;
ænne, 111/13; anne, 19/6; 95/18;
143/13; enne, 135/3.
(2) *pron. indef. art. an, a.* an, 3/7;
5/7, 24; 9/21; 11/2; 13/12,29; 15/
18; 19/27; 23/9; 27/22, 23; 29/15,
30; 37/22; 47/24; 51/6, 27; 53/
19; 57/20; 59/19; 63/2, 11; 65/
10; 67/25; 71/6; 81/12; 85/28;
91/8, 11; 101/1, 2, 27; 103/9, 12;
105/2; 107/5, 11, 18, 27; 111/24;
121/29; 123/25; 127/26; 129/13;
133/4, 23; 135/10; 137/2; 139/14;
141/2; on, 125/27; 143/29; 149/
19; 151/20; a, 19/6; 31/19; 39/
27; 93/12; 97/29, 31; 101/2; 135/
23; 147/22; ane, 3/22; 7/15; 29/
18; 39/21; 51/4; 59/12; 61/24;
65/24; 101/1; 109/14; 143/11;
145/32; anne, 5/22; are, 31/25.
anald, *see* onalen.
anaon, *adv. anon, even until (with
to),* 9/3; anoan, 135/24; anon, 5/3;
7/32; 33/29; 39/4; 51/8; 81/26;
87/12; 95/5; 101/31; 109/7; 111/
31; 113/1; 115/7; 117/21; 119/6;
131/5.
anbidende, *part. pres. awaiting,* 31/8.
and, *conj. and,* 3/19; 5/31; 7/21, 28;
9/7, 31; 11/27; 15/13, 21, 29; 17/
11; 19/2 (2); 21/15 (2), 28, *etc.*
ænde, *sb. end, sg. nom. d. ac.* 5/1;
25/3; 89/26; 141/28; ande, 19/8;
33/10.
ande, *sb. indignation, d. sg.* 89/27.
ænde-dai, *sb. end-day, sg. nom.* 19/16;
d. ænde-daiȝe, 33/12; ande-daiȝe,
5/3.
andetnesse, *sb. confession, nom. d. ac.*
121/28; andetetdnesse, 121/30;
andettednesse, 123/8.
andetten, *v. to confess, pres. opt.* 3 *sg.*
andette, 123/16; *imp. pl.* andettið,
123/11.

andȝeat, *sb. intellect, understanding,
nom. d. ac.* 85/29; 125/13, 14; and-
ȝet, 85/27; 89/31; 127/23; anȝeat,
85/33.
andin, *v. to end, finish,* 149/23; *pres.
ind. pl.* andieð, 139/1; *pret. pl.*
andeden, 149/25.
andlicnesse, *see* anlicnesse.
andsware, *sb. answer, sg. d. ac.* 17/
14; answere, 57/34.
andswerien, *v. to answer,* 17/25;
-swerizen, 89/2; *pres. ind.* 2 *sg.*
andswerest, 59/26; 3 *sg.* -swereð,
23/5; 47/7, 19; 93/1; 97/16;
-swered, 95/15; *imp. sg.* -swere,
17/17; *pret.* 3 *sg.* -swarede, 25/33;
-swerede, 67/29, 33; 79/2; 113/16,
20.
ane, *adv. alone, only,* 9/24; 51/11;
73/20; 89/3, 21; 121/24; 123/18;
135/5; 141/23; 143/11; one, 15/
32; 71/10; 105/12; 115/2; 129/1;
135/11; 141/5.
anȝeat, *see* andȝeat.
ængel, *sb. angel, sg. nom. ac.* 55/17;
angel, 5/9; 7/17; 103/25; 105/16;
117/29; *nom.* angle, 53/26; *d. ac.*
angele, 105/20; *pl.* angles, 15/3;
43/19; 121/2; aingles, 15/11; 31/
13; 55/8; 113/16.
angelich, *adj. angelic,* 129/23.
angin, *sb. beginning, sg. nom.* 115/7;
anginn, 25/7, 19; 59/20; 91/13;
101/21; anȝinn, 5/8; 101/26; *d.*
anginne, 25/19.
anginnen, *v. to begin,* 27/23; agin-
nen, 101/23; *pres. ind. pl.* anginn-
neð, 91/12; *pret. ind.* 3 *sg.* agann,
111/32; *pl.* agunnen, 149/24; *pret.
part.* agunnen, 151/5; aȝunnen,
3/11.
æni, *pron. any, anybody,* 3/2; 75/32;
ani, 5/31; 11/26, 31; 13/20; 35/6;
41/8; 45/22, 28; 51/29; 59/4; 65/
5; 67/16; 69/30; 77/21; 83/4;
85/3; 93/26; 99/28; 101/14, 28,
31; 105/31; 141/22; 145/9; 147/
14; 151/2; aniȝe, 31/20; 39/9;
aniȝere, 101/11.
anker, *sb. anchorite, sg. nom. ac.* 73/
30; ancer, 73/29; *pl. d.* ancres, 35/
2; 137/10; 143/14.
anlepine, *see* onlepi.
anliche, *adv. lonely,* 139/5.
anlicnesse, *sb. likeness, face, nom. d.
ac.* 23/10, 14, 18; 39/14; 95/22,
23; 113/23, 24; andl. 97/3; 115/
9.
annesse, *sb.* (1) *oneness, unity, d. ac.*

GLOSSARY.

25/12; onnesse, 151/20; (2) lone-
liness, solitude, annesse, 143/8, 14,
15; 149/16; onnesse, 73/25; 137/
10, 11.
anoan, anon, see anaon.
ansæte, adj. solitary, 73/30.
ansiene, sb. face, d. ac. 31/24; 83/
15, 17; 95/30.
answere, see andsware.
apostel, sb. apostle, sg. nom. ac. 13/4;
27/19, 29; 29/26; 35/8; 39/15;
49/3, 13; 65/17; 67/14; 89/5;
93/22; 97/21; 105/22, etc.; apostele, 65/32; 73/15; 89/17; 93/28;
pl. apostles, 35/31.
ær, adv. conj. ere, before, 15/2; 31/31;
39/24, 26; 43/23; 47/2; 53/15, 18;
55/30; 57/10; 59/3; 61/13; 63/
33; 73/29; 81/25; 83/20; 89/18;
91/24; 103/21, 22; 111/4, 7; ar,
83/20; 103/10; 145/7; comp.
ærrer, 83/31; arrer, 45/29; 51/16;
71/18; 73/21; 123/1, 8; arer, 117/
32; harrer, 133/20; superl. arst,
adv. first, 3/3; 13/16; 15/32; 35/
22; 47/28; 63/23; 73/28; 83/6;
87/32, 34; 89/4, 25; 101/22; 115/
25; 121/5, 9; 133/11; 143/19.
aræren, to rear, raise, 83/25; araren,
27/4; 83/19; pres. ind. 3 sg.
araröð, 41/27; pl. aræreð, 101/15;
pret. 3 sg. ararde, 91/10; arearde,
111/27; pret. part. arard, 97/
30.
arche, sb. ark, ac. sg. 43/23, 28.
are, sb. mercy, pity, grace, sg. ac. 15/
33; 19/19; 21/10, 20, 21; 23/1;
113/33; 123/19; 145/13; 147/1;
ore, 57/24; 81/28; 83/28; 115/4,
6, 21.
aredde, v. to save, 3 sg. opt. pres.
103/19.
arewen, sb. arrows, pl. nom. ac. 63/
16, 17.
arfastliche, adv. piously, 31/8.
arisen, v. to rise, arise, 77/2; pres.
ind. 3 sg. arist, 95/3, 5; pret. ind. 3
sg. aras, 25/25; aros, 33/20; 119/
26; 121/1.
arme, adj. see earm.
armes, sb. arms, d. pl. 103/1.
arnde, sb. errand, ac. sg. 57/9.
ærrer, arrer, see ær.
arst, see ær.
art, see bien.
arvednesses, sb. difficulties, 95/24.
asolkenesse, sb. sloth, 3/23; asolk-
nesse, 3/21.
asse, sb. ass, d. sg. 93/10.
astored, pret. part. stored, 97/32.

astrecchen, v. to stretch down, 3 sg.
pret. astrehte, 113/32.
at, sh. meal, eating, d. ac. pl. ates,
127/12; 135/11; 137/24; 139/23;
aten, 137/29.
at, prep. at, in; of, from, 11/25; 19/
27; 25/3, 8; 33/10; 49/7, 10, 24;
71/10; 75/5; 77/19; 79/15; 81/
18; 89/26; 91/12; 117/9; 141/
15, 21; 143/30; 145/9; 149/7, 12;
hat, 141/27.
atbersten, v. to escape, 105/19.
atempren, v. to temper, regulate, 3 sg.
ind. pres. atempreð, 107/21, 24.
atter, sb. poison, venom, sg. nom. 123/
10; d. attre, 119/23.
að, sb. oath, sg. d. aðe, 9/15, 16; g. (or
ac. pl.) oðes, 9/5.
auȝen, see aȝen.
auht, see aȝen and awht.
auhte, adj. worthy, excellent, 79/28.
auwen, see aȝen.
ævre, adv. ever, always, 3/14; 9/27;
11/26; 15/18, 19; 17/32; 19/8,
10; 23/25, 28; 29/7, 16, 20; 31/
13; 33/22; 35/6, 11; 39/11; 51/
28, 32; 55/6, 18; 59/14; 61/3,
21; 63/3, 20; 65/31; 67/5, 6, 9;
87/19, 29; 89/24; 97/4; 101/21,
26; 103/31; 109/8; 113/3, 10;
115/5; 117/4; avre, 9/29; 13/15;
15/16; 19/4; 27/4; 85/7; 97/2;
113/15, 27; 115/29; 117/3; 121/
3, 26; 125/16; 129/16; 133/20;
137/21; 139/24; 143/18, 19; 149/
26; 151/21; evre, 93/9; evre,
21/25; 55/15, 21; 105/33; 107/
22; 121/16; havre, 137/17; aver,
11/31; 25/2.
ævrilch, pron. every, 109/8; avrich,
39/14; 105/4; avriche, 63/11;
151/1.
awecchen, v. to raise, pret. ind. 2 sg.
aweihtest, 21/26.
awei, adv. away, 11/17; 19/32; 23/
16; 69/3, 7; 73/20; 81/29; 91/
6; 99/30; aweiȝ, 19/30.
aweiward, adv. wayward, 47/3.
awen, see aȝen.
awerȝede, pret. part. cursed, 3/12,
28; 91/4; awerȝhede, 7/23.
awht, (1) pron. aught, anything, 145/
6; auht, 133/12; (2) adv. possibly,
anyhow, auht, 39/4; aut, 61/13;
ouht, 53/18.

B.

badd, see bidden.
bafte, prep. behind, 11/8.

GLOSSARY. 213

baften, *adv. behind,* 21/16.
baftespache, *sb. backbiting, nom. ac. sg.* 11/1, 3.
bam, *see* baðe.
bar, *see* beren.
bare, *adj. bare,* 63/19.
barnen, *v. to burn,* 39/18; bernen, 33/5; barnin, 65/34; *pres. part.* barnende, 35/31; 73/13; barninde, 49/18; 143/21.
bat, *see* beaten.
baþ, *sb. bath, ac. sg.* 107/19.
baðe, (1) *num. both, nom. d. ac.* 9/10 (2); 11/7; 29/3; 95/13; 97/21, 27; 125/17; boðe, 95/18 ; *g.* beire, 25/16; 37/2; 81/7; *d.* bam, 25/15; 97/13; (2) *conj.* baðe ... and, 11/16; 17/27; 25/22; 53/4, 5; 55/14; 61/14, 31; 71/33; 93/27; 115/4; 119/17; 133/31; bade, 71/11; boðe, 43/20; 51/26.
be, *see* bi.
beames, *sb. weaver's beams,* 39/22.
beaten, *v. to beat, pres. ind.* 3 *sg.* bat, 29/20.
bebod, *sb. commandment, sg. d.* bebode, 9/11; 41/5; 61/1; 77/23; *pl. ac.* bebode, 19/24, 32; 61/33; bebodes, 67/30, 32; 71/31.
bedæld, *pret. part. deprived,* 41/9.
bedd, *sb. bed, bed-room, sg. ac.* 147/10; *d.* bedde, 143/2, 5.
bede, *sb. prayer, sg. d. ac.* 127/1; 141/18, 20, 27; 143/25, 28; 149/15.
beden, *see* bidden.
befallen, *v. to fall, pres. opt. pl.* 121/11.
befasten, *v. to entrust, pres. ind. pl.* befasteð, 79/11.
befelen, *v. to defile,* 43/11; *pres. ind.* 3 *sg.* bifeleð, 93/26; *pl.* befeleð, 121/20; *pret. pl.* befielde, 43/6; *part.* befeld, 83/6.
befelen, *v. to commit, urge, pres. ind.* 2 *sg.* befelst, 139/3; *pret. ind.* 3 *sg.* bevall, 51/12; 139/4; *part.* bevolen, 9/21; 11/22; 15/31.
beforen, *prep. before,* 93/13; 113/28; 123/29; 139/5; before, 113/31.
beforen, *adv. before,* 51/21; 103/10.
biȝeate, *sb. gain, possession, sg. d. ac.* 79/12, 13; *pl.* biȝeates, 43/33.
beȝelpen, *v. to boast,* 127/19; *pres. ind.* 3 *sg.* biȝelpð, 5/28.
biȝeten, *v. to get, gain, beget,* 17/6; 33/8; 63/25; 79/30, 34; 99/24; beȝeten, 141/2; *pres. ind.* 2 *sg.* beȝiethst, 125/20; 3 *sg.* beȝett, 123/13; beȝiet, 137/7; *pl.* biȝeteð, 79/

27; *opt.* 3 *sg.* beȝete, 79/26; 149/26; beȝiete, 125/19; *pret. ind.* 1 *and* 3 *sg.* beȝat, 145/12; biȝatt, 17/7; 93/17; *opt.* 1 *sg.* biȝate, 11/26; *part.* biȝeten, 17/20, 23; 31/32; 77/26; (biȝetenð *MS.*), 79/31, 34; 111/13; beȝeten, 143/25.
beggen, *v. to buy, pres. ind.* 3 *sg.* beið, 121/18; *pret.* 1 *sg.* bouhte, 11/26.
behat, *sb. promise, sg. d.* behate, 31/24; *pl. ac.* behotes, 31/11.
behaten, *v. to promise,* 129/21; *pres. ind.* 2 *sg.* behatst, 9/29; 71/17; 3 *sg.* behat, 87/25; *pl.* behoteð, 31/18; behoteþ, 31/19; *pret. ind.* 1 *and* 3 *sg.* behet, 11/25; 37/5; 125/18; 129/16; behiet, 31/11; 55/5, 14; 2 *sg.* behete, 115/30, 32; *pret. part.* behaten, 8/16; 33/23; 71/16; 129/21; 131/19; behoten, 9/4; 97/8; 109/25; bihoten, 121/1.
beheve, *adj. profitable, useful,* 99/25; 101/23; 109/8; 149/9; biheve, 141/30; behieve, 107/28.
behofde, *sb. behoof, use, d. sg.* 51/26; behofte, 87/17; beofte, 135/5.
behoten, *see* behaten.
behoven, *v. to behoove, belong, pres. ind.* 3 *sg.* behoveð, 39/13; 63/8; 99/22; beoveð, 128/9; bihoved, 121/27; behoveþ, 39/25; *pl.* behoveð, 39/24; *pret.* 3 *sg.* behofde, 53/17.
beið, *see* beggen.
beire, *see* baðe.
becaht, *pret. part. deceived,* 33/14.
becam, *see* becumen.
bicleped, *pret. part. accused,* 9/17.
becleppen, *v. to encircle, pres. ind.* 3 *sg.* beclepð, 95/4.
becnawe, *pret. part. confessing,* 7/6; 13/8; 145/13; bicnawe, 83/13.
becumen, *v. to become,* 83/31; 117/7, 17; *pres. ind. pl.* becumeð, 107/22; *opt.* 3 *sg.* becume, 67/16, 20; *pret. ind.* 3 *sg.* becam, 97/3.
becweðen, *v. to bequeath, sg. imp.* becweð, 147/17.
belæven, *v. to remain,* 99/19; beleaven, 75/3; *pres. ind.* 3 *sg.* belæfð, 73/14; 81/18; *pret.* 3 *sg.* bileafde, 11/27.
beleave, *sb. belief,* 51/33; 93/27.
belemð, *see* belimpen.
beli, *sb. ac. sg. belly,* 137/34.
believen, *v. to believe, pres. ind. pl.* believeð, 27/5, 12; 31/17; 51/33; 95/2; believen, 25/9; *pret.* 1 *sg.*

E

GLOSSARY.

beliefde, 55/16; *pret. part.* beliefde, 29/16.
belimpen, *v. to belong, pres. ind.* 3 *sg.* belemð, 101/12; *pl.* belimpeð, 101/5.
bilokin, *v. to belook, look after,* 99/23; *pres. ind.* 3 *sg.* belokeð, 95/9; *opt.* 3 *sg.* belokie, 123/19.
bemanen, *v. to complain, bemoan, pres. ind.* 3 *sg.* bemaneð, 137/30; *imp. sg.* bemæn, 113/29; *pret.* 3 *sg.* bemande, 115/7.
bemone, *sb. ac. sg. complaint, bemoaning,* 21/29.
ben, *see* bien.
bene, *see* biene.
benemen, *v. to take away, bereave, prevent, deprive,* 15/8; 41/23; 143/13; binemen, 51/19; *pres. ind.* 3 *sg.* benemð, 13/13; benimð, 127/30; *pl.* benemeð, 79/25; 105/30; *opt.* 3 *sg.* beneme, 69/5; benime, 15/2; 111/7; *pl.* benime, 133/27; *imp. sg.* benem, 83/18.
benen, *sb. ac. pl. beans,* 43/13.
beneðen, *prep. adv. beneath,* 95/8; 123/27.
beplaiten, *v. to tax, pres. ind. pl.* beplaitið, 81/4.
bereaven, *v. to bereave, pret.* 3 *sg.* bereavede, 115/26; *part.* bireaved, 25/3.
beren, *v. to bear,* 53/28; 55/3, 13; 71/22; 95/2; 125/1; *ger.* berene, 33/24; *pres. ind.* 2 *sg.* berest, 33/31; 3 *sg.* berð, 39/14; 47/27; 53/6; 59/16; 97/19; 101/25; 121/18; 141/5; berþ, 41/5; *pl.* bereð, 123/33; 135/22; *opt.* 3 *sg.* bere, 33/26; 57/8; *imp. pl.* bereð, 71/29; *pret. ind.* 2 *sg.* bere, 103/32; 3 *sg.* bar, 49/18; 51/29; 87/23; 119/27; 125/4, 6; 119/27 (up); *pl.* baren, 119/11; *pret. part.* ȝeboren, 15/11; iboren, 21/12; 109/34.
bereusinge, *see* berewsinge.
birewnesse, *sb. repentance, d. ac.* 21/2; 105/23; ber., 145/19.
berewsen, *v. to repent,* 121/14; biriwsin, 121/14.
berewsinge, *sb. repentance, nom. d. ac.* 7/1; 121/16; 145/29; beriwsinge, 125/32; bereusinge, 85/13.
berȝen, *v. to save,* 81/10; 101/20; 151/12; bergen, 73/7; berȝin, 151/10; *pres. ind.* 3 *sg.* berhð, 101/29; *pret. part.* ȝeborȝen, 41/14; 53/22; 129/28, 29; 149/21; ȝeborȝwen, 15/20; iborȝen, 19/4; 129/22; 151/5; ȝeboreȝen, 27/17; 41/16; 71/19; 73/5; 77/5, 9; ȝeboregen, 119/1; iboreȝen, 37/17; 39/20; 63/12; 109/8; iborewen, 107/3.
berieles, *sb. burying-place, d.* 139/4.
biriwsin, *see* berewsen.
beriwsinge, *see* berewsinge.
berken, *v. to bark,* 109/22.
bernen, *see* barnen.
bersten, *v. to burst, pres. ind.* 3 *sg.* bersteð, 73/13; *pl.* bersteð, 73/17.
berðen, *sb. burden, sg. nom.* 71/30; *ac.* berðene, 71/29.
besantes, *sb. Bezants, pl.* 17/5, 11, 20, 21.
beseken, *v. to beseech, entreat, beg,* 141/22; 143/19; 145/9; 147/28; besechen, 141/27; *pres. ind.* I *sg.* besieche, 21/30; beseche, 47/14; besieke, 145/30; 3 *sg.* besekð, 81/18; besekeð, 145/6; *pl.* besecheð, 11/30; besekeð, 109/18; beseceð, 141/15; *opt.* 2 *sg.* besieke, 21/6; beseke, 149/7; *imp. sg.* besiec, 39/6; besiech, 117/9; *pret.* 3 *sg.* besohte, 143/30; 145/2; besouhte, 147/15; *pl.* besohten, 111/26, 27; 113/31.
besett, *pret. part. beset,* 95/32.
besmiten, *pret. part. polluted,* 9/23.
beswiken, *v. to deceive, pres. ind.* 3 *sg.* beswikð, 3/29; 23/18; 33/10; 79/5; beswicð, 133/17; *pl.* beswikeð, 79/22; *imp. sg.* beswic, 41/2; *pret. ind.* 3 *sg.* beswoc, 51/20; *part.* beswiken, 3/8, 24; 5/19, 21, 23, 25; 11/22; 25/4; 51/11; 89/21; 93/9; 137/22; 139/4; beswikene, 49/7; 61/24; 67/13; 69/22; 137/33.
beswonken, *pret. part. toiled,* 151/8.
bet, *adv. better,* 97/32; 105/11; bett, 5/25; 73/26.
betachen, *v. to deliver, entrust, assign, bestow,* 75/18; 83/25; *pres. opt.* 3 *sg.* betæche, betache, 75/11; *pret.* I *and* 3 *sg.* betahte, 17/2, 6, 21; *part.* betaht, 43/26.
betellen, *v. to maintain,* 75/19; 77/3.
betere, *adj. adv. comp. better,* 27/23; 29/23; 37/22; 57/20; 65/4; 67/21; 69/4; 73/7; betre, 29/21; bettre, 129/3; 139/12; 143/19.
betide, *v. to betide,* 3 *sg. opt. pres.* 37/31.
betowen, *pret. part. bestowed, applied,* 13/2.
betst, *adj. adv. best,* 21/31; 35/10;

GLOSSARY. 215

65/21; 71/12; 137/33; betste, 147/20.
bette, *see* **bieten.**
betwen, *prep. between,* 97/26; 115/19; 149/13; betwenen, 51/15; betwienen, 23/21.
beðenchen, *v. to think of, consider,* 51/14; *pres. ind.* 2 *sg.* beþencst, 65/8; beþeincð, 133/17; *imp. sg.* beþenc, 118/20; beðenc, 135/24.
bevall, bevolen, *see* **befelen.**
bewænt, *v. to turn, sg. imp.* 101/21.
bewedded, *pret.part.wedded,married,* 5/24; 81/24; 131/24.
bewepen, *v. to beweep, pres. ind.* 3 *sg.* beweopð, 5/26; *pret. ind.* 3 *sg.* beweop, 85/16; bewop, 145/25.
bewerien, *v. to defend,* 79/23.
bewunden, *part. pret. wrapt,* 49/28.
bewune, *adj. wont,* 139/6, 7; bewunen, 139/9.
bi, *prep. by, of, through, about, with,* 17/15; 55/16; 67/22; 71/24; 75/25; 85/7; 89/3; 91/30; 93/10; 113/8; 133/15; bie, 9/12; 29/24; be, 3/27; 9/12, 22; 13/25; 19/17; 23/10; 31/25, 32; 35/13, 26, 32; 39/10; 47/2; 49/13; 55/4, 19; 67/25; 69/6; 79/13, 14; 85/25, 26; 89/3; 97/1, 21; 105/7; 111/13; 115/28; 119/29; 123/4; 137/26; 147/15; 151/23.
bi-, *cf.* **be.**
bidden, *v. to beg, pray,* 143/11, 17; 147/30; 151/23; *pres. ind.* 1 *sg.* bidde, 7/21; 15/33; 21/5, 13; 47/8, 14; 69/32; 83/14; 89/10; 93/2; 97/12; 109/23; 117/8; 3 *sg.* bitt, 77/10; 95/11; 109/11; *opt. pl.* bidden, 141/29; *imp. sg.* bide, 39/6; 101/13; 145/8; bidde, 143/3; 1 *pl.* (*adhort.*), bidde we, 7/31; 2 *pl.* biddeð, 19/19; biddeþ, 21/18; *pret. ind.* 1 *sg.* badd, 97/17; *pl.* beden, 145/2.
bien, *v. to be,* 3/28; 5/13; 7/25; 9/2, 14, 26; 15/4, 20; 19/4, 7; 21/28; 25/31; 27/5, 6, 17; 31/30; 33/5; 37/7; 17; 39/20, 22, 23; 41/16; 47/29; 49/22; 51/30; 53/22, 29; 55/7, 17; 61/4, 18; 63/12; 67/17, 24; 69/1; 71/1, 19; 73/4, 5, 12; 75/14, 27, 35; 77/5, 9; 79/30; 81/8; 87/3, 4, 31; 97/13, 18, *etc.*; ben, 53/12; 61/30; 125/9; 127/13; 129/22, 29; 137/5; 139/29; beon, 121/10; be, 41/14; *ger.* benne, 71/12; 123/34; bene, 105/5; 143/6; *pres. ind.* 1 *sg.* am, 5/13; 7/6, 7, 29; 9/17;

11/7; 13/8, 15; 21/29; 23/9; 27/1, 21; 33/28, *etc.*; ham, 95/23; 2 *sg.* art, 25/33; 29/11; 41/15; 49/19; 51/23; 61/3; 65/25; 67/34, *etc.*; biest, 103/20; best, 135/7; 3 *sg.* is, 3/7, 8, 9, 22, 23, 28; 5/1, 4, 7, 10, 18, 19, 21, 23, 24, 26; 7/15, 16, 25; 9/6, 14, 22, 24, 25, 32; 11/3, 14, 18, 20; 13/12, 30; 15/2, 6, 7, 19, 24; 17/3, 4, 28, 30, 32; 19/1, 2, 7, 16, 34; 21/14, 15; 23/8, *etc.*; ys, 51/26; 81/28; his, 59/8; 119/24; 121/16, 30; 123/25; 129/3, 14; bieð, 3/11; 29/33; 97/4; 139/12; 143/21; 147/30; *pl.* bieð, 8/2; 5/11, 31; 7/2; 13/5; 15/3, 4; 19/5, 25; 21/2, 4, 13, 14, 22; 25/3, 9, 20; 27/9; 29/17, 27; 31/23; 33/13; 41/32; 43/20, 21; 45/14; 47/11; 49/30; 51/24; 53/23, 25; 55/24, 29, 33; 57/22, 25, 33; 59/15; 61/23; 65/12, 14; 67/13; 71/27; 73/19, 21, 23; 77/30; 79/18, 21; 85/12; 87/6, 7; 89/21, *etc.*; bieþ, 25/16; bied, 103/18; beoð, 15/23; 49/26; beð, 87/29; 123/29; 141/9; bið, 103/23; berð, 19/14; bien, 63/15, 17; 69/22; 79/7, 10, 28; 95/3; 109/16; 133/21; ben, 123/28; bie (ʒit), 97/31; *opt. sg.* bie, 3/9; 7/3; 9/32; 15/20; 23/6; 27/18, 22, 28; 29/28; 33/16, 18; 35/8; 39/2, 11, 13, 24, 26, 28; 53/15; 55/3; 57/28; 59/13; 65/1, 31; 67/5, 6, *etc.*; be, 97/30; 141/29; 149/3; *pl.* bien, 19/24; 23/30; 43/30; 45/1; 133/25; 149/7; ben, 135/18; bie, 109/31; *imp. sg.* bie, 59/2, 8; 61/8; 71/16; 73/10; 75/9; 89/35; 91/23; 103/6; 107/8; be, 45/27; *pl.* bieð, 89/30; 101/18; 113/4; 139/16; *pret. ind.* 1 *and* 3 *sg.* was, 5/8; 7/17 (2), 32; 9/27 (2); 11/9, 26; 13/21, 23; 15/11; 23/10; 25/23, *etc.*; 2 *sg.* ware, 17/8; 23/21; 87/16; 109/34; 145/23; were, 25/1; *pl.* wæren, 7/24; 73/21, 31 (2); 111/33; waren, 19/10; 21/12; 55/4; 83/31; 99/7; 103/1; 115/3; 119/12, 14; 123/1; 133/7; 137/16; 143/12, 32; 147/8; 149/12, 13; weren, 103/13; ware, 43/14; *opt. sg.* wære, 21/11; 47/17; 67/9; 85/3; 109/15; ware, 9/17; 11/10; 27/14; 99/25; 119/9; 123/15–18; 151/1; *pl.* wære, 81/7; *part.* ʒeben, 5/14; ibien, 7/30; 15/22, 25; 117/3; bien, 15/28. (*Cf.* ne.)

biene, *sb. prayer, sg. d. ac* 85/20;
141/16; bene, 147/27; *pl.* bienes,
61/6; 65/3; benes, 133/30.
bieten, *v. to mend, repay, atone,
repair,* 67/8; 117/19; *pres. opt.*
3 *sg.* biete, 133/20; *pl.* biete,
77/32; *imp. sg.* biet, 67/8; *pret.
opt.* 3 *sg.* bette, 67/8; *part.* ibett,
25/30.
bilif, *sb. sustenance, sg. nom.* 91/
29; *d.* bilive, 93/17.
binden, *v. to bind,* 17/27; *pres. ind.
pl.* bindeð, 133/1; *pret. part.* ʒebunden, 85/31; ibunden, 41/33;
49/29; 53/11; 101/9; ibunde,
41/15.
biscop, *sb. bishop, sg. d.* biscope, 109/
9; *g.* biscopes, 53/12.
bismeres, *sb. insults,* 51/16; 59/4.
bisne, *adj. short-sighted,* 125/17.
biterliche, *adv. bitterly,* 85/17.
bitt, *see* bidden.
bitter, *adj. bitter,* 33/31; 89/26;
bitere, 41/27; 45/9; 57/16, 34;
89/24; bitre, 119/16; bittere, 145/
25.
bladdre, *sb. bladder, nom. sg.* 73/19.
blanden, *v. to blind, sg. imp.* bland,
127/7.
blast, *sb. blast, breath, sg. nom.* 95/20;
pl. blastes, 45/13.
blescien, *v. to bless,* 83/30; *pres. opt.
pl.* bledscin, 151/19; *imp. sg.* blesci,
13/19; *pret. part* iblesced, 13/7;
51/27; 109/25, 26; 115/32; 117/
29, 30, 32; iblescede, 51/18; 119/
3.
bleðeliche, *see* bliðeliche.
blind, *adj. blind,* 127/4; blinde, 49/
22; 75/34; 109/19; 127/10 (2).
blindfallen, *v to blindfold,* 3 *sg.
pret.* blindfallede, 119/10.
blisse, *sb. bliss, sg.* 13/24; 17/9; 21/
24; 31/9, 14, 26, 27, 28, 29, 30;
33/3, 7; 35/4, *etc.*; *pl.* blisses, 57/
18.
bliðe, *adj. blithe,* 83/21; 91/23;
141/6.
bliðeliche, *adv. blithely,* 11/29; 23/
2; 35/33; 47/20; 59/28; 69/20;
109/18; 133/26; 141/8; 147/21;
bleðeliche, 13/6; 37/14, 16; 47/
23; 77/19; 87/2; 113/29; *comp.*
bliðelicor, 9/18; 55/6; –liker, 23/
3; bleðelicher, 23/19.
blod, *sb. blood, sg. nom. ac.* 21/10;
53/1, 14; 119/21; *d.* blode, 119/
22; 131/27.
bodien, *v. to proclaim, pret. pl.* bode-
den, 15/13.

boc, *sb. book,* 61/32; *d.* boke, 19/9;
37/33; 141/20; boche, 65/12.
bonen, *sb. bones, d. pl.* 93/6.
borde, *sb. board, table, d. sg.* 43/33;
53/9.
borʒin, *v. to borrow,* 77/19.
bot, *sb. boat, d. sg.* bote, 43/32.
bote, *sb. penance, amendment, nom. ac.*
39/4; 77/32.
boðe, *see* baðe.
bouhte, *see* beggen.
bowes, *sb. boughs,* 45/32.
brǽde, *sb. breadth, d.* 45/32.
bread, *sb. bread, nom. ac.* 51/35; 53/
2, 9; 89/3; bred, 147/8; *d.* breade,
149/1.
bredale, *sb. bridal, d.* 95/33.
bredgume, *sb. bridegroom, ac.* 95/33.
breken, *v. to break,* 137/27; *ger.*
brekene, 11/20; *pres. ind.* 2 *sg.*
brekst, 89/15; 3 *sg.* brecþ, 37/28;
brekð, 73/14.
brene, *sb. burning, heat, d.* 19/1;
63/32; 119/24.
bried, *sb. bride, nom.* 103/29.
briht, *adj. adv. bright,* 31/13; 105/
16; brihte, 33/5; 139/7; *superl.*
brihteste, 5/9.
brihtnesse, *sb. brightness,* 31/12.
bringen, *v. to bring,* 23/32; 43/27;
bringe, 33/20; *pres. ind.* 3 *sg.*
bringþ, 35/32; 115/4; bringð, 129/
10; brinkgð, 83/1; brigþ, 37/30;
101/14; *opt. pl.* bringen, 103/22;
pret. 1 *and* 3 *sg.* brohte, 5/8; 9/10;
35/22; 51/20; 57/1; 85/21; 97/
6; 99/6; 105/17; *part.* ibroht,
21/18.
broðer, *sb. brother, sg. d. ac.* 3/4;
11/6; 63/28; 111/27; *pl. ac.*
breðren, 75/31.
bruken, *v. to enjoy,* 139/3.
brusel, *adj. frail,* 91/28.
buʒen, *v. to bow, turn,* 65/13; *pres.
ind. pl.* buʒeð, 51/3; *imp. pl.* buʒeð,
19/18.
buhsum, *adj. obedient,* 51/4; 75/14,
27; 97/13.
buhsumnesse, *sb. obedience,* 107/26
(*note*).
buc, *sb. belly, d.* buce, 53/10.
burh, *sb. city,* 103/11, 13; burʒh,
137/4.
buten, *prep. conj. except, save, but,*
129/20; 137/24; 139/31; 143/13;
bute, 7/25; 9/13; 15/1, 5, 14, 16,
20; 17/16, 31; 19/20, 28; 27/17,
28; 29/3; 31/15; 39/20; 41/33;
43/7, *etc.*
buven, *adv. above,* 103/24.

GLOSSARY. 217

Ch.
(for c see k.)

chapmann, *sb. chapman, merchant,* *nom.* 121/18.
charite, *sb. charity,* 35/14; 39/19, 25; 41/1, 24; 65/19; 95/31; 99/13 (*see* karite).
cheas, *see* chiesen.
cheastes, *sb. strifes,* 41/27.
chele, *sb. chill,* 19/1; 63/33.
chepinge, *sb. bargain,* 11/27; chiepinge, 79/5.
cherche, *sb. church, sg.* 27/4, 6; 43/28; chereche, 51/27; *pl.* chierches, 77/28.
chierche-þinges, *sb. church-things,* 139/30.
chiesen, *v. to choose, pret. ind.* 1 *sg.* cheas, 23/1; *part.* ȝekorene, 17/31; ȝecorene, 49/18; 77/7; 107/10; 131/26; 145/19; icorene, 73/16; ikorene, 119/32.
child, *sb. child, sg. nom. ac.* 49/27, 31; 55/3; 67/19; 87/23; chilt, 85/21; *pl.* childre, 41/16; 55/13; 75/3; children, 35/4; 41/18; 51/24; 59/22; 89/21; 133/7.
childhad, *sb. childhood, d.* -hade, 67/33.
chirch-landes, *sb. church-lands,* 77/28.
chiverinde, *part. pres. shivering,* 63/33.
chiveringe, *sb. gnashing,* 19/1.

D.
dade, *sb. deed, sg.* 127/14; 147/23, 29; *pl.* dades, 15/21; 17/26; 141/6; dædes, 103/11.
dai, *sb. day, sg. nom. ac.* 11/7; 17/12; 19/13, 26; 27/22; 31/31; 61/7; 83/19; 89/32; 113/18; 117/3; daiȝ, 137/26, 32, 34; 147/8; 151/23; *d.* daiȝe, 3/27; 9/22; 35/32; 39/10; 51/23; 55/4; 85/26; 89/18; 117/4; *g.* daiȝes, 17/16; 39/33; 145/23; *pl. g. ac.* 137/4, 9, 15; daȝas, 27/22; daȝes, 137/13; *d.* daiȝen, 67/26.
dæl, *sb. deal, part, sg. ac.* 35/13; dale, 5/17; 21/9.
dælen, *v. to deal, divide, pres.* 1 *sg.* dale, 39/17; deale, 65/33; 2 *sg. ind.* dalst, 45/24; *pret. pl.* dælden, 77/25.
dead, *adj. dead,* 29/25; 147/18; deaðe, 15/23; 77/18; 111/27.
deadbote, *sb. satisfaction, d.* 105/24.

deadliche, *adj. mortal,* 51/4; 61/14, 24; 109/15; dedlich, 143/29.
deale, *see* dælen.
deað, *sb. death, sg. nom. ac.* 3/10; 7/19, 24; 9/18; 25/25; 51/14, 31; 69/5; 105/19, 31, 33; 109/2; 111/7, 30; 113/18, 21; 117/18, 19; *d.* deaðe, 7/32; 9/3; 21/26; 25/26; 33/20, 29; 51/9, 13; 53/7; 87/13; 105/17; 109/7; 111/29; 117/22; 119/2, 7, 26; 121/1; 123/15; 127/19; *g.* deaðes, 51/24; *pl.* 111/28.
deave, *adj. deaf,* 75/34.
dede, *see* don.
dedlich, *see* deadliche.
deme, *sb. judge, nom.* 77/18.
demen, *v. to judge,* 25/27; 53/14; *pres. ind. pl.* diemeð, 57/32; *opt. pl.* demen, 105/23; *pret. part.* idemd, 77/31; 105/25; 119/2.
depnesse, *sb. depth,* 5/10.
derewurðe, *adj. precious,* 15/12; 43/14; 81/26; 85/18; 91/15; derwurðe, 129/13; derworðe, 135/22; *superl.* derewurðeste, 51/28.
derien, *v. to harm, hurt,* 101/30; deriȝen, 61/5.
derne, *adj. secret,* 3/7; dierne, 3/9.
derneliche, *adv. secretly, concealedly,* 141/4; 143/17.
dest, *see* don.
deð, *see* don.
deules, *sb. griefs,* 29/22.
devel, *see* dievel.
diemeð, *see* demen.
diepliche, *adv. deeply, truly,* 7/26.
dier, *sb. beast, sg. nom.* 93/12; *pl.* 139/19; 149/30.
dierne, *see* derne.
diest, *see* don.
dieð, *see* don.
dievel, *sb. devil, sg. nom. ac.* 9/25, 28; 27/10; 39/5; 51/11, 18, 19; 89/29; 101/30; 105/33; 113/20; 115/2; 119/5, 6; devel, 23/18; 29/26; 49/6; 77/3; 131/3; 139/20; *d.* dievle, 11/17; 29/2, 22; 37/21; 41/22, 27; 57/4; 87/7; 89/24; 99/30; 103/2; 119/23; 135/26; dievlen, 57/1; devele, 75/18 (*note*); *g.* dievles, 19/15; 39/7; 41/26; 63/18; 73/19; 83/11, 31; 89/35; 101/2; 111/2, 4; 119/17, 25; 127/19; devles, 45/13; 135/27; *pl. d.* dievlen, 19/5, 33; 91/2.
dievliche, *adj. devilish,* 43/30.
discipline, *sb. discipline,* 125/29; 127/23.

GLOSSARY.

dohter, *sb. daughter, sg.* d. 63/28;
pl. voc. dohtren, 53/33.
dole, *sb. deal, part, ac. sg.* 111/22.
dom, *sb. doom, judgment, sg. nom.
ac.* 59/2; 67/23; 105/7, 10, 30,
31; 115/19, 30; *d.* dome, 51/21;
53/15; 67/10; 105/14, 32; 113/
28; 115/28; 117/18; 137/5.
domesdai, *sb. doomsday, d. sg.* 25/
27; domesdaiȝe, 11/11.
domesmann, *sb. judge, nom.* 121/22.
don, *v. to do,* 3/2, 19; 23/15; 29/
3, 13; 33/33; 57/23; 59/5, *etc.*;
donn, 71/17; *ger.* donne, 3/12,
17, 18; 15/1, 10; 17/19; 21/27;
27/31; 33/13; 35/6, 23; 87/4,
31; 39/3; 43/8; 61/34; 63/10;
73/27; 75/6, 17; 81/14; 83/7;
109/11; 113/19; 135/12; 137/6;
done, 61/21; 129/4; *pres. ind.*
1 *sg.* do, 7/28; 103/18; 2 *sg.* dost,
33/31; dest, 41/1; 45/23; 77/3;
133/12; 135/28; diest, 9/28; 41/
2; 103/5; 3 *sg.* doð, 3/14, 16; 5/
28; 13/21; 35/2; 45/20, 30; 63/
22; 65/3; 71/21; 73/26; 77/4;
103/14; doþ, 37/15; deð, 3/15;
29/26, 27; 73/15; 107/19; 109/
14; 127/11; 133/19, 30; 139/19;
dieð, 5/20, 28; 25/10; 33/7; 37/
17; 63/23; 85/29; 109/15; 113/
3; 133/17; dieth, 143/24; *pl.*
doð, 5/31, 32; 35/5, 6; 57/21, 22;
61/12, 24; 89/33; 137/21; deð
(?), 125/29; don, 77/14, 15, 16;
opt. sg. do, 37/20; 39/9; 57/20,
21; 59/12; 69/31; 75/7; 99/14;
121/14; 133/19; *pl.* don, 35/7;
69/23; 143/17; *imp. sg.* do, 13/
19; 27/29; 37/33; 59/31; 71/8,
etc.; *pl.* doð, 19/15, 18; 123/5;
doþ, 27/31; — *pret.* 1 *and* 3 *sg.*
dede, 5/16; 7/27; 9/10; 11/10,
32; 13/20; 17/7; 33/27, 32, 33,
34; 45/29, *etc.*; 2 *sg.* dedest, 11/9;
23/12; 145/26, 27, 31; *pl.* deden,
51/15; 99/19; 149/23, 24; *part.*
ȝedon, 17/14; 29/17; 51/21; 101/
24; 117/24; 121/25; 133/16;
145/29; ȝiedon, 145/25; idon, 3/
15, 25, 26; 7/7, 24, 25; 9/7; 13/
2, 15; 15/31; 17/10, 18; 25/29,
30; 47/1; 51/16; 67/35; 78/13;
75/10; 85/7; 105/27, 29; 111/33;
113/2, 17; 147/22; don, 151/5.
drǣden, *v. to fear, pres. ind.* 3 *sg.*
drat, 63/5, 6; *pl.* drǣdeð, 63/1;
dradeð, 61/24; 69/15; *imp. sg.*
drǣd, 61/33; *pl.* drǣdeð, 61/29;
part. dradinde, 59/15.

drǣdnesse, *sb. fear,* 59/17, 24; 61/
3; 63/2; dradnesse, 59/18; 61/12;
63/3, 5, 7, 8, 10; 73/11; 91/13;
141/24.
draȝen, *v. to draw, go, pl. ind. pres.*
draȝeð, 57/26.
dranc, *see* drinken.
drench, *sb. drink, sg. nom.* 89/7;
dat. drenkch, 87/29; *pl.* drenches,
43/10; 127/12; 135/12; 137/24,
35; 139/9, 23.
drieri, *adj. dreary,* 3/13.
drifst, drifð, *see* driven.
drihten, *sb. lord, nom. ac. sg.* 43/3;
67/29.
drinke, *sb. drink, sg. d. ac.* 137/28;
drinken, 149/2 (*inf.* ?).
drinken, *v. to drink,* 37/15; 43/14;
107/14; 139/6; *pres. ind. pl.*
drinkeð, 137/26; *pret. ind.* 3 *sg.*
dranc, 51/10.
drinkeres, *sb. drinkers,* 139/2.
driven, *v. to drive,* 41/32; *pres. ind.*
2 *sg.* drifst, 87/18; 3 *sg.* drifð,
83/16; drifþ, 99/30; *pl.* driveð,
29/9; *pret. ind.* 3 *sg.* drof, 91/6;
part. ȝedriven, 7/17; 111/6; i-
driven, 181/6.
drope, *sb. drop, sg. ac.* 145/32; *pl.*
dropes, 43/31.
drunkenesse, *sb. drunkenness,* 23/
26.
dumbe, *adj. dumb,* 75/34; 109/20,
21.
dune, *sb. hill, nom. d. ac. sg.* 103/
12, 15; 111/12, 21 (ðune); 143/
11.
dure, *sb. door, sg. ac.* 143/3, 6; *pl.
ac.* duren, 99/23.
dust, *sb. dust, sg. nom. ac.* 47/27;
95/21; *d.* duste, 39/18; 67/1.
dwel, *sb. error, sg. ac.* 29/9; *d.*
dwele, 39/28; 83/10.
dwellen, *v. to refrain, pres. ind.* 2
sg. dwellest, 135/28.
dwelmenn, *sb. heretics, pl.* 27/18.

E.

eadi, *adj. blessed,* 25/9, 33; 29/15,
21; 31/8, 14; 33/13; 35/3, 18;
37/4; 49/24; 55/15; 59/25; 95/
9; 99/9; 107/21; 113/3, 6; 117/
35; 121/10; 123/25; 125/8; 133/
10; 141/2, 12, 17; eadie, 81/9;
eadiȝe, 103/4; 111/22; 113/32;
eadiȝen, 35/23.
eadinesse, *sb. happiness,* 25/7; 33/
22; 43/1, 19; 113/24; 115/1, 19;
145/14; ædinesse, 95/34.

GLOSSARY. 219

eadmode, *adj. humble, meek,* 49/10;
57/25; 59/1, 10.
eadmodliche, *adv. humbly,* 39/6;
113/31; 129/23; 141/26.
eadmodnesse, *sb. humility, sg.* 7/1;
31/12; 47/26; 49/3, 5; 51/9;
53/20, 34; 55/11; 57/5, 8, 30;
59/3, 13; 85/12; edmodnesse, 49/
1; *pl.* edmodnesses, 125/18.
ealch, *see* elch.
ealde, *adj. old,* 7/28; 109/4; 111/
30; 119/6; 149/29; elde, 27/26;
superl. eldest, 149/19.
ealleshwer, *see* elleshwar.
eard, *sb. land, sg. ac.* 35/5; *d.* earde,
23/32.
eare, *sb. ear, sg. ac.* 13/18; 127/29;
pl. earen, 51/1; 61/5; 133/26;
145/5.
earme, *adj. poor,* 17/24; 63/31;
89/34; 103/16; arme, 21/15.
earninge, *sb. merit,* 21/19, 21; 29/5.
earres, *sb. earnest,* 31/28; erres, 19/
28.
eavre, *see* œvre.
ech, *see* eo.
eche, *sb. addition,* 51/32.
eche, *adj. eternal,* 9/3; 19/31; 25/
29, 30; 31/28; 33/21, etc.
echen, *v. to increase, add,* 51/15;
pres. ind. 3 *sg.* ecð, 5/26; *pret.
part.* ieiht, 147/28.
edmodnesse, *see* ead-.
eft, *adv. conj. again,* 11/25; 18/4;
15/1; 19/33; 27/28, 32; 29/6,
23, etc.
eftsones, *adv. conj. again,* 31/10;
71/16; 89/14; 123/20; efsones,
99/14; 111/9.
eifulle, *adj. awful,* 19/5.
eiȝe, *sb. terror, awe, fear,* 19/29;
127/16; 141/25; heiȝe, 61/21;
eiȝhe, 55/26; 81/21.
eiȝe, *sb. eye, sg. d. ac.* eiȝen, 69/9; *pl.*
49/17; 61/4; 81/30; 125/9, 16,
17; eiȝene, 51/2; 85/14; 119/9;
125/10, 11, 14, 23; 127/18; 133/
25; eieȝene, 87/2; eiene, 91/28.
eihte, *sb. property,* 17/12, 14; 33/
15; 37/15, 21, 23; 69/23, 28; 75/
22; 77/19, 27; 79/6, 26, 27, 30,
33; heihte, 41/19.
eilen, *v. to do harm, pres. ind.* 2 *sg.*
eilest, 133/11; *pret.* 3 *sg.* eilede,
133/6; *pl.* eileden, 133/8.
eisliche, *adj. awful,* 19/25; 105/32.
eisliche, *adv. awfully,* 93/24.
eo, *conj. also,* 9/7; 13/22; 35/12;
41/14, 21; 43/21; 47/17; 51/13;
53/7; 55/18; 71/11; 73/5, 20;

75/5; 93/2; 109/34; 119/18;
127/11; 133/2; ech, 127/27; 129/
27; iec, 3/16; 7/28; 21/4; 41/
19; 51/15; 61/15; 65/15.
ecnesse, *sb. eternity,* 21/25.
elch, *pron. each, every,* 61/33; 123/
19; ealch, 77/24; ællch, 19/15 (?);
ælche, 11/7; 17/12; 77/10; 89/
14; ællche, 19/26; alche, 19/13;
21/16; 35/27; 61/7; 133/23;
139/17; 151/11; ælchen, 99/16;
alchne, 39/34; elchere, 75/19;
77/20; alchere, 131/25; 141/27.
elde, *see* ealde.
eldren, *sb. parents,* 103/23; 109/4.
ele, *sb. oil,* 33/3.
elles, *adv. conj. else,* 27/16, 27;
89/23; 135/28; 151/5.
elleshwar, *adv. elsewhere,* 19/21;
ealleshwer, 123/14.
embe, *prep. about,* 41/23; 49/2;
53/23, 24; 69/21; 73/29; 99/2;
109/19; 147/4.
embehwile, *adv. sometimes,* 63/32.
embeþanc, *sb. consideration, care,
sg. nom. ac.* 39/26; -ðanc, 69/14;
d. -ðanke, 103/15; -þanke, 141/24;
pl. -ðankes, 69/16.
emcristen, *sb. fellow-Christian, sg.
ac.* 11/23; 77/20; 79/13; 81/5;
133/12; -cristenn, 79/4; *g.* em-
cristenes, 67/12.
emlich, *adj. like, even,* 31/13; emliche, 25/16.
engelisc, *adj. English,* 63/14.
enne, *see* an.
eordlic, *see* ierðlich.
eorða, *see* ierðe.
eremite, *sb. hermit, sg. nom.* 73/27;
hermite, 73/30; *pl.* eremites, 35/
3; hermites, 137/10; heremites,
143/14.
erres, *see* earres.
erðliche, *see* ierðlich.
ervename, *sb. inheritance,* 117/10.
eten, *v. to eat,* 3/25; 37/15; 43/13;
107/14; *pres. ind.* 2 *sg.* etst, 51/
23; *pret. ind.* 3 *sg.* att, 51/10.
eu, *see* ȝe.
evel, *sb. evil, sg. nom. ac.* 9/14; 13/
19; 27/33; 29/6, 14; 51/26; 53/
6; 61/21; 67/7; 79/7; 103/26;
129/4; 133/17, 19; *d.* evele, 19/
18; 59/30; 61/23; 65/13; 87/3
(*pl.* ?); 135/6; *g.* eveles, 29/12;
pl. eveles, 39/11; 103/2.
evel, *adj. evil,* 11/3; 29/8; 59/31;
101/31; evele, 11/4; 15/25; 31/
7; 41/21; 43/17; 45/13; 59/1;
67/3; 71/27, 33; 75/2; 79/17,

22; 87/1; 95/29; 109/34; 115/4; 123/31; 125/15; 133/15; 141/7, 8; hevele, 11/1; evle, 147/12; eveles, 9/6.
evele, *adv. evil*, 11/8; 25/30; 57/22; 61/12; 133/16; 149/24, 25.
evelnesse, *sb. evilness*, 11/14; 113/26; 127/9.
evre, *see* ævre.
euwȝ, *see* ȝe.

F.

fader, *sb. father, sg.* 7/18, 32; 9/25; 11/7; 13/21; 15/11; 25/11, 13, 15, 26; 27/2; 35/3; 37/3, 6; 41/8; 49/15; 51/8, 31; 63/5, 7, 28; 91/20; 93/2; 97/7; 109/7, 28; 111/1; 113/5; 117/6, 12; 119/6, 28; 143/3; 151/19; *pl.* faderes, 7/30; 15/1; 27/15; 73/32; 149/10, 12.
fair, *adj. fair*, 91/24; 109/5; faire, 11/23; 29/34; 43/30; 95/31; 139/7.
fællen, *v. to fell*, 21/15.
fallen, *v. to fall, pres. ind. pl.* falleð, 109/19; *pret. ind.* 1 *sg.* fel, 13/29; fell, 83/24.
fand-, *see* fond-.
fare, *sb. drive*, 137/4.
faren, *v. to fare, go, drive*, 73/24; fare, 23/22; *pres. ind.* 3 *sg.* farð, 5/27; 17/29; 27/10; 57/11; 61/22; 127/5; *pl.* fareð, 35/5; 45/8 (2); 73/20; 79/13; *opt.* 2 *sg.* fare, 103/21; 3 *sg.* fare, 15/2; *pl.* faren, 55/31; *imp. pl.* fareð, 89/23.
fast, *adj. fast, firm*, 29/31; faste, 15/27; 89/1; 45/15; 51/29; 95/6; feste, 29/29.
faste, *v. to fasten, strengthen, sg. imp.* 83/22.
1. fasten, *sb. fast, fasting (jejunium), sg. nom. dat. ac.* 33/29; 93/16; 125/31; 137/1, 3, 6, 9, 18, 28; 149/15; *d.* fastene, 89/11; *pl. nom.* fasten, 137/16.
2. fasten, *v. to fast*, 3/17; 137/12, 25; *pres. ind.* 3 *sg.* fast, 5/27; *pl.* fasteð, 137/25; *imp. pl.* fasteð, 19/17; *part.* fastinde, 137/17; *pret.* 3 *sg.* faste, 137/9, 15; fastede, 137/13.
fastliche, *adv. firmly*, 21/10; 27/16; 29/32; 37/23; 39/5; 69/34; 97/2; 135/25.
fatt, *sb. vessel, sg. nom. ac.* 123/34; 135/21, 22; *pl. ac.* faten, 123/33.

feawe, *adj. few*, 25/2; 45/27; 57/12; 133/21.
feden, *v. to feed*, 139/24; 149/17; *pres. ind.* 3 *sg.* fett, 53/3; *pl.* fedeð, 53/2; *imp. sg.* fed, 149/1; *pret. part.* ifedd, 43/12; 109/34.
fel, *see* fallen.
felauscipe, *sb. fellowship, sg. ac.* 41/31.
felawȝes, *sb. fellows*, 139/5.
fele, *adj. many*, 21/16; 23/27; 29/27; 91/2; 125/16, 17; 139/24.
fellen, *v. to fill*, 137/34; 139/9; *pres. ind.* 3 *sg.* felð, 83/33.
felste, *sb. help, d. sg.*, 151/12.
felðes, *sb. filths*, 131/9.
ferr, *adv. far*, 45/32; 73/31.
ferrene, *adv. from afar*, 103/15.
ferst, *see* first.
fet, *see* fot.
fett, *see* feden.
fier, *sb. fire, sg. nom. ac.* 29/1; 35/31; 61/31; *d.* fiere, 19/31; 25/30; 35/21; 63/32; 139/7.
fiet, *see* fot.
fif, *num. five*, 17/1, 2, 5, 7, 11, 20, 21.
fiftene, *num. fifteen*, 147/27.
fihten, *v. to fight, pl. ind. pres.* 89/35.
finden, *v. to find*, 49/11; 73/33; 75/2; 87/32; 129/10; *pres. ind.* 2 *sg.* finst, 45/27; 3 *sg.* fint, 95/8; *pl.* findeð, 13/4; 15/5; 73/27; 85/22; 121/17; 123/14; findeþ, 103/24; finden, 37/33; finde we, 147/14; *pret. ind.* 3 *sg.* fond, 111/10; *pl.* funden 99/18; *part.* ȝefunden, 61/2; ȝefunde, 9/28.
fingre, *sb. finger, d. sg.* 49/25.
firliche, *adv. suddenly*, 123/15.
first, *sb. respite, time, sg. ac.* 17/19; fierst, 89/16; ferst, 147/22; *d.* firste, 17/23.
fiteres, *sb. rags*, 49/29.
fiðeres, *sb. wings*, 101/34.
flasch, *see* flesc.
flen, *v. to flee, ger.* flene, 137/11; 3 *sg. ind. pret.* fleih, 137/12.
flesc, *sb. flesh, sg. nom. ac.* 21/9; 53/13; 109/32; flesch, 93/16; flæsch, 97/23; flasch, 53/1; *d.* flesce, 87/7; 131/27; flesche, 87/7; 97/24; *g.* flesces, 89/29; flesches, 23/24; 39/8; 135/15; flasches, 109/32.
flesliches, *adj. carnal*, 43/5.
fliȝen, *sb. flies*, 89/33.
flode, *sb. flood, d. sg.* 43/24.
flotten, *v. to float*, 33/4.

GLOSSARY. 221

flowinde, *part. pres. flowing*, 81/33.
flum, *sb. river, d. sg.* 121/6.
folȝien, *v. to follow*, 107/2; folȝin, 15/6; 23/19, 20; 33/27; 41/17; 43/1, 16; 45/31; 49/8, 19; 61/17; 75/20; 77/5; 81/9; 87/18; 97/11, 13, 27; 101/27; 119/32; 139/22; 149/11; 151/11; *pres. ind.* 3 *sg.* folȝeð, 23/23; 71/25; 111/3; folȝið, 129/14; folȝid, 99/8; *pl.* folȝieð, 57/1; folȝið, 15/14; 41/26; 43/3, 21; 99/9; 109/18; *opt.* 2 *sg.* folȝe, 109/33; 111/20; folȝhi, 27/18; *pl.* folȝin, 15/5; *imp. sg.* folȝe, 69/3; 75/12; 133/10; folȝih, 77/9; *pret.* 1 *and* 3 *sg.* folȝede, 13/27; 83/11; 2 *sg.* folȝedest, 23/11, 17; *pl.* folȝeden, 57/5; *part.* ifolȝed, 15/15; 93/9.
folȝeres, *sb. followers*, 41/26; 57/2.
folk, *sb. folk, people, sg. nom. ac.* 79/22; 137/4; folc, 117/9; *d.* folke, 55/12; 85/20; 143/30; *g.* folkes, 127/8.
fond, see finden.
fondin, *v. to try, tempt*, 73/17; *pres. ind.* 3 *sg.* fandeð, 3/18; *imp. sg.* fonde, 139/10; 1 *pl.* fondie we, 21/1; *pret.* 3 *sg.* fondede, 111/9; *part.* ȝefanded, 73/28; ȝefonded, 73/12; ifonded, 71/11; fonded, 41/19.
fandinge, *sb. temptation, d. sg.* 43/29, 30; *pl.* fandinges, 73/11; fondinges, 29/22; 39/8; 103/3; 107/23.
for, *prep. for, on account of, because of, through*, 3/11, 13; 5/26, 34; 7/4, 17, 18, 19, 22 (2), 23; 9/29; 11/30; 17/32; 19/1, 2; 21/5, 8, 13, 18, 19, 30; 27/28; 29/5 (2); 33/9, 13, 28, 29; 35/3; 37/15, 17; 39/5, 10, 18; 41/9; 43/22, 29 (2), *etc.*
for, *conj. for, because*, 27/9.
forbeden, *v. to forbid, pres. ind.* 3 *sg.* forbiet, 81/22; forbett, 11/4, 27; 39/3; 135/12; forbettt, 37/23; forbet, 87/30; *imp. sg.* forbet, 59/29; *pret. part.* forboden, 7/26; forbodene, 41/28; 119/11.
forberen, *v. to forbear, pl. pres. opt.* 97/12.
forbisne, *sb. example, nom. d. ac.* 13/16; 15/10; 29/18; 33/6; 39/21; 47/24; 49/6, 21, 24; 51/10; 65/30; 79/22; 113/11; 127/11, 27; 129/18; 135/5; 137/11; 141/28; 143/14, 29; forbysne, 49/12; *pl.* forbisne, 49/24.

forbod, *sb. prohibition, forbidding, sg. ac.* 11/20; 37/29; *d.* forbode, 5/22; 11/4; 113/18; *pl.* forbodes, 67/31; 81/22.
forboden, see forbeden.
forbuȝen, *v. to avoid, imp. sg.* forbuh, 39/3.
fordemen, *v. to condemn, pres. ind.* 3 *sg.* fordemþ, 53/14; *pret. pl.* fordemden, 51/13; 59/2; *part.* fordemd, 5/4.
fordruȝede, *part. pret. dried up*, 83/1; 85/1; 145/33.
forealded, *part. pret. grown old*, 83/10.
forenammde, *part. pret. foresaid*, 15/29.
forfaren, *v. to perish*, 113/24; 149/11, 21; *pres. ind.* 3 *sg.* forfarð, 45/30; *opt. pl.* forfaren, 125/30; *pret. part.* forfaren, 137/5.
forȝaf, see forȝiven.
forgaud, *part. pret. despised*, 145/14.
forgelt, *adj. guilty*, 145/11, 14, 18; forgilt, 7/29; forȝelt, 7/7; 13/15; 21/29; 67/6; 83/28; forȝilt, 67/9; forȝielt, 11/4; 85/15; forȝeilt, 119/9; forgilte, 63/18; 113/13, 33; 145/27; fogelte, 145/26; forȝelte, 79/24; 95/29; forȝeltes, 95/23.
forȝeten, *v. to forget*, 7/11; 87/23; *pres. ind.* 1 *sg.* forȝete, 47/17; 87/24; *pl.* forȝiteð, 7/4; *opt.* 3 *sg.* forȝete, 87/23; *pl.* forȝeten, 69/12; *imp. sg.* forȝeit, 151/21; *pret. part.* forȝeten, 87/21.
forȝielden, *v. to repay*, 75/32, 35; *pret. part.* forȝolden, 75/35.
forȝifnesse, see forȝivenesse.
forȝiven, *v. to forgive*, 27/12; 123/21; *ger.* forgivene, 21/7; *pres. ind.* 2 *sg.* forȝifst, 39/34; *pret. ind.* 3 *sg.* forȝaf, 111/30, 31; 2 *sg.* forȝave, 85/17; 145/26; *part.* forȝiven, 51/31; forȝivene, 111/33.
forȝivenesse, *sb. forgiveness*, 15/33 (*MS.* forȝivesse); 19/19; 21/6; 39/6; forȝifnesse, 123/6; 137/7; 145/2, 11.
forȝivenlich, *adj. pardoning, pardonable*, 145/16; -liche, 123/8.
forȝolden, see forȝielden.
forhaten, *part. pret. promised*, 8/15.
forholen, *part. pret. concealed*, 123/10.
forhowen, *v. to contempt, despise, pres. ind.* 2 *sg.* forhowest, 65/28; 3 *sg.* forhoweð, 65/20; *pret.* 3 *sg.* forhowede, 123/17.

foriswel3en, *v. to swallow*, 45/26;
forswole3en, 139/18, 19.
forcuð, *adj. bad, ignominious, comp.*
forcuðere, 73/21; *superl.* forcupeste,
51/13.
forlai3, *see* forliggen.
forlaten, *v. to leave, forsake*, 111/7;
pres. ind. 2 *sg.* forlatst, 65/28;
103/21; 3 *sg.* forlat, 71/22, 24;
pl. forlætep, 5/33; forlateð, 35/3;
55/27; 103/22; *opt.* 2 *sg.* forlate,
93/4; 3 *sg.* 67/18; *pl.* forlaten,
141/19; *imp. sg.* forlat, 73/4; 103/
20; *pret. ind.* 1 *and* 3 *sg.* forliet,
23/11; 85/19; 2 *sg.* forliete, 23/
17; *part.* forlaten, 3/13; 23/23;
43/2, 16; 87/1, 21.
forleie(3)en, *see* forliggen.
forleire, *sb. copulation, d. sg.* 131/
17.
forliesen, *v. to lose, destroy*, 11/16;
39/32; 41/10; 55/7, 32; 61/14,
15; 69/15; 93/26; *pres. ind.* 2
sg. forliest, 65/23, 29; 127/3; 3
sg. 5/29; 65/21; *pl.* forliesseð, 9/1;
61/26; 67/11; *opt.* 2 *sg.* forlies,
61/4; 3 *sg.* forliese, 63/6; *pl.* forliesen, 43/28; *pret. ind.* 3 *sg.* for-
leas, 43/26; 81/23; *opt.* 3 *sg.*
forlure, 11/27; *part.* forloren, 17/
12; 27/21; 59/13; 61/18; 67/2;
73/14; 81/1; 83/22; 117/35;
127/14; 131/22; 145/14; forlorene,
139/1.
forliggen, *v. to commit adultery, de-
flower, imp. sg.* forli3e, 67/31;
pret. ind. 3 *sg.* forlai3, 81/24; *part.*
forlei3en, 131/11; forleiene, 111/
29.
forloren, forlure, *see* forliesen.
forme, *num. first*, 7/18; 9/27;
superl. formeste, 49/12.
forsaken, *v. to forsake*, 31/6; *pres.
ind.* 1 *sg.* forsake, 9/31; 3 *sg.* for-
sakþ, 45/6; *pl.* forsakeð, 29/26;
pret. ind. 3 *sg.* forsoch, 145/24;
part. forsaken, 23/29; 85/16; 111/
31; forsakene, 3/2; 73/23.
forsceawin, *v. to foreshow*, 17/29.
forsceawnesse, *sb. foresight*, 103/8,
9.
forswald, *part. pret. scorched*, 119/
24.
forsweri3en, *v. to forswear*, 9/16;
forssweren, 9/7; *pres. ind. pl.* for-
swerieð, 61/26.
forto, *conj. in order to*, 15/10; 17/
6; 35/7; 45/11, 12, 17; 57/30;
73/26; 79/12; 101/20; 113/15;
117/22; 143/13, 30; 151/9, 10,
18; for te, 11/13; 45/13; 57/30;
73/20; 85/24.
forð, *adv. forth, along, ever*, 9/3; 11/
17; 19/33; 21/1, 24; 23/13, 24;
25/12, 31; 85/21; 95/28; 113/16;
121/25; 143/21; 147/31; forþ, 25/
15; *comp.* forðer, *further*, 47/1;
55/27; 59/28; 79/28; furðer, 57/
3; 75/28.
forðan, *conj. because, for*, 3/10; 5/
11, 13, 25; 15/4, 5, 20; 19/16, 20,
28; 23/11; 31/24; 33/1; 35/11;
37/22, 28, 31; 43/31, *etc.*; forþan,
129/4; 131/18, 25; forðan ðat,
123/32; forðan ðe, 9/15; 23/17;
25/8; 27/1; 29/12; 35/15; 45/
30; 51/19; 59/13; 61/16; 63/4;
75/20; 123/12; forðan þe, 123/
34.
forðat, *conj. because, for*, 75/13; 99/
33.
forðbringe, *v. to bring forth*, 2 *sg.
opt. pres.* 47/10.
forðdra3en, *v. to draw forth*, 147/29.
forðen, *adv. even*, 33/15.
forði, *conj. because, therefore*, 11/9,
16; 13/24; 15/28; 17/7; 25/3,
9; 31/15; 33/2, 24; 47/28, *etc.*;
forþi, 129/5; 133/9; 147/24; forði
ðat, 7/29; 13/7; 15/27; 47/21;
49/4; 51/21; 55/10; 67/11; 85/
34; 91/26; 105/17; forði þat,
145/17; forþi ðat, 55/12; 149/21.
forðsceawin, *v. to show*, 147/23.
forðsið, *sb. departure, death, d. sg.*
-siðe, 17/24.
forwurpen, *v. to reject, cast away*,
83/13; *pres. ind. pl.* forwerpeð,
73/22; *opt.* 2 *sg.* forwerp, 83/15;
pret. ind. 1 *and* 3 *sg.* forwarp, 83/
11, 14; *part.* forworpen, 13/31.
forwurðen, *v. to perish, be wasted
away, pres. ind. pl.* forwurðeð, 83/
12; *pret. part.* forwurðen, 83/10.
fot, *sb. foot, sg. ac.* 29/8; *d.* fote,
135/2; *pl. nom. ac.* fiet, 17/27;
85/18; 89/35; 119/11, 12; fet,
145/10; fett, 133/31.
fowerti, *num. forty*, 137/9, 13, 15.
fram, *prep. from*, 5/9; 11/17; 17/
24; 19/15, 18, 30, 32; 23/12, 17,
23, 31; 37/1; 41/32; 43/17; 57/
10; 59/29; 61/23; 63/27, 30, 31;
65/13; 67/32; 73/31; 75/18; 81/
21, 22, 30; 83/15, *etc.*; from, 61/
22; 95/27; fro, 43/14; 55/22;
59/31; 103/2.
framde, *sb. strangers*, 13/9; 19/4;
41/22; 65/6.
fram ðat, *conj. since*, 9/21.

GLOSSARY.

freme, *sb. profit, advantage,* 47/30; 87/17.
frend, *see* **friend**.
frevreð, *see* **frievrien**.
frie, *adj. free,* 135/30.
friend, *sb. friend, sg. voc.* 21/26; *d.* frend, 115/31; *pl. nom. ac.* friend, 65/6; 75/31; 81/7; *d.* friende, 9/8; friennden, 41/22.
frievrenesses, *sb. consolations,* 57/18.
frievrien, *v. to console,* 85/24; *pres. ind.* 3 *sg.* frievreð, 87/26; frevreð, 105/22; *pret. part.* ʒefrievred, 83/32.
fro, from, *see* **fram**.
frovre, *sb. comfort, nom. sg.* 97/1.
frovre-gost, *sb. spirit of consolation, paraclet, ac. sg.* 83/33.
ful-, *see* **full-**.
fule, *adj. foul,* 53/9, 10; 63/30; 83/6; 87/15; 123/30; 131/5; 139/8; full, 93/26.
fulfremed, *pret. part. finished,* 39/23.
full, *adj. full, quite,* 15/24, 25; 53/27; 63/31; 73/18; 101/8; 139/8; fulle, 65/22.
fullʒewiss, *adv. certainly, surely,* 45/6; 49/19; 77/30; 91/16; 103/21; -ʒewis, 121/8; 129/9; -iwis, 27/9; fulʒewis, 65/29; 105/3; 133/1; fuliwis, 57/23.
fulliche, *adv. fully,* 51/8.
fullwroht, *pret. part. finished,* 39/24.
fultume, *sb. help, d. sg.* 23/32; 47/3, 13; 71/3, 31; 81/10; 95/33; 97/32; 113/29; 121/11.
funden, *see* **finden**.

G, ʒ.

gaderen, *v. to gather, pres. ind.* 3 *sg.* gadereð, 47/26; *pret. part.* igadered, 91/14; 149/13; 151/17; ʒeigadered, 91/24.
ʒaf, *see* **ʒiven**.
ʒalle, *sb. gall, ac. sg.* 119/16.
galnesse, *sb. lechery, luxury, fornication, sg.* 23/27; 89/27; 131/4; 135/19; *pl.* galnesses, 48/11, 18.
gan, *v. to go, ger.* gonne, 127/31; *pres. ind.* 2 *sg.* gost, 85/34; 3 *sg.* gað, 127/4; 139/17, 19; *pl.* gað, 89/3; *opt.* 3 *sg.* go, 89/18; 143/23; *imp. sg.* ga, 3/3; 11/17; 17/9; 69/2; 109/27, 31, 32; 127/32; 139/4; 143/2, 5; go, 91/4; 105/13; *pl.* gað, 19/30; 53/34; *pret.* 3 *sg.* ʒiede, 69/3, 7; 83/2, 11; 85/16; 119/22; 121/5; *part.* ʒegan, 121/26 (*see* **wenden**).
gann, *see* **ʒinnen**.
ʒapnesse, *see* **ʒeap-**.
ʒarke, *v. to prepare, imp.* 2 *sg.* 73/10; *pret. part.* iʒarked, 103/31.
gast, *sb. ghost, spirit, sg. nom. ac.* 3/12; 7/6; 23/11, 15; 35/30; 41/29; 59/21; 61/7, 9; 73/1; 79/2; 83/9, 17; 85/10, 11; 89/21; 135/23; gost, 83/9, 22, 25; 93/3; 95/21; 97/23; *d.* gaste, 21/21; 25/24; 89/8; 131/2; goste, 91/23; 97/23; *g.* gastes, 41/31; *pl.* gastes, 23/20, 26, 31; gostes, 91/5; 103/23.
gastlich, *adj. spiritual,* 73/29, 34; gastliche, 7/30; 15/1; 43/19, 27; 45/11; 53/24; 57/15, 19; 73/29; gostliche, 85/30.
gate, *sb. gate, sg. nom. ac.* 91/17; 119/31; *pl. nom. ac.* ʒaten, 27/7, 9; gaten, 99/23.
gavele, *sb. usury, d. sg.* 77/24, 26; goule, 79/6.
gaveleres, *sb. usurers,* 77/24, 32; 121/21; gouleres, 77/31.
gawrinde, *pres. part. looking,* 133/26.
ʒe—ʒe, *conj. as well—as,* 95/17.
ʒe, *pron. ye, you, nom.* 5/32; 19/20; 27/30; 31/18; 41/26, 30, 32 (2); 49/11; 51/24, 32, 34, 35; 53/1, 33; 61/30; 69/20 (2), 21, 22, 23; 71/29, 31; 79/24, 25; 81/4; 93/23; 97/12; 125/29; ʒie, 7/22; 19/14, 30, 31, 33; 21/14, 22; 31/19; 41/33; 69/10, 12, 14, 15; 79/22, 23, 27; 81/7; 89/21; 97/1; 123/4, 5; 125/30; 135/19, 20, 22; 139/33; hie, 135/18; *d. ac.* eu, 59/23; 71/28; euwʒ, 41/32; ʒew, 15/9; 21/17, 18, 21, 24; 27/31; 45/6; 89/23; 123/33; 131/24; 135/14, 19; 139/20; ʒeu, 19/16, 21; 21/4, 14, 20; 27/22; 41/31; 51/30; 53/34; 59/26; 69/10, 19, 22; 71/30; 73/1, 2; 79/21 (3), 23, 29, 32; 81/3, 4; 91/1; 95/13; 97/12, 21; *g.* ʒeure, 67/16.—ʒewselven, *yourselves, nom. d. ac.* 123/5; ʒeuselven, 53/33; 79/21; 93/23; 95/28.
ʒeald, *see* **ʒielden**.
ʒeap, *adj. prudent, crafty,* 81/14; 89/35; 99/26; ʒeape, 79/11, 18, 22; 101/17, 18.
ʒeapnesse, *sb. prudence,* 99/25; 101/4, 19, 27; ʒepnesse, 99/21; ʒapnesse, 103/8, 9.

ȝear, *sb. years, pl.* 147/27; hier, 143/32.
ȝeave, *see* ȝiven.
ȝebede. *sb. prayer, sg. nom.* 143/20, 23; *d. ac.* ibede, 135/28; 143/16.
ȝebidden, *v. to pray (refl.)*, 143/2.
ȝedett, *part. pret. concealed*, 123/1.
ȝediht, *part. pret. ordained*, 39/27.
ȝedweld, *part. pret. deceived*, 15/19.
ȝedwoll, *sb. error, nom. sg.* 27/27.
ȝefele, *v. to feel, pres. ind.* 1 *sg.* 83/32; 2 *sg.* ȝefelst, 127/15.
ȝefostred, *pret. part. nourished*, 43/12.
ȝegunnen, *see* ȝinnen.
ȝȝherhþs, *sb. hearing, nom. sg.* 17/4.
ȝeheveȝed, *pret. part. made heavy, heavy laden*, 71/27; iheveȝed, 69/16.
ȝehieren, *v. to hear*, 69/20; ȝeheren, 133/28; 143/5; iheren, 17/17; 27/14; *pres. ind.* 2 *sg.* iherst, 61/8; ihierst, 87/15; 3 *sg.* ȝeherð, 41/12; 45/29; iherð, 57/15, 17; 103/28; ȝehiereð, 123/31; 139/12; *pl.* ȝehiereð, 7/21; 51/2; 79/16; ihereð, 19/11; *opt.* 2 *sg.* ȝehiere, 53/21; ȝehire, 125/21; *pret.* 1 *and* 3 *sg.* ȝeherde, 147/24; iherde, 147/26; ihierde, 143/31; *part.* ȝeherd, 11/13; 37/10; 85/23; iherd, 21/29; 71/9; 85/20; 147/5; 149/20.
ȝekynd, *sb. kind, nature, shape, state, quality, sg. nom.* 117/25; *d. ac.* ȝekynde, 19/7; 25/21; 67/7; 97/9, 10; 119/28; ȝekinde, 27/28; ikynde, 21/8; 27/25; 97/5; 105/11; ikinde, 71/14; ikende, 95/18; *pl.* ȝekynden, 33/3; ȝekyndes, 69/34.
ȝecnawen, *v. to know*, 35/19; 57/11; 71/3; 127/24; icnawe, 87/5; icnowen, 101/3; *pres. ind.* 1 *sg.* icnawe, 31/25; 2 *sg.* ȝecnoust, 67/30; 3 *sg.* icnauð, 99/3Q; *pret. part.* icnawen, *conscious*, 87/4; icnawe, 21/28.
ȝekoren, *see* chiesen.
ȝecweme, *adj. agreeable*, 43/22; 65/32; 111/19; 141/29; 143/20; icweme, 77/27; 85/3; 101/22; 111/25; 119/29; 141/9; icueme, 21/2; *sup.* icwemeste, 85/11.
ȝecwemen, *v. to please*, 127/24; 133/22; icwemen, 137/33.
ȝelasten, *v. to last, perform, accomplish*, 35/11; ilasten, 63/3; *pres. ind.* 3 *sg.* ȝelast, 55/21; ilast, 33/21; *pret.* 3 *sg.* ȝelæste, 11/25; ȝelaste, 129/17; 137/4.

ȝeleave, *sb. belief, faith, sg. nom.* 25/6; 29/32; ileave, 29/24; *d. ac.* ȝeleave, 25/5; 27/31; 39/1; ȝeleven, 131/27; ileave, 15/27; 25/31; 27/8, 11; 31/7; 45/15; 51/29; 73/25; 101/32; ileaven (?), 109/24.
ȝelich, *adj. like*, 9/27; 29/19; 49/15; 89/31; ilich, 11/10; 47/27; 81/19; iliche, 13/25; 15/23.
ȝelieven, *v. to believe*, 83/29; ilieven, 25/10, 13; 59/5; 93/8; 95/1; *pres. ind.* 1 *sg.* ilieve, 21/10; 25/18; 31/25; 145/15, 22; 2 *sg.* ȝeliefst, 27/5; 103/5; iliefst, 39/2; 3 *sg.* iliefð, 25/8; 29/26; *pl.* ȝelieveð, 29/28; ilieveð, 29/25; leveð, 119/32; *opt.* 2 *sg.* ilieve, 41/3; 3 *sg.* ilieve, 31/15; *pl.* ilieven, 27/17; *imp. sg.* ȝelief, 27/16; 29/7; ilief, 27/32; 29/5; lief (?), 89/30; *pl.* ilieveð, 51/35; *pret.* 3 *sg.* iliefde, 109/30; *pl.* ȝeliefden, 29/8.
ȝelimpen, *v. to happen, befall, speed*, 27/32, 33; 143/19; ilimpen, 41/11; *pres. ind.* 3 *sg.* ȝelimpð, 101/2; ilimpþ, 29/4; ilimpð, 99/33.
ȝelome, *adv. frequently*, 151/24.
ȝelp, *sʰ. boasting, sg. nom.* 5/20; *d. ac.* 89/28.
ȝelpen, *v. to boast*, 3 *sg. ind. pres.* ȝelpð, 5/22.
gelt, *sb. guilt, sg. nom.* 51/31; *ac.* gylt, 39/34; *d.* gelte, 115/11; 117/8, 15; *pl.* geltes, 117/26.
ȝemanlich, *adj. common*, 41/19; ȝemaneliche, 21/4.
ȝemarked, *pret. part. marked*, 31/24.
ȝemartired, *pret. part. martyred*, 133/7.
ȝeme, *sb. heed, ac. sg.* 5/1, 4; 27/22; 135/4; ȝieme, 5/2; 11/19; 87/28; 89/19, 32; 103/17; 109/5; 135/7.
ȝemeleaste, *sb. carelessness, d. ac. sg.* 3/23; 17/11; -leste, 63/9; -laste, 121/24; *pl.* -leastes, 43/32.
ȝemeten, *v. to meet, pl. pret.* ȝemetten, 113/10; imetten, 29/8; 113/12.
ȝemeðe, *sb. sobriety, d. ac. sg.* 139/13; imeðe, 139/24.
ȝemiend, *sb. remembrance, mind, nom. sg.* 61/17; imiend, 23/13.
ȝemoane, *sb. company, intercourse, sg. d.* 127/13; *ac.* imone, 55/13.
ȝeond, *adv. thither*, 133/26.
ȝeorne, ȝerne, *see* ȝierne.
ȝeplanted, *pret. part. planted*, 51/26.
ȝepnesse, *see* ȝeap-.

GLOSSARY. 225

ȝerard, pret. part. reared, raised, 93/22.
ȝerihte, sb. judgment, ac. sg. 105/3.
ȝernde, see ȝiernen.
ȝesali, adj. blessed, 135/3; isæli, 75/35; isali, 97/31; 107/20; 129/25.
ȝescafte, sb. creature, sg. nom. 105/4; pl. d. iscafte, 105/4.
ȝesceppen, v. to shape, form, create, pret. ind. 3 sg. ȝescop, 69/31, 32; iscop, 47/8; 49/26; part. gescapen, 25/1; 87/16; 105/11; 127/13; iscapen, 23/10, 14, 16; 63/21; 73/15; 105/5; 113/15, 25; 115/1, 3, 9; iscapene, 19/10; 25/20.
ȝesen, v. to see, 125/8, 13, 23; isien, 19/3; 31/18; 49/19; 51/1, 7; 69/20; 81/16; 91/2; 103/17; 131/1; 141/4; ger. ȝesiene, 35/23; pres. ind. 2 sg. ȝesikst, 49/22; 61/7; ȝiesichst, 125/16; ȝesiest, 125/23; 3 sg. ȝesikþ, 139/11; isikð, 49/23; 143/4; isiecþ, 57/17; ȝesieð, 103/27; isieð, 57/14; ȝeseðh, 41/12; pl. ȝesieð, 53/1; 79/16; isieð, 7/21; 15/22; 51/2, 34; ȝeseð, 135/6; ȝesien, 19/33; opt. pl. ȝeseo, 81/31; pret. ind. 1 and 3 sg. iseih, 119/9; 147/26; neg. n'iseih, 25/9; pl. iseiȝen, 23/21; ȝeseiȝe (we), 149/25; opt. 3 sg. iseiȝe, 19/6; part. ȝesiȝen, 125/9; iseȝen, 149/20.
ȝesihthe, sb. sight, nom. sg. 17/4.
ȝespused, pret. part. espoused, 131/22.
gestninge, sb. dinner, ac. sg. 75/30, 33.
ȝesund, adj. sound, 73/15.
ȝeswæint, pret. part. afflicted, 85/12 (cf. swaint).
ȝeswiken, v. to cease, desist, 47/13; iswiken, 61/12; pres. opt. 2 sg. iswik, 87/19; imp. pl. ȝeswikeð, 41/30; iswiked, 41/30; pret. ind. 3 sg. ȝeswoc, 81/25.
ȝeswink, sb. labour, toil, trouble, sg. nom. ac. 27/22; 79/15; iswink, 75/4; iswinch, 47/4; d. ȝeswinke, 137/19; iswinke, 27/20; pl. ȝeswinkes, 151/17.
ȝet, ȝete, see ȝiet.
ȝeþanc, sb. thought, mind, sg. ac. 33/18; 35/21; 47/13; iþanc, 39/5; iðang, 35/28; d. ȝeþanke, 19/3; 131/13; iþanke, 47/24; 51/35.
ȝeu, see ȝe.
ȝeuer, ȝeuwer, see ȝewer.
ȝew, see ȝe.
ȝewar, adj. aware, 29/28.

ȝewer, pron. your, 5/32; 21/19; 121/7; 123/11; 135/21; 139/17; ȝeuwer, 45/5; ȝeuer, 69/11; 71/28, 29; 81/5, 6; 113/4; ȝuer, 7/22; ȝewere, 45/6; 51/26; ȝeuere, 79/23; ȝeure, 21/23; 41/29; 49/11; 51/35; 69/12, 13, 14, 23; 79/22, 23, 27; 81/4; 89/32; ȝure, 11/7; 19/16; 61/29.
ȝewill, sb. will, sg. nom. ac. 97/27; iwill, 15/15; 23/12; 93/9; 89/29.
ȝewinne, sb. strife, d. ac. sg. 97/27.
ȝewiss, adv. certainly, truly, 13/30; 91/18; iwiss, 97/31; 129/25; iwis, 23/8; 41/1; 63/23; 77/6, 22; 105/8; 133/5; 135/17; 139/1; 147/5.
ȝewit, sb. wit, sense, sg. nom. iwitt, 65/18; d. iwitte, 19/7; pl. gewittes, 17/21.
ȝewitnesse, sb. witness, d. ac. sg. 41/5; 59/16; 141/5; iwitnesse, 73/26; 97/19; 101/25; 119/29.
ȝewrite, sb. writ, d. ac. sg. 73/27; 93/19.
ȝewundred, part. pret. surprised, 95/15.
ȝewune, sb. custom, sg. d. 79/17; nom. iwune, 113/27.
ȝie, see ȝe.
ȝiede, see gan.
ȝielden, v. to repay, requite, pay, give, 31/10; 77/33; pres. opt. 3 sg. ȝielde, 21/28; 91/32; imp. sg. gield, 89/14; pret. ind. 3 sg. ȝeald, 117/33.
ȝieme, see ȝeme.
ȝierne, adv. eagerly, willingly, 29/13; 57/7; 69/32; 93/18; 103/18; 125/22 (ȝiere MS.); ȝerne, 135/25; ȝeorne, 19/19.
ȝiernen, v. to long for, yearn, 117/9; pres. ind. 1 sg. ȝierne, 59/27; pret. 3 sg. ȝernde, 43/7.
ȝiernfull, adj. eager, 109/16.
ȝiernliche, adv. eagerly, 23/9.
ȝiet, adv. conj. yet, still, even, again, 3/22; 9/21, 28; 21/30; 27/27; 35/2; 39/18; 49/23; 53/20; 55/27; 57/2; 59/5, 28; 61/7; 65/34; 67/33; 73/33; 75/28; 79/28; 88/4; 97/31, 32; 101/27; 113/2, 20; 117/35; 135/2, 16; 137/26; 147/22, 27; Giet, 8/7; 7/15; 9/6; 11/22; 17/2; 29/18; 59/7; 61/17, 19; 133/13, 19; 135/16; 141/2; ȝet, 5/26; 121/24; ȝiete, 5/34; 7/31; 17/30; 51/28; 83/28; 133/8; ȝete, 11/31; 133/5.

ȝieven, *see* ȝiven.
ȝif, *conj. if, whether*, 5/23; 7/2, 3, 4;
9/17; 11/31; 13/1, 20; 17/19,
23; 19/6, 20; 21/11; 23/3; 31/
28, 30; 33/30; 35/19 (2); 37/14,
32; 39/3, 14; 45/19, 22, 26, 29;
47/5; 49/7; 53/18; 57/22, 33;
59/2, 9, 26, 28; 61/8; 65/8; 67/
7, 16; 69/21; 71/14, 17, 29; 73/
3, 4 (ȝis *MS.*), 6 (2), 14, 24; 75/
2, 4, 12, 14, 22; 77/11, 12, 19,
etc.; Gif, 5/26; 11/25; 13/19;
23/1; 25/31; 33/21; 35/33; 37/
19, 23; 39/17, 31; 41/2; 49/19,
20; 63/25; 65/33; 67/8; 69/1;
73/13, 25; 75/32; 77/2, 10, 14,
21; 103/5; 125/11; 131/9; 135/
6, 25, 27; 141/13, 21; 149/4;
151/10; gif, 101/10.
ȝif, *see* ȝiven.
gilden, *adj. golden*, gildenene, 17/5.
gylt, *see* gelt.
gyltleas, *adj. guiltless*, 133/15.
ȝimstanes, *sb. gems*, 95/32.
ȝinc, ȝing, *see* ȝit.
ȝinker, *pron. of both of you*, 97/30.
ȝinnen, *v. to begin*, *pret. ind.* 3 *sg.*
gann, 121/5; *part.* ȝegunnen, 47/9;
101/27; iȝunnen, 47/2.
ȝise, *adv. yes*, 31/23.
ȝit, *pron. ye two, nom.* 97/24, 26, 27,
31; *d. ac.* ȝing, 97/13; ȝinc, 97/30;
ȝung, 97/26; *g.* ȝunker, 95/13;
97/26.
ȝitsin, *v. to covet, lust, ind. pres.* 3
sg. ȝitsið, 97/23; *pl.* 69/15.
ȝitsinge, *sb. covetousness*, 23/27; 43/
5; 89/27.
ȝive, *sb. gift*, *sg.* 63/11, 23, 25; 65/
8, 10, 15; 69/33; 71/6; 81/12;
85/28; 87/5; 91/8; 147/5; give,
21/20; *pl.* ȝives, 53/25, 27; 131/2.
ȝiven, *v. to give*, 11/29; 15/9; 17/
14; 33/6; 45/28; 67/21; 77/10,
13; 85/33; 107/1; 117/10; 139/
26 (2); 145/21; ȝive, 71/28;
given, 91/31; *ger.* ȝivene, 139/31;
143/14; ȝievene, 145/30; *pres. ind.*
1 *sg.* ȝive, 39/18; 65/34; 2 *sg.* ȝifst,
37/20; 77/12; 3 *sg.* ȝifð, 35/22;
37/3, 14; 77/7; 79/6; 109/12;
149/4; *pl.* ȝiveð, 77/29; 139/25;
opt. 2 *sg.* ȝive, 139/27; 3 *sg.* 9/2;
39/7; *imp. sg.* ȝif, 69/2; 83/20;
127/31; 147/22; 149/2; *pret. ind.*
1 *and* 3 *sg.* ȝaf, 13/16; 17/19, 23;
65/16; 99/6; ȝaif, 137/10; gaf, 77/
12; 2 *sg.* ȝave, 81/26; ȝeave, 147/
2; *part.* iȝiven, 21/9; 31/25, 28;
57/23; 69/30; 83/17; 139/27, 29.

ȝivere, *sb. giver, ac. sg.* 139/28.
givernesse, *sb. avidity, greed*, 23/26;
ȝivernesse, 89/26.
glad, *adj. glad*, 83/21; 107/18; 141/
6; gladd, 91/23; gladne, 139/28;
comp. gladdere, 147/30.
gladien, *v. to gladden*, 69/19.
gladliche, *adv. gladly*, 139/27.
gladnesse, *sb. gladness*, 137/8.
gleues, *sb. glees, amusements, joys*,
69/18.
glewmen, *sb. gleemen, nom. pl.* 121/
21.
god, *sb. God, sg. nom. d. ac.* 7/7; 11/
16; 13/25; 15/33; 17/2; 19/29;
37/18; 43/8; 71/17; 77/21; 81/
22; 89/12; 111/19; 123/30; 147/
15; godd, 5/10, 12, 16; 7/26; 11/
27; 13/20, 31; 19/12; 21/28; 23/
6, 14, 16; 25/11, 18, 22; 29/3;
35/15, 17–20; 37/3, 10, 13, 23;
39/6, 30, 31; 43/26; 49/15; 51/7,
21; 55/11; 57/22, 24; 61/11, 21,
22, 33; 65/5; 69/12, 17, 21, 23,
28, 31, *etc.*; goðð, 127/26; gode,
19/3; 125/18; *d.* gode, 3/16; 7/
22, 30; 9/29, 30; 13/15; 15/7, 28;
21/4, 13, 17, 30; 25/8; 29/4, 13;
31/13; 35/17; 37/11, 13, 21, 24,
33; 39/9, 12; 43/9, 22; 45/15, 30;
47/23; 55/6; 57/9 (*note*); 59/32;
63/9; 65/31, *etc.*; godde, 143/17;
gen. godes, 3/2, 5, 11, 13, 14, 25,
27; 5/11, 22; 9/7; 11/2, 4, 19,
20; 13/7, 31; 15/5, 14, 16, *etc.*;
ȝodes, 9/11 (*cf.* godalmihtin).
god, *sb. good, sg. nom. ac.* 3/16, 17;
5/31, 32; 11/8; 13/19; 17/10,
20; 23/15; 25/29; 27/33; 29/4,
27; 35/6, 23; 37/20; 39/2; 45/26,
27; 49/31; 51/26; 53/5; 59/31;
65/31; 71/17; 81/15, 19, 20; 87/
4; 93/19; 111/33; 121/25; *d.*
gode, 8/11; 11/30; 25/3; 29/14;
39/12; 47/30; 65/17; 89/11; 109/
10; 135/5; 151/5, 22; ȝode, 103/
7; *pl.* gode, 81/18; 85/5; 143/24;
ȝode, 119/20.
god, *adj. good*, 27/14; 37/22; 45/
22, 29; 47/5, 17; 65/13; 67/34;
69/1, 13; 73/4; 75/5; 77/7; 79/
30; 81/9; 95/30; 99/8; 109/6;
127/22; 135/1; 145/22; 147/23,
29; 149/7; ȝod, 123/12; gode, 8/
18; 9/2; 15/4; 17/7, 8, 22 (3);
23/13(2); 27/11, 31; 29/10, 23;
33/6; 35/33; 43/15, 21; 45/22;
59/10; 63/26; 65/12, 14; 69/5;
71/9, 18, 33; 73/2; 75/1; 79/28;
85/8; 93/4; 95/32; 97/1, 14;

GLOSSARY.

99/7, 26; 101/32; 103/27, 31; 109/24; 111/2; 115/4, 11; 125/15; 129/18, 21; 131/25; 133/24, 27 (2); 135/4; 137/10, 32; 139/9; 141/5, 6, 8; 143/26; 147/8, 11, 23, 29; godne, 75/4.
godalmihtin, *sb. almighty God, nom. d. ac.* 7/7; 11/16; 13/25; 35/7; 43/2; 61/25; 91/32; godd-, 55/32; 111/17; 123/12; 125/24; 143/4; 145/6; godalmihti, 29/31; *g.* godalmihtines, 41/8.
goddfrihti, *adj. God-fearing*, 71/11.
goddcundnesse, *sb. Godhead*, 25/18, 25; 97/10.
godnesse, *sb. goodness*, 11/15; 25/17; 29/5; 59/12; 83/15, 18; 113/25; 115/8, 21; 117/20; 127/22; 145/17, 21, 31; 147/22; 149/29; 151/4.
godspell, *sb. gospel, sg. nom. ac.* 5/29; 71/19; 75/12; 143/10; goddspell, 37/7; 149/19; *d.* godspelle, 15/8; 47/22; 71/22; 75/28; 91/19; goddspelle, 55/24; 67/25; 75/26.
godspellere, *sb. evangelist, nom. sg.* 35/24; 41/6.
ʒoc, *sb. yoke, ac. sg.* 71/22, 30.
gold, *sb. gold, sg. ac.* 17/16; 67/19; *d.* golde, 33/14.
ʒomes, *sb. palates*, 119/23.
ʒon, *see* gan.
gost, *see* gast.
grace, *sb. grace*, 21/23, 27; 23/29; 31/5, 30; 35/13; 59/16; 65/30; 67/11; 83/30.
grady, *adj. greedy*, 139/15.
grislich, *adj. grisly*, 19/6.
griđ, *sb. peace, ac. sg.* 131/7.
grundwall, *sb. ground-work, foundation, nom. ac.* 47/9; 93/28; grunnd-, 93/30; *d.* grundwalle, 95/4.
ʒuer, *see* ʒeuwer.
ʒung, *see* ʒit.
ʒunge, *adj. young*, 69/3; 109/4; (*cf.* iung-).
ʒunker, *see* ʒit.
ʒure, *see* ʒeuwer.
gylt, *see* gelt.

H.

habben, *v. to have*, 17/15, 23; 21/11; 23/2; 27/10; 29/17; 31/14, 19, 20; 35/7; 39/15; 41/29, 31; 43/23; 45/26; 51/32; 53/22; 55/3, 13; 57/28–30; 63/21, 23; 67/12; 77/31; 79/12; 83/24; 85/21, *etc.*; habbe, 11/28, 32; haven, 15/3; 27/8; 59/25, 28; 63/26; 65/6; 67/28; 69/21; 75/3, 4, 10; 77/13, 17, 20; 95/11; 113/7; 115/21; *ger.* habbene, 31/2; habbenne, 113/15; *pres. ind.* 1 *sg.* habbe, 5/14; 7/15, 30; 9/21; 11/22, 23; 13/9; 15/15, 22, 25, 31; 17/10, 12, 14, 16; 27/21; 39/17, 19, 20; 47/12; 53/17; 55/23, *etc.*; have, 15/28; 83/22; 2 *sg.* havest, 29/12; 31/28, 29; 39/11, 12; 41/4; 47/9; 75/4, 6; 87/1, 4; 91/24; 145/29; 147/1; hafst, 11/13; 17/18, 20; 21/29; 23/29; 27/3; 31/20; 35/20; 37/9; 41/1; 45/24; 59/3, 10; 61/2; 65/7; 69/2; 71/9, 13; 77/11; 81/29; 83/17, 27, 33; 85/4, 7, 25; 89/16; 93/21; 127/16; 3 *sg.* haveđ, 3/14 (*MS.* haved), 22–26; 5/18, 19, 22; 11/3; 13/15; 15/18; 21/17; 29/22; 33/2, 17; 35/18; 39/29; 43/2, 19; 47/1; 57/5, 24; 63/10; 65/19; 67/35; 73/1; 77/11; 81/1; 101/27, 28; 103/30; 105/11; 117/3, 20; 119/31; 127/9, 11, 13; 131/2, 22; 133/16; 147/12; hafđ, 3/7, 13; 5/23, 29; 7/3, 7, 26; 9/3, 6, 23; 11/31; 13/7, 31; 21/7–9; 23/23; 31/25; 33/3; 45/22; 57/3, 18; 63/27; 69/30; 73/26; 79/33; 81/17, 22; 87/20; 91/29, 31; 93/8; 95/6, 31; 97/7; 99/9; 113/2, 34; 115/2; 119/32; 121/24; 127/33; 131/10, 12, 19 (hafd *MS.*); 187/2, 6; 145/14; 151/4, 6; hafþ 111/22; *pl.* habbeđ, 3/15, 16; 5/30; 11/30; 15/13; 19/11, 34; 23/27; 25/29, 30; 27/31; 33/10; 35/16; 43/2, 16 (habbed *MS.*); 57/6; 59/14, *etc.*; habben, 7/24; 77/33; haven, 69/21; 79/15; 81/4; *opt.* 2 *sg.* habbe, 31/31; 53/23; 65/1, 30; 81/15; 89/12; 99/22; 129/9; have, 59/32; 89/10, 15; 99/4; 3 *sg.* habbe, 5/17; 21/21; 101/24; 105/3; have, 39/29; 101/16; *pl.* habbe, 131/21; haven, 55/26; 77/30; *imp. sg.* have, 33/14; 39/5; 61/3; 63/28; 81/28, *etc.*; ave, 145/13; *pret.* 1 *and* 3 *sg.* hafde, 13/23; 23/14; 81/25; 133/20; hadde, 13/2, 24; 21/20; 23/16; 27/20; 31/32; 43/8, 26; 47/1, 2; 51/21; 53/15; 55/12; 57/8; 67/20; 79/34; 83/20; 85/3, 15; 97/29; 105/18, *etc.*; 2 *sg.* hafdest, 71/18; 77/12; 83/21; hafdst, 31/31; haddest, 65/4; 71/16; *pl.* hafden, 109/2; 127/20; hadden,

GLOSSARY.

33/12; 83/28; 95/19; hadde, 51/16; *part.* ȝeafd, 147/1; ihafd, 15/27; 47/12; 81/29 (*cf.* nabben).
hadde, *see* habben.
hadede, *pret. part. ordained ones, clerics,* 19/26, 31; 45/25; 79/17; hodede, 18/9.
hades, *sb. persons,* 25/11.
haf, *see* habben.
hafde, *see* heaved.
haht, *sb. danger, peril, risk, sg. nom.* 11/20; hauht, 87/27; hauth, 71/16; *d.* hahte, 45/8; 79/14.
hail, *int. hail!* 53/27; hoal, 117/20.
hal, *adj. whole,* 78/14.
halden, *see* healden.
hæle, *sb. health, salvation, sg. d ac.* 69/12; 71/14; hale, 29/1; 69/18; 83/21; 85/6.
halen, *v. to heal,* 71/2; *pret.* 3 *sg.* halde, 119/25.
halend, *sb. saviour, sg. nom. ac.* 21/31; 119/25; *d.* halende, 33/19.
half, *adj. half,* 51/6; halve, 79/13.
half, *sb. side, part, behalf, d. ac. sg.* 27/18; 81/7; 99/29, 32; 117/30; halve, 107/13.
halȝen, *v. to hallow, pres. part.* halwende, 47/15; *pret.* 3 *sg.* halȝede, 137/8; *part.* ȝehalȝed, 87/17; 129/15.
hali, *adj. holy, saint,* 5/34; 7/4; 15/6, 16; 19/21; 21/21, 23; 23/15, 25; 25/6, 10, 12, 15, 24; 27/14; 29/18, 30; 33/24, 34; 35/1, 8, 15, 29, 30, 33; 37/14, 26; 41/14, 29; 43/4, 16, 28; 47/2, 10, 14, 22, 29; 49/2, 3; 51/27, 33; 53/3, 10, 19, 23, 31; 55/19, 23, 24, 32; 57/9; 59/17, 19, 20; 61/8, 19; 63/3, 14; 67/14, 25; 71/2, 19; 73/1, 12, 32; 75/14, 28; 77/6, 24; 79/2; 81/23; 83/3, 17, 30; 85/10; 87/1; 89/5, 8; 91/12, 25; 93/2, 7, 23, 27; 95/4, 6, 9, 12; 97/29; 101/24; 103/1, 9, 13; 105/2, 9, 22, 25; 107/1, 11; 113/10, 32, 33; 119/14, 20, 22, 27; 121/17, 29; 123/14; 125/24, 27; 127/26; 129/14, 15, 27; 131/2, 4, 8, 10; 133/7, 10, 13, 21; 135/10, 18; 137/3, 7; 141/18; 143/20, 25, 27; 149/9, 12, 19, 26, 27; 151/20; holi, 39/15; 75/7; 88/2; 85/25; 99/24; 109/3, 24; 113/8, 28; haliȝe, 13/16; 29/32; 33/7; 35/9, 28; 41/23; 53/16; 77/7; 79/2; 85/22; 89/20; 107/9, 19; 133/1; holiȝe, 91/18, 19; halie, 33/32,
34; 35/17; 61/6; 85/29; 103/5; 119/2; 131/20; 151/13; holie, 83/2; 95/8; 99/22; halȝe, 3/17; halȝen, 5/27; 9/7, 31; 19/4; 21/12; 65/5; haliȝes, 151/17.
halidom, *sb. holiness, ac. sg.* 129/31.
haligast, *sb. Holy Ghost, sg. nom. ac.* 19/22; 25/11; 37/2; 61/8; 135/23; 151/20; haligost, 91/3; *g.* haligastes, 41/30; *d.* haligaste, 131/2; haligoste, 91/23.
[h]alle, *sb. hall, d. sg.* 141/22.
halp, *see* helpen.
halsiȝe, *v. to conjure,* 1 *sg. ind. pres.* 93/2.
halsume, *adj. wholesome,* 135/16; holsum, 111/18.
halt, *see* healden.
halte, *adj. halt,* 75/34.
halve, *see* half.
halwende, *see* halȝen.
ham, *sb. home, sg. ac.* 35/4; 67/18; *d.* at ham, 79/15.
ham, *adv. home (domum),* 23/32; 27/24; hom, 89/23.
hamward, *adj. homeward,* 147/25.
hand, *sb. hand. sg. d. ac.* 23/8; 71/21; 97/7; 127/20; 133/18; hande, 133/15 (2), 31; *pl.* handes, 119/14; handen, 17/27; 133/31; honden, 119/13.
handeweorc, *sb. handiwork, sg. nom. ac.* 21/22; handiwerc, 13/7; 115/5.
handiswink, *sb. hand-work, d. sg.* handiswinke, 91/30.
handsselle, *sb. handsel, ac. sg.* 29/10.
hangen, *v. to hang,* 3 *sg. pret.* hangede, 51/28; 119/22.
harde, *adj. hard,* 45/18; 61/22; 127/9.
hardnesse, *sb. hardness, d. ac. sg.* 45/21; ardnesse, 33/7.
harkien, *v. to hearken, hear, listen, pres. ind.* 3 *sg.* harkeð, 47/23; *pl.* harkieð, 7/5; *imp. sg.* harke, 25/32; 37/10; 49/11; hærce, 31/31; *pl.* harkieð, 19/27; 53/33 (2); harkið, 19/22.
harm, *sb. harm, sg. nom. ac.* 29/10; 101/28; 103/6; 115/25; 117/33; *d.* harme, 9/10; 101/23; 103/6; hearme, 65/16; *pl.* harmes, 59/4.
harrer, *see* ær.
hæte, *sb. heat, sg. d. ac.* 17/32; hate, 103/4.
haten, *v.* (1) *to bid, command, pres. ind.* 3 *sg.* hat, 17/26; 109/11; 123/32; 125/27; *pret. ind.* 3 *sg.*

hiet, 99/16; 101/17; *pl.* hieten, 129/20; *part.* ʒehote, 43/8; ioten, 149/30.
(2) *to be called, pres. ind.* 3 *sg.* hatte, 3/8; 11/2; 13/12; 15/18; 35/10; 49/2; 63/4, 14; 69/33; 99/24; 103/12; 111/24; 135/10; 149/8, 27; *pret. part.* ʒehaten, 123/25; ʒehoten, 107/27; ihoten, 45/16.
hatien, *v. to hate,* 99/13; *pres. ind.* 1 *sg.* hatie, 67/1; 3 *sg.* hateð, 37/28; 141/14; *opt. pl.* hatien, 7/22; *imp. sg.* hate, 67/7; *pret.* 1 *sg.* hatede, 5/15; 39/19; 2 *sg.* hatedest, 33/2.
hatte, *see* haten.
hæðendom, *sb. heathendom, d. sg.* -dome, 31/7.
haðene, *sb. adj. heathen,* 51/12; 79/12; heðene, 77/16.
haðenesse, *sb. heathendom,* 27/27.
hauht, *see* haht.
have, *see* habben.
havekes, *sb. hawks,* 69/19.
he, *pron. he, sg. nom. m.* 3/14, 15, 18; 5/2, 3, 21, 23-29; 7/3, 19, 27; 9/1, 3, 26; 11/6, 9, 27, 31; 13/7, 13, 18, 19, 26; 15/1, 2, 6, 20; 17/15, 16, 18, 26, 29; 19/7, 14; 21/3, 8, 20, 21; 25/15, 19-21, 23, 25, 26, 33, *etc.*; hie, 3/12, 16; 31/1, 2 (?); 37/32 (?); 45/23; 143/18; *f.* heo, *she,* 99/26; hie, 3/8, 9, 24-26, 29; 5/1, 8, 17, 18; 7/25; 11/3; 13/12-14; 15/19; 23/23, 24; 25/6-8; 29/19, 25, 32, 33; 31/1, 2 (?); 33/7, 32, 34; 35/2, 11, *etc.*; ʒie, 123/26; he, 131/12; *n. (nom. and ac.)* hit, *it,* 3/28; 11/10, 20; 13/1, 2; 19/20; 21/3, 11; 27/2, 27, 28, 31, 32; 29/3, 5, 7, 12, 20, 32; 31/15, 21; 33/4, 5, 15, 31, 32; 35/7; 37/33; 39/3, 24, 27; 41/11; 45/16, 19; 47/4, 18, 21; 53/8, 13, 18, 19, 24; 55/1, 31; 57/22, 28; 59/1, 5, 27; 61/13, 23; 65/14; 67/7, 8, *etc.*; hitt, 135/25; 143/11; it, 9/14; 11/9; 31/20; 59/8, 13; 69/4; 75/2, 6; 79/30; 89/29; 101/5; 109/24; 129/17; 151/6, 8; *gen. m. and n.* his, 5/3, 21, 23, 26; 7/32; 9/4, 7, 25, 31; 11/30; 13/21, 31; 15/1, 6-8; 17/6, 7, 14, 26, 31; 19/4, 7, 16; 21/9, 10, 22, 23; 23/1, 14; 25/14, 21, 24-6, *etc.*; is, 121/24, 31; 133/16, 18; 135/5; 137/34; 147/24; hise, 119/11; 121/24; 133/24, 25, 31; 139/5;
141/23; 145/10; *f.* hire, 15/19; 23/24; 29/31; 37/22; 43/33; 55/5, 6, 32; 57/7, 9; 85/18, 20; 87/23; 95/7; 101/19, 28, 29; 103/11; 107/14; 111/30; 113/27; 125/4, 6; 129/18; 131/8, 10, 12; 133/29; 147/12; *d. m. and n.* him, 7/20; 9/2; 11/8, 23-26; 15/2, 8, 32; 17/7, 14; 21/2, 25; 25/33; 27/12; 29/10, 17, 22, 33; 33/4, 8; 35/20; 37/5, 6, 10, 13, 31; 39/6, 9, 29, *etc.*; *f.* hire, 3/11, 29; 5/10, 16, 18, 21; 7/19, 23; 13/15; 23/23, 25; 29/18, 24, 32; 35/1, 12; 49/5, 23; 53/20, 31; 65/11; 83/7; 85/21; 91/11, *etc.*; her, 31/5; *ac. m.* hine, 13/19; 31/5, 25; 37/6; 51/13, 20; 65/27; 73/15; 83/19; 99/33; 111/11, 31; 113/23; 135/6, 28; *f.* hie, 35/32; 43/24; 141/19; hes, 15/2; 17/15; 31/31, 32; 33/8, 23; 39/20; 41/13; 49/3; 57/10; 65/18; 75/24; 81/25; 88/8, 22; 85/17; 95/13; 97/7; 99/6; 101/9; 107/20, 21; 109/1; 111/7; 131/3; 133/30; 141/2, 4; his, 125/20, 22; 149/28; *pl. nom.* hie, 3/2; 5/11, 12, 30; 7/2, 4; 13/6, 7; 15/4, 5; 17/5; 19/3, 10, 24, 26; 21/3; 23/16, 19, 21, 30; 25/3; 27/5; 29/3, 8, 9, 17; 33/9, 10, 12, 13, *etc.*; hi, 25/29; 57/33; 79/12; 87/29; 105/7; 115/14; he, 25/30; 29/26; 59/30; 61/24; 79/28; 89/35; 95/3; *g.* here, 5/30; 7/1; 13/27 (2); 15/3; 23/19, 28 (2), 32; 25/16, 18; 27/5; 33/11, 12; 35/8; 37/2, 4, 32; 45/1, 11, 17; 55/30; 57/32; 61/17, 25, 26, *etc.*; heare, 127/9; her, 35/5; 137/21; *d.* hem, 9/15; 13/26, 27; 17/11, 26; 19/9; 23/21; 25/1, 15; 27/9, 12; 29/3; 33/6, 10, 33, 34; 35/17; 47/13; 53/25; 57/24, 28, 30, 31, 32, *etc.*; him, 137/23; heom, 145/3; *ac.* hes, 3/19; 5/28, 29 (?); 7/4; 15/32; 23/29; 33/34; 37/1; 47/6, 10, 12; 49/26; 55/32; 57/33; 65/18; 71/2, 3; 75/33; 77/29; 91/2; 93/18; 99/30; 103/21; 107/24; 128/30, 32; his, 127/18; 141/8; is, 131/22; *with* self, *sg. nom. m.* himselfe, 5/12; 19/29; 33/20; 37/16, 18; 101/7; 113/5; 117/34; 119/7; 141/28; 145/6; -selv, 111/25; *f.* hireself, 55/24; 59/15; *d. ac. m.* himselven, 5/2, 25; 13/14, 16; 25/19; 31/10; 39/28; 49/16;

51/1; 53/14, 30; 57/1, 20; 63/20, 23; 65/20; 97/3; 115/25, 27; 133/5; 135/4; *pl. d. ac.* hemselven, 5/12, 33; 7/2, 5; 51/2; 55/29, 30; 57/32.
healden, *v. to hold, keep, esteem,* 37/6; 47/13, 17; 53/22; 55/6, 15; 71/17, 18, 31; 99/3; 105/28; 107/20; 109/1; 129/17, 20, 22; 135/20; 143/15; ealden, 151/11; *pres. ind.* 2 *sg.* haldst, 73/6; 3 *sg.* halt, 63/19; 67/17; 77/4; 81/21; 89/29; 107/21; 129/23; 133/18; *pl.* healdeð, 5/34; 7/4; 79/21; 95/28; 105/11; 131/19; healdeþ, 5/34; healden, 77/29; 79/11; *opt.* 2 *sg.* healde, 59/32; 3 *sg.* 121/16; 129/25; *imp. sg.* hald, 61/33; halt, 45/27; 1 *pl. (adhort.)* healde (we), 23/24; *pret. ind.* 1 *and* 3 *sg.* hield, 7/31; 51/8; eald, 145/11; *pl.* hielden, 73/33; helden, 97/2; *part.* ihealden, 55/4; 65/15; 67/16; 79/18; 129/5; ihealde, 67/32; 79/25; ihelden, 57/6.
hearme, *see* harm.
heaved, *sb. head, sg. nom. ac.* 27/6; 91/28; 101/20, 21; 131/26; *pl.* hafde, 19/31.
heaved-senne, *sb. cardinal sin, sg.* 5/15; 37/16; 101/9; 121/22; 123/8; eaved-, 139/18; heved-, 53/11; 67/34; *pl.* heaved-sennes, 7/27; 111/1; heved-, 3/9, 29; 27/9; 81/21.
heden, *v. to hide,* 1 *sg. pret.* hedde, 125/3.
hei, *adj. high,* 7/3; heih, 55/17; 71/17; 125/18; heiʒe, 7/2, 3; 65/26; 95/22; 97/7; 111/21; heie, 109/13; *comp.* heiʒer, 49/19; heier, 115/29; heigere, 75/17; heiʒere, 127/20; *sup.* heiʒest, 35/10; 53/29; 145/16; heiʒeste, 67/4; heisten, 9/27.
heiʒin, *v. to exalt,* 5/12; *pret. part.* iheiʒed, 57/5; 73/32.
heih, *sb. height, d. sg.* 95/7.
heiliche, *adv. exaltedly,* 57/29.
heinesse, *sb. height,* 5/9.
held, *see* healden.
helle, *sb. hell, d. ac. sg.* 7/20; 17/30; 19/9; 27/8–10; 57/2; 61/31; 75/20; 105/26; 113/34; 115/4; 127/5.
helle-depnesse, *sb. depth of hell, d. sg.* 5/9.
helle-grund, *sb. ground of hell, d. sg.* -grunde, 57/4.
helle-pine, *sb. pain of hell, d. ac. sg.* 5/4; 37/30; 63/22; 77/32; 145/15; *pl.* -pines, 87/25.
helpe, *sb. help, d. ac. sg.* 21/23; 23/15; 47/8; 55/25; 63/26; 101/1; 125/22; help, 93/4.
helpen, *v. to help,* 9/9; 23/16; 47/18; 57/30; 63/33; 65/21, 29; 103/25; 151/10; *pres. ind.* 3 *sg.* helpð, 53/19; 143/28; *pl.* helpen, 101/14; *imp. sg.* help, 97/28; 101/12; *part.* helpinde, 137/7; *pret. ind.* 1 *sg.* halp, 9/9; *part.* iholpen, 65/4.
helpend, *sb. helper, nom. sg.* 39/12.
helpleas, *adj. helpless,* 23/21.
henen, *adv. hence,* 17/29.
heng, *see* hon.
her, *adv. here,* 19/19; 21/24; 51/5; 75/15; 91/16; 105/21; 117/14; 123/13; hier, 9/6; 19/20; 21/12, 14; 27/3; 31/18; 35/8; 37/14; 53/32; 55/1, 7; 57/4, 8; 65/7, 29; 67/26; 69/3, 19; 75/16; 91/14; 97/6; 103/20, 21, 27; 111/6; 123/13; 145/8; 151/16.
herberʒin, *v. to harbour,* 67/22; herborʒin, 149/16.
herde, *see* hieren.
heremites, *see* eremite.
herfore, *adv. conj. therefore,* 5/4; 109/23; hierfore, 5/13.
herien, *v. to praise,* 21/25; 151/15; heriʒen, 83/30; 151/24; herʒen, 57/1; *pres. ind. pl.* herieð, 21/17; *opt.* 2 *sg.* heriʒe, 151/22; *pl.* heriʒen, 151/19.
herienge, *sb. praise, ac. sg.* 5/29, 31.
hermite, *see* eremite.
hermitorie, *sb. hermitage,* 73/25.
herof, *adv. hereof, hereabout,* 5/32; 7/6; 13/8; 31/21; 39/15; 65/17; 67/23; 71/7; 77/2, 34; 93/28; 97/19; 99/10; 113/3; 123/3; 133/14; 135/7, 12; 139/10, 15; 141/12; hierof, 41/5; 51/29; 71/19; 75/7; 85/32; 87/8, 27, 28; 123/1, 10; 129/30; 133/13; 139/33.
hersum, *adj. obedient,* 5/19; 7/30, 32; 9/2; 45/1; 51/8; 109/3, 7, 9, 10, 12, 14, 30, 31; 111/17; 117/21; 119/6.
hersumen, *v. to obey,* 137/33.
hersumnesse, *sb. obedience,* 7/21; 43/22; 71/30; 107/26 (*corr. into* ibuhs.); 109/2; 111/21; 119/5; 149/16.
herte, *see* hierte.

GLOSSARY. 231

herten, *v. to hurt,* 3 *sg. ind. pres.* hert, 45/22.
hes, *see* he.
heŏene, *see* haŏŏen.
heved, *see* heaved.
hevele, *see* evel.
heven, *sb. Heaven, d. sg.* hevene, 9/12; 15/12; 25/14, 26; 27/2; 33/26; 43/19; 45/11; 49/25; 53/29; 87/26; 99/6; 105/14, 16, 25; 113/5; 117/5; 119/27; 127/4; 129/23.
hevene-heinesse, *sb. height of Heaven, d. sg.* 5/9.
hevene-riche, *sb. Kingdom of Heaven, sg. d. ac.* 7/17; 31/2; 45/12; 69/8; 71/24; 99/15; 103/30; 121/8; 127/9; 139/3; hevenriche, 13/6; 75/26; 145/15; heveriche, 77/25; *g.* heveneriches, 57/6; 79/2 (!); 91/17; 113/16; 119/31; hevneriches, 151/12.
hevenlich, *adj. heavenly,* 95/21; hevenliche, 111/9.
hevi, *adj. heavy,* 3/13; 95/19; 109/6; hevy, 3/24.
heviliche, *adv. heavily,* 47/3.
hider, *adv. hither,* 41/25, 26; 97/8; 133/26.
hie, *see* ʒe.
hield, *see* healden.
hier, *see* her.
hier, *see* ʒear.
hierabuten, *adv. here about,* 91/31.
hierafter, *adv. hereafter,* 5/7; 29/30; 65/10; 71/6; 81/12; 85/28; 91/8; 99/22; 121/29.
hieraʒean, *adv. here against,* 37/18; 105/12.
hierbuven, *adv. here above,* 103/23.
hierdes, *sb. shepherds,* 43/20.
hierembe, *adv. here about, hereof,* 85/26.
hieren, *v. to hear, pres. ind. pl.* hiereŏ, 135/6; *pret.* 3 *sg.* herde, 11/9; (*cf.* ʒehieren).
hieron, *adv. hereon, herein,* 39/21; 139/1.
hierte, *sb. heart, sg. nom. d. ac.* hierte, 11/3; 17/28; 31/29; 35/22, 31; 45/18; 49/11; 55/30; 61/22; 69/16; 83/1; 85/12; 119/17, 19, 24; 125/2, 5, 6, 10, 11; 127/8, 9; 131/6; 135/2, 26; 137/21; 141/4, 11, 13; 143/5, 21; 145/30, 33; 147/30; herte, 13/27; 17/2; 27/3; 31/27; 33/17; 35/21, 33; 41/29; 53/9; 57/21; 59/1, 5, 27; 63/15, 26; 69/25, 26; 73/18, 26; 75/23; 83/6, 32, 34; 85/13, 26; 87/6, 15; 89/32; 101/8; 103/3; 121/31; 123/1; 147/13; hirte, 123/34; *g.* herte, 45/21; 69/13.
hierteforen, *adv. here before,* 59/14; 91/12; 95/3; -fore, 91/1.
hierto, *adv. hereto, for this,* 117/21.
hiet, *see* haten.
hyrde, *sb. retinue, d. sg.* 43/12.
hlaverd, *sb. lord, sg. nom. ac.* 17/6, 7; 31/26; 45/3; 47/8; 51/5; 67/27; 77/35; 81/27; 83/20; 85/2, 8; 93/15; 105/13; 107/8; 115/4, 30; 117/12; 125/3; 127/17, 21; 141/31; 143/23; 145/12, 30; 147/20; 149/1; laverd, 7/32; 13/20; 19/24; 33/3, 23; 55/11; 63/17; 83/4, 12, 16, 31; 87/10; 101/34; 113/33; 115/7, 16; laverde, 121/9; hlaveerd, 67/32; *d.* hlaverde, 21/4; 151/15; laferde, 7/7; laverde, 15/28; 21/13; 23/1; 25/8; 29/4; 55/6; loverde, 109/10; 111/19; loverd, 115/25; *g.* laverdes, 17/9, 12.
hleitres, *sb. laughters,* 101/15.
hlesten, *v. to listen,* 19/22, 32; 23/3; 45/24; 61/17; 67/14; 71/29; 97/11; lhesten, 47/5; leshten, 107/14; lesten, 45/31; 69/7; 75/14; 87/10; 101/11; *pres. ind.* 3 *sg.* hlest, 45/5; *pl.* hlisteŏ, 109/18; *opt.* 3 *sg.* (2 *sg. imp.!*), hlest, 61/9; *pl.* hlesten, 133/26; *imp. sg.* hlest, 67/3; 69/6; 75/21, 28; 77/9; 101/4; lihst, 73/8; 1 *pl.* (*adhort.*) hleste (we), 67/23; 2 *pl.* hlesteŏ, 41/25, 26; 45/3; 59/23.
hlustes, *sb. lusts,* 135/15; 137/24.
hlutter, *adj. pure, clear,* 73/26; 83/8; 123/9; 127/2; 131/14; 141/3.
hoal, *see* hail.
hodede, *see* hadede.
hoʒiʒen, *v. to care,* 137/20.
hol, *sb. hole, sg. ac.* 101/28; *d.* hole, 101/29, 32.
holi, *see* hali.
holsum, *see* halsum.
hom, *see* ham.
hon, *v. to hang,* 3 *sg. ind. pret.* heng, 53/10; 119/3; 145/27.
hond, *see* hand.
hope, *sb. hope,* 15/27; 29/29, 31; 31/9, 14; 33/10, 13, 14, 17, 19, 32; 35/38; 39/1; 45/15; 51/29; 55/25; 63/28; 89/10; 95/6; 115/5; ope, 97/2.

232   GLOSSARY.

hopien, *v. to hope*, 145/34 ; *pres. ind.* 3 *sg.* hopeð, 29/32 ; 31/2 ; 37/17 ; *pl.* hopieð, 67/13 ; 115/12 ; 131/18.
hord, *sb. hoard, sg. nom. ac.* 69/25 ; 75/26 ; *d.* horde, 151/17.
hordom, *sb. whoredom, adultery, sg. d.* hordome, 121/21 ; *pl.* hordomes, 67/31.
hore, *sb. filth, d. sg.* horewe, 31/1.
hors, *sb. horse, d. sg.* horse, 89/31.
hot, *adj. hot*, 107/19 ; 109/6 ; hote, 63/32.
hoten, *see* haten.
houhfull, *adj. anxious*, 87/31.
hu, *adv. how*, 3/18 ; 11/19 ; 19/12 ; 23/5 ; 35/18 ; 37/10, 24, 25 ; 41/12, 13 ; 47/7 ; 57/10 ; 65/5, 13 ; 77/8 ; 83/27 ; 87/22 ; 89/21 ; 105/21 ; 111/33 ; 113/15 ; 137/32 ; 139/5, 6 ; 141/32 ; hwu, 137/34.
hucche, *sb. coffer, nom. sg.* 75/25.
hundes, *sb. hounds, dogs,* 69/19 ; 109/20, 22.
hundred, *sb. hundreds,* 113/34.
hunger, *sb. hunger, sg. ac.* 143/32 ; *d.* hungre, 95/24.
hure, *adv. at least*, 143/16.
hus, *sb. house, sg. nom. ac.* 35/4 ; 67/18 ; 91/11, 17 ; 111/4 ; *d.* huse, 27/24 ; 33/6 ; 41/15 ; 73/10 ; 79/1 ; 95/5 ; 99/16, 18 ; 107/28 ; 109/29 ; 111/1 ; 123/26.
hus, *see* we.
hute, *see* wuten.
hwa, *pron. who, m. f. sg. nom.* 11/18 ; 59/24 ; 77/4 (2), 35 ; 79/1 ; hwo, 81/17 ; 109/24 ; *g.* hwos, 99/32 ; *d.* hwam, 47/29 ; 49/27, 30 ; 51/1 ; 85/22 ; 95/23 ; 109/26 ; wham, 139/18 ; *ac.* hwan, 21/10 ; wan, 127/22 ; *n.* hwat, 7/28 ; 17/14, 18 ; 19/22 ; 23/30 ; 25/32 ; 31/20, 32 ; 39/32 ; 45/3, 23 ; 61/9 ; 63/22 ; 67/3, 28 ; 69/6 ; 75/21, 28 ; 87/10 ; 89/4 ; 97/21 ; 99/27 (2) ; 101/4 ; 113/13 ; what, 111/16 ; wat, 125/20, 21 (2).
hwanene, *adv. whence*, 129/8 ; hwannen, 69/34.
hwanne, *adv. when*, 69/34 ; 81/33 ; 87/20 ; whanne, 57/25.
whar, *adv. where*, 109/12.
hwarfore, *adv. wherefore*, 45/28.
hwarliker, *see* warliker.
hwarof, *adv. whereof*, 69/29 ; 73/18.
hwarto, *adv. whereto*, 113/14.
hwa se, *pron. whoever, m. sg. nom.* 53/10 ; *d.* hwam swo, 85/22 ; *n.* hwat swa, 75/16 ; hwat swo, 67/5 ;

hwat swo ævre, 37/31 ; hwat so, 141/15.
hwat, *see* hwa.
hwat hwat, *pron. whatsoever*, 151/6.
hwatliche, *adv. quickly, bitterly*, 99/32 ; *comp.* hwatliker, 87/19.
hweðer, *conj. whether*, 111/17 ; hwaðer, 69/27 ; 109/5 ; whaðer, 101/22 ; hweðer, 31/19 ; 141/29.
hwaðer, *pron. which, m. sg. nom.* 95/13 ; *n.* hwaðer swo, *whichsoever*, 113/19.
hwi, *adv. why*, 13/22 ; 75/25, 27 ; 77/5 ; 87/12, 13 ; whi, 77/4.
hwider, *adv. whither*, 17/29.
hwile, *sb. while, time, sg. g.* 19/26 ; 41/3 ; 47/16 ; 53/2 ; 65/4 ; 75/9 ; 87/16 ; 89/33 ; 111/1 ; wile, 121/19 ; 125/20 ; 137/19 ; *ac.* hwile, 19/19 ; 75/15 ; 85/31 ; 87/11 ; 97/14 ; 129/7.
hwile, *adv. formerly*, 73/31.
hwilc, *pron. which, sg. nom. m. and ac. n.* 29/11 ; hwilch, 27/22 ; 29/10 ; 71/11 ; whilch, 77/13 ; *gen.* hwilches, 29/6 ; hwilche, 71/34 ; *d. m.* hwilche, 51/23 ; 113/18 ; *f.* hwilliche, 149/13 ; hwælche, 21/31 ; *pl.* hwilche, 87/6, 7 ; wilke, 125/11.
hwittere, *adj. comp. whiter*, 83/4.
hwo, *see* hwa.
hwu, *see* hu.

I.

i-, *cf.* ȝe-.
i, *see* ic.
ia, *adv. yea*, 9/13 (2).
iattred, *pret. part. poisoned*, 103/3 ; 119/17.
ibiete, *v. to repair, pres. opt.* 2 *sg.* 77/23.
ibroiden, *part. pret. woven*, 45/14.
ibuhsumnesse, *sb. obedience*, 107/27 (*footnote*).
idel, *adj. idle, vain*, 5/20 (2) ; 89/28 ; 133/18 ; idele, 7/5 ; 23/22.
idelnesse, *sb. idleness, vanity, sg.* 3/25 ; 87/30 ; ydelnesse, 5/3 ; 57/14 ; *pl.* idelnesses, 101/14 ; ydelnesses, 133/27.
ieiht, *see* echen.
iec, *see* ec.
ielde, *sb. age*, 25/16 (ilelde, *MS.*) ; 49/16, 27 ; 111/14.
ierlich, *see* ierðlich.
iernen, *v. to run*, 81/32 ; *pres. imp. pl.* ierneð, 51/25 (2) ; *part.* ierninde, 85/1, 14 ; 95/27 ; ierniende, 131/7.
ierðe, *sb. earth*, 9/12 ; 25/15 ; 33/

GLOSSARY. 233

27; 35/22; 49/25; 53/30; 63/19, 20, 30; 75/27; 95/19; 99/6; 105/15, 27; 109/32; 117/6, 25, 27, 32; 129/23; eorða, 27/29.

ierðlich, *adj. earthly*, 95/22; ierlich, 63/29; eordlic, 27/1; ierðliche, 89/20; erðliche, 11/29.

ifastned, *pret. part. fastened*, 95/6; 103/1.

iflhte, *sb. fight, d. sg.* 89/34.

iflite, *sb. conflict, d. sg.* 67/24.

iforðin, *v. to perform*, 71/15; iforðen, 109/5.

ihalden, *v. to keep, pret. pl.* ihelden, 129/18.

iheren, *see* ȝehieren.

ihwited, *pret. part. whited*, 15/24.

ic, *pron.* I, 3/27; 5/13-16; 7/6, 7, 15, 28, 29; 9/9, 10, 17 (2), 18, 21 (2), 26, 30; 11/9, 10, 12, 22, 23, 25, 26, 31, 32; 13/1, 2, 8 (2), 10, 15, 20, 21, 27, 29; 15/9, 15, 21-23, 25, 28, 29, 32, 33; 17/9, 10, 12-14, 17, 19, 21, 23; 19/8; 21/4, 5, 11, 13, 28, 30, 31; 23/1, 2, 9 (2), 11, 12; 25/18; 27/1, 13, 17, 21; 33/27, 28; 39/17 (2), 19, 20; 41/12, 13; 47/1, 2, 11, 12, 14-16; 49/10; 53/16, 17 (2), 18, 20; 55/11, 13, 15-17, 23; 57/11; 59/6 (2), 16, 23, 27 (2), 28; 65/33 (2); 67/1, 2 (2), 3, 28 (2), 32, 33; 69/32; 71/28 (2); 73/8; 75/24, 25; 81/32; 83/3, 4, 6, 7, 13, 14 (2), 19 (2), 20 (2), 23, 26, 31, 32; 85/2, 3 (2), 5 (2), 24, 34; 87/3, 10, 24; 89/10; 91/1, 24; 93/4, 6, 9, 10, 13, 17; 95/17, 19, 21, 23 (2); 97/1, 9, 11-13, 17 (2), 21; 103/16, 19; 105/31; 109/23, 29; 111/12; 113/12, 29; 115/14, 20; 117/1, 5, 8, 10, 13-15, 21; 145/34; 151/8; ich, 5/16; 11/22, 25, 31; 13/26; 15/27, 31; 17/16; 21/10, 29; 27/4, 5, 21; 31/25; 39/19, 20; 47/2, 8; 53/15; 75/25; 83/12, 21; 85/33; 87/13, 14, 16; 93/2, 12; 95/15, 21, 27; 113/17, 29; 125/3, 19; 127/18, 22-24; 131/24; 141/31; 145/8, 13, 15, 19, 20, 22, 30; 147/10, 21, 26 (2), 27; 149/3; ihc, 23/1; ic ham, *I am*, 95/23; i, 7/21; 15/10; 83/24; 103/18; im (+ min), 15/15; *d. ac.* me, 3/4, 7, 23-26; 5/12, 17, 19; 7/6; 9/6, 8, 15, 16, 29, 30; 11/3, 4, 5, 9, 10, 11, 17, 26; 13/1, 15-17, 20, 22, 25; 15/16, 18, 22, 25; 17/2, 12, 17 (2), 25 (2), 26, 27 (2); 19/14, 15, 30, 32, 33; 21/1, 3, 6, 26, 30, *etc.*; *with self, nom.* me self, *myself*, 7/6; me selv, 53/17; *d. ac.* meselven, 5/12; 9/8; 83/24.

ich, *see* ic.

icynde, *adj. natural*, 57/28.

ikyndelich, *adj. natural*, 27/27.

iclensed, *see* clansien.

icnowen, *see* ȝecnawen.

ilche, *see* ilke.

ilesten, *to listen*, 107/22.

ilieve, *v. to believe*, 105/31.

ilke, *pron. same*, 17/11; 21/8; 29/32; 31/3, 32; 37/23; 41/8; 51/5; 63/8; 93/14; 101/8; 123/5; 127/11; 129/15; 135/3, 22; 139/11; 145/2; 151/1 (*each*); ilche, 5/17; 11/12, 30; 13/31; 23/13; 47/8; 53/6; 57/22; 77/15; 83/20; 89/18, 23; 99/2; 105/9, 15; 107/9; 109/30.

imængd, *part. pret. mingled, mixed*, 63/4; imaingd, 63/7.

imered, *pret. part. refined*, 17/16.

imett, *sb. measure, sg. ac.* 11/28; *d.* imete, 149/3.

imeðfull, *adj. sober*, 139/16.

imotet, *pret. part. coined*, 17/15.

in, *prep. in*, 17/27, 28; 43/20; 73/28; 75/26; 87/10, 23; 89/8; 91/23; 95/4; 133/18; 149/4, 12; 151/20.

inede, *adj. needy*, 147/5.

infare, *sb. entrance, ac. sg.* 99/31.

inȝehied, *sb. understanding, conscience*, 65/11; 141/1, 3; inȝied, 147/11, 13, 23.

inne, *prep. adv. in, within*, 35/17 (2), 30; 37/11; 63/1; 83/9; 99/5; 105/5; 123/26; 135/22.

inohȝ, *adj. enough*, 81/17; inowh, 13/24.

inreste, *adj. sup. inmost*, 17/28.

into, *prep. into*, 5/4, 9; 9/3, 10; 13/29; 17/9; 19/31; 25/26, 30; 27/2, 10, 24; 31/12; 33/26; 35/5; 37/30; 43/32; 45/17; 57/2, 4, 6; 61/31; 69/8; 78/2, 25 (2); 77/25; 95/33; 99/15, 16; 101/29, 31, 32; 103/25; 105/14, 25, 26; 109/19, 29; 113/1; 115/3, 4; 141/22; 143/2, 5, 7.

iradi, *adj. ready*, 117/15, 21.

is, *v. see* bien.

is, *pron. his, them, see* he.

iscapen, iscop, *see* ȝesceppen.

isene, *adj. iron*, 119/12.

isetnesse, *sb. ordinance*, 95/16.

isien, *see* ȝeseń.

ismered, *pret. part. anointed*, 33/3.

GLOSSARY.

ysope, *sb. hyssop, d. sg.* 83/2.
israelisce, *adj. Israelitish,* 55/12.
istreiht, *pret. part. stretched,* 63/19.
istriend, *pret. part. begotten,* 117/5, 6.
it, *see* hit.
itrand, *pret. part. rolled up,* 101/19.
iðolien, *v. to suffer,* 123/26; *pret. part.* ipoled, 59/6; iðoled, 113/34.
iprowen, *pret. part. thrown, made* (?), 95/31.
iungman, *sb. young man, youth, nom. sg.* 67/25.
iwæiȝen, *see* weiȝen.
iweven, *pret. part. woven,* 39/22.
iwinnen, *v. to gain,* 151/13.
iwiten, *v. to know,* 99/28.

J.

justise, *sb. justice, judge,* 105/5, 16.

C, K.

kæie, *sb. key, nom. sg.* 7/25.
cam, *see* cumen.
kandeles, *sb. candles,* 139/7.
cann, *see* cunnen.
kanunekes, *sb. canons,* 35/2.
carefull, *adj. full of care, sorrowful,* 87/31.
karf, *see* kerven.
karite, *sb. charity,* 37/13, 24, 33; 39/14, 23; 51/30; carite, 45/16, 32; cariteð, 47/14; 95/3; kariteð, 19/34; 21/14; 63/4; 67/2 (cf. charite).
casteles, *sb. castles,* 129/4, 6.
kastin, *v. to chasten,* 143/30.
kedde, *see* keðen.
kelien, *v. to cool,* 21/1; *pres. ind. pl.* kylieð, 119/23; *imp. sg.* kiel, 103/3, 4; *pret. part.* ikeled, 137/2.
kenesmen, *sb. kinsmen, ac. pl.* 75/31.
kenne, *sb. kin, kind, kindred, family, generation, sg. d. ac.* 7/2; 55/12, 22 (2); 65/26; 95/22; 109/13, 26, 28, 33; 115/31; 117/32; *gen.* kennes, 9/6, 8; 11/32; 25/17; 29/7; 33/33; 43/11, 18, 31; 49/16; 71/28, 34; 78/11; 75/1; 95/25; 103/2; 107/12; 119/23; 127/33; 129/8, 19; 131/4; 137/16; 141/5, 6; 147/9; 149/3, 18.
kere, *sb. choice, ac. sg.* 113/19.
kerven, *v. to carve,* 27/26; 3 *sg. ind. pret.* karf, 91/11.
kessen, *v. to kiss, pl. pret.* kesten, 117/24.
keðen, *v. to tell, show, declare, make known,* 35/13; kyðen, 23/4; 83/

27; *pres. ind.* 3 *sg.* kydh, 109/12; *pl.* cyðeð, 57/34; *pret.* 3 *sg.* kedde, 53/31; 55/21; *part.* ȝekydd, 11/24.
kiel, *see* kelien.
kydh, *see* keðen.
kiertel, *sb. coat, ac. sg.* 127/30.
kylieð, *see* kelien.
king, *sb. king, sg. nom.* 141/26; 147/18; kyng, 81/23; 95/10; *gen.* kynges, 43/12; *d.* kinge, 15/7; 141/21; 147/15, 25; kynge, 43/15; kyng, 115/32; *pl. nom.* kinges, 49/27; *gen.* kinge, 141/26; kiningene, 95/10.
kyðeð, *see* keðen.
clane, *adj. clean, pure,* 123/33; 125/10, 20, 22; 127/1; 131/8, 12, 24; 143/21; clene, 83/8; 95/31; 121/8.
clane-hierte, *adj. pure in heart,* 125/8, 19, 25.
clannesse, *sb. purity, chastity,* 43/17; 123/25; 129/15, 18, 26, 27, 29; 131/1, 15; 135/22; clennesse, 123/24.
clansin, *v. to cleanse, sg. imp.* clanse, 123/34; *pret. part.* iclansed, 83/3; iclensed, 65/1.
claðes, *sb. clothes,* 57/26, 27, 32; 73/22; 87/30; cloðes, 5/33.
clene, *see* clane.
clepien, *v. to call, cry,* 103/19; clepiȝen, 65/28; *pres. ind.* 1 *sg.* clepie, 21/13; clepiȝe, 21/4; 3 *sg.* clepeð, 17/26; 49/3; 53/34; 141/17; *pl.* clepieð, 11/7; clepeð, 73/30; *opt.* 2 *sg.* clepiȝe, 145/8; *imp. sg.* clepe, 57/7; 75/30, 33; 127/16; *pret.* 3 *sg.* clepede, 31/5; 109/20; *part.* ȝecleped, 7/16; icleped, 3/9, 22; 5/7; 9/24, 25, 32; 18/30; 25/6; 29/30; 35/15, 27, *etc.*
clepienge, *sb. calling, d. sg.* 71/32.
clereo, *sb. clerk, nom. sg.* 81/16.
cloðes, *see* claðes.
cnelin, *v. to kneel, ind. pres. pl.* cnelið, 51/3; *imp. sg.* cnyle, 145/9.
cnewes, *sb. knees,* 51/3.
cnewlinge, *sb. kneeling, d. sg.* 127/1.
cniht, *sb. knight, nom. sg.* 121/17.
cnyle, *see* cnelin.
cold, *adj. cold,* 107/19; 109/6.
com, *see* cumen.
confessores, *sb. confessors,* 35/1.
corn, *sb. corn, d. sg.* corne, 29/19.
costninȝes, *sb. temptations,* 119/25.
craftes, *sb. crafts,* 65/12.

GLOSSARY.

craven, *v. to accuse, prosecute,* 75/19.
craviere, *sb. accuser, calumniator, d. sg.* 75/11, 18.
crepen, *v. to creep, ind. pres.* 3 *sg.* crepþ, 101/29; *imp. sg.* crep, 101/31.
crewlinde, *pres. part. crawling,* 139/8.
cristendom, *sb. christendom, christianity, baptism, sg. ac.* 7/31; 73/6; *d.* cristendome, 25/7.
cristene, *sb. Christians, nom. pl.* 95/2.
cristeneman, *sb. Christian, nom. sg.* 9/17.
cumen, *v. to come, go,* 13/22; 17/13, 25; 21/18; 27/33; 33/26, 27; 43/18, 32; 45/2; 61/13; 69/8, 9; 79/10; 91/21, *etc.*; *pres. ind.* 2 *sg.* cumst, 25/2; 73/10; 75/17; 3 *sg.* cumeð, 29/33; 121/29; cumþ, 5/7; 11/8; 19/3, 27; 25/15, 27; 29/4, 6, 7, 11, 30; 31/10; 35/27, 30; 37/1, 3, *etc.*; cumð, 19/17; 35/28; 57/11; 63/2; 71/6; 85/28; 91/8; 135/23, 25; *pl.* cumeð, 9/3; 17/13; 45/13; 49/28; 63/25; 71/33; 87/6, 7, 24, 28; 89/24, 26, *etc.*; cume (3e), 43/1; cumen, 77/25; *opt.* 3 *sg.* cume, 53/15; cumen, 81/33; *pl.* cumen, 71/1; 103/10; *imp. sg.* cum, 103/29; 109/29; 1 *pl.* (*adhort.*) cume (we), 113/27; 2 *pl.* cumeð, 59/22; 71/26; *pret. ind.* 1 *and* 3 *sg.* cam, 13/24; 15/9, 10; 17/30, 31; 59/1; 67/25; 97/8; 109/2; 119/3; 145/3; com, 35/31; *opt.* 2 *sg.* come, 141/22; 3 *sg.* come, 111/4; *pret. pl.* comen, 15/11; 23/26; 43/14; 95/27; 99/16; 113/31; 119/20; *part.* ʒecumen, 117/33; 141/17; icumen, 99/33.
cunnen, *v. to know, to be able,* (*I can*), *pres. ind.* 1 *and* 3 *sg.* cann, 49/31; 81/17, 21; 99/32; 107/11, 20; 109/17; *pl.* cunnen, 49/12; 65/20; 77/14; 79/23; 81/19; 109/22; 135/21; 139/24; *opt.* 2 *and* 3 *sg.* cunne, 71/2; 99/23; kunne, 71/3; *pret.* 1 *sg.* cuðe, 9/21; *pl.* cuðen, 9/23.
curune, *sb. crown, ac. sg.* 15/8.
cuðe, *see* cunnen.
cwelleres, *sb. killers,* 75/12.
cweðen, *v. to say,* 11/13; *pret. ind.* 3 *sg.* cwað, 53/32; 67/28, 32; 69/8, 10; 81/27; 109/28; 117/27; 147/25, 26.
cwide, *sb. legacy, ac. sg.* 147/17.

L (Cf. Hl.).

læche, *sb. doctor, d. sg.* 27/25.
laczste, *adj. last,* 19/28.
laden, *v. to lead,* 21/24; 71/12; 73/8; leden, 27/24; 65/13; *pres. ind.* 3 *sg.* latt, 127/10; *pl.* lædet, 73/34; *pret.* 3 *sg.* ladde, 5/3; *part.* iladd, 53/18.
lafdi, *sb. lady, sg. d. ac.* 5/24; 21/5; 53/26, 34; 57/7; *pl.* lafdies, 53/34.
laʒe, *sb. law, sg. nom. d. ac.* 99/12, 13; 109/16; 149/29; 151/3; laʒhe, 137/13; 145/5; laʒwe, 7/28; lauʒe, 111/30; *pl.* laʒwes, 51/8.
laʒeliche, *adj. lawful,* 43/8.
lahfulnesse, *sb. word of honour,* 11/24.
lai, *see* liggen.
lac, *sb. sacrifice, sg. nom. ac.* 85/14; loac, 111/19; 117/13; 119/27; loc, 85/2, 5, 11, 17, 19, 23; 117/8; 119/29; *pl. d.* (?) lake, loke, 21/2 (*see foot-note*).
lampe, *sb. lamp, d. sg.* 33/5.
land, *sb. land, country, sg. nom. ac.* 61/16; 75/3; 109/32; lond, 111/9; *d.* lande, 5/27; 35/6 (*ac. pl.?*); 41/11; 45/2; 61/14; 109/28, 31; 111/8; londe, 43/27; 79/13; 85/2; 97/28; 109/29.
lanen, *v. to lend, inf.* leanen, 11/29; *pres. ind.* 2 *sg.* lanst, 77/21; *pl.* laneð, 77/27; læneð, 79/12; *imp. sg.* lean, 77/19; *pret.* 2 *sg.* lændest, 77/22; *pl.* 77/30; *part.* ilænd, 11/31.
lang, *adj. long,* lange, 17/23; 59/25; lagne, 17/19; *comp.* lengere, 89/16.
lange, *adv. long,* 17/18; 33/21; 43/12; 47/12; 103/20; longe, 15/19; 23/28; 87/4; 93/9; *comp.* lenger, 77/29.
længe, *sb. length, ac. sg.* 39/33.
lare, *sb. lore, discipline, instruction, g. d. ac. sg.* 19/15; 23/20; 45/6, 21, 31; 61/8, 17; 63/18; 73/19; 83/11, 14; 127/14; lore, 47/13, 15, 20; 77/6; 83/14; 125/26.
laren, *v. to teach, pres. ind.* 3 *sg.* lærð, 111/6; lareð, 127/12; *pret. ind.* 2 *sg.* lardest, 21/28.
lasse, (1) *adj. less,* 45/30; (2) *adv.* 71/18.
last, *see* lasten.
læste, *conj. lest,* 75/10; ðe laste, 109/18; þe las te, 125/29 (*cf.* naðelæs).

236 GLOSSARY.

lasten, *v. to last*, 3 *sg. ind. pres.* last, 59/14.
laten, *v. to let, think, appear, behave, forbear, forsake, leave, restrain*, 3/15; 33/30; 53/20; 67/22; 147/19; 149/28; læten, 37/17; 55/5; 69/4; 115/21; læte, 91/27; leten, 47/12; *pres. ind.* 2 *sg.* latst, 47/4; 59/9; 3 *sg.* latt, 63/9; 65/19; lat, 5/24; 13/31; 61/21; 133/31; *pl.* lateþ, 35/5; lateð, 71/33; læteð, 55/29; læted, 7/2; *opt.* 2 *sg.* lat, 111/20; 143/6; 3 *sg.* læte, 37/30; 57/20; *imp. sg.* lat, 77/17; 113/25; læt, 69/23; 105/30; let, 81/31; latt, 109/23; 113/23; *pret. ind.* 1 *sg.* let, 13/26; *part.* ilaten, 5/14.
latt, *see* laden.
lað, *adj. loathsome*, 147/19.
laðliche, *adj. loathsome*, 19/5; loðlich, 109/6; *superl.* laðlicheste, 51/14.
lauȝe, *see* laȝe.
laverd, *see* hlaverd.
lean, *sb. reward, ac. sg.* 5/31; 11/32; 35/7; 57/28; 75/5; 77/13, 17, 31; 135/29; 139/32.
leanen, *see* lanen.
lease, *adj. false*, 9/28; 41/4, 9; 65/27; 73/2; 81/3.
leasinge, *sb. leasing, lying, nom. d. ac. sg.* 9/22, 26, 27, 32; lesinge, 9/20; *pl.* leasinges, 9/31.
leawede, *adj. laic*, 13/9; leeavede, 79/17.
leden, *see* laden.
lef, *see* lief.
left, *sb. air, nom. sg.* 95/20.
leiȝe, *sb. lye, nom. sg.* 95/30.
leiȝen, *v. to lay*, 93/30; leien, 105/28; *pret. part.* ȝeleid, 137/3; ileid, 47/9; 93/31.
leihen, *v. to laugh, pres. ind.* 3 *sg.* leicheð, 57/14; *pl.* leiheð, 81/3; *part.* leiȝinde, 127/5.
leme, *sb. gleam, nom. sg.* 23/9.
lemen, *sb. limbs, pl.* 27/5; 131/26; lemes, 131/4; 133/25.
lenger, *see* lang.
lengðe, *sb. length*, 45/32.
lernin, *see* liernien.
lesinge, *see* leasinge.
leste, *v. to lust*, 3 *sg. pret.* 13/27.
lesten, *see* hlesten.
leten, *see* laten.
letten, *v. to let, hinder*, 3/18; 137/12.
leðebeih, *adj. compliant, buxom*, 109/3; -bei, 113/26; -beiȝe, 45/1.

leðre, *adj. wicked*, 51/12.
leve, *see* lief.
leveð, *see* libben *and* lieven.
libben, *v. to live*, 31/8; 57/29; 67/22; 75/5; 139/11; 147/18, 19, 27; *ger.* to libbenne, 91/30; *pres. part.* libbende, 55/1; liviende, 45/2; 61/16; 63/30; 77/18; liviȝende, 41/11; *g. sg.* liviendes, 27/2; *pres. ind.* 3 *sg.* leveð, 89/3; 135/5; liveð, 151/21; *pl.* libbeð, 57/26, 27; *pret.* 2 *sg.* livedest, 33/21.
lief, *adj. dear*, 3/4; 43/22; lef, 147/19; lieve, 7/22; 21/7, 26; 23/10 (2); 31/28; 53/19; 57/6, 9; 69/32; 73/9; 83/34; 85/24; 89/10; 91/23; 93/21; 95/34; 99/2; 115/31; 119/2; 127/15; 129/6; 151/8; leve, 83/12; 119/30; 145/30; *comp.* levere, 11/26; 43/12.
lien, *v. to lie* (*mentiri*), 2 *sg. ind. pret.* luȝe, 9/28.
liernien, *v. to learn*, 59/23; liernin, 23/20; 47/21; 109/17; 151/11; liernen, 49/24; lernin, 49/8; *pres. ind.* 2 *sg.* liernest, 87/2; *opt.* 2 *sg.* lierne, 69/34; *imp. pl.* liernið, 49/10; lierneð, 63/34; *pret. part.* ilierned, 69/4; 71/10.
lierning-cnihtes, *sb. disciples*, 99/14.
liesen, *v. to release*, 3 *sg. ind. pret.* liesde, 7/20.
lif, *sb. life, sg. ac.* 5/3; 9/1; 21/24; 33/21; 41/33; 51/32, *etc.*; *g.* lives, 39/25; 53/11; 75/1; 105/14; 139/10; *d.* live, 9/3; 15/2; 19/12; 21/12, 15; 25/29; 35/27; 43/26; 51/5, *etc.*; *pl. nom.* lif, 73/30.
liggen, *v. to lie* (*jacere*), *pres. ind.* 3 *sg.* lið, 87/16; 63/19, 29; 101/19; 111/1; 121/21, 22; 139/5, 7; *pret. ind.* 3 *sg.* lai, 49/28, 31.
liht, *sb. light* (*lux*), *sg. nom. ac.* 17/30; 31/24; 35/22, 26; 49/18, 19; *d.* lihte, 35/23; 49/21; 63/31; 127/18.
liht, *adj. light* (*levis*), 71/30; 95/19; 109/6.
lihten, *v. to lighten, light, to make easy*, 71/29.
lihten, *v. to enlighten, illumine, pres. ind.* 3 *sg.* lihteþ, 35/26; *imp. sg.* liht, 127/18; *pret.* 3 *sg.* lihte, 49/18.
lihtliche, *adv. lightly, easily*, 21/15; 57/14, 15; 81/20; -lich, 93/8.
lichame, *sb. body, sg. nom. d. ac.* 11/16; 17/3, 25; 25/22; 27/6; 31/

GLOSSARY. 237

11; 33/19; 39/18; 43/28; 45/3;
47/16; 49/17; 53/2, 4; 55/14,
33; 57/10; 61/30, 31; 63/29;
75/18; 85/31; 91/27; 93/5, 8;
95/15, 17; 101/12; 111/28; 117/
14; 119/28; 121/2; licame, 61/
14; 93/27; 95/12; likame, 65/34;
123/27; 129/7; 131/12, 15; 133/
25; 135/21; *g*. lichames, 9/18;
23/19; 71/14; likames, 137/24.
lichamliche, (1) *adv. bodily*, 67/26;
(2) *adj*. likamliche, 131/21.
likin, *v. to please, like*, 85/25; *pres.
ind.* 3 *sg.* likeð, 47/21; 119/31;
137/23; *pl.* likeð, 69/15; *pret.* 3
sg. likede, 11/10; 119/10, 18.
likinge, *sb. liking, d. ac. pl.* 119/19.
lyon, *sb. lion, nom. sg.* 139/19.
lippen, *sb. lips, ac. pl.* 59/30.
litel, *adj. little*, 5/1; 17/8, 20; 29/
19; 45/29; 49/22, 26; 71/13;
91/29; 97/29, 31; 107/13, 15, 16;
147/22; 149/24; litle, 19/19;
27/13; 43/31; 75/14; 97/14;
little, 151/8.
litlen, *v. to humble*, 3 *sg. pret.* litlede,
49/16.
lið, see liggen.
lipien, *v. to soften*, 3 *sg. ind. pres.*
liþegað, 33/7.
live, see lif.
liven, see libben.
loac, see lac.
lofsang, *sb. praise, ac. sg.* 19/27.
loc, see lac.
lokin, *v. to look after, keep*, 17/3;
19/6; 43/20; 71/13; 91/20; 99/
25; 121/11; 133/30; 149/18;
pres. ind. 2 *sg.* lokest, 47/3; 3 *sg.*
loceð, 27/25; 71/23; lokeð, 61/11;
103/10, 15; *pl.* lokieð, 43/33;
lokið, 115/13; *opt.* 2 *sg.* lokie,
145/31; 3 *sg.* loki, 133/24; *imp.
sg.* loce, 89/19; loke, 53/32; 69/
27; 85/25; 111/16; 117/15; 145/
8; *pret. ind.* 2 *sg.* lokedest, 145/
24; 147/1; 3 *sg.* lokede, 55/11;
111/32; *pl.* lokeden, 103/13; 149/
30.
lomb, *sb. lamb, d. sg.* lombe, 129/
14.
lond, see land.
long, see lang.
lore, see lare.
lott, *sb. lot, part, sg. nom. ac.* 21/9;
111/22; 123/6; loth, 5/17.
loð, see lað.
loverd, see hlaverd.
luʒe, see lien.
lust, *sb. lust, sg. nom. ac.* 135/23, 28;
pl. lustes, 31/7; 39/8; 43/6; 109/
33; hlustes, 135/15; 137/24.
lustfull, *adj. lustful*, 51/24.
luve, *sb. love, sg. nom. d. ac.* 3/5, 11,
13; 7/22; 11/2, 30; 15/28; 19/
34; 21/8, 30; 25/16; 33/4, 28,
etc.; *d.* luven, 33/5; 37/18; *pl.*
luves, 39/23.
luvien, *v. to love*, 19/32; 21/25;
69/30 (livien *MS*.), 109/1; 137/
11, 18; luviʒen, 37/5, 6, 25; 41/
13; 91/21; 101/5; 107/1; luviʒe,
67/3; luven, 65/24; 143/14; *pres.
ind.* 2 *sg.* luvest, 37/23, 26; 39/
32; 41/5; 69/29; 77/15; 91/26;
101/6; 111/11, 16, 17; 3 *sg.*
luveð, 35/20; 37/10, 27; 89/30;
41/7; 45/16; 91/20; 101/9; 111/
3; 139/28; luvieð, 121/23; 133/
31; 141/15; luviʒeð, 107/20; *pl.*
luvieð, 5/31; 15/14; 69/15; 99/
12; 131/20; 137/10; 139/33;
luviʒeð, 59/26; 61/15; 63/1; 77/
15; 107/28; *opt.* 2 *sg.* luviʒe, 39/
13; 3 *sg.* luvie, 31/15; *pl.* luviʒen,
41/33; luven, 69/23; *imp. sg.* luve,
67/5, 7; 77/16; 125/24; *pl.* luvieð,
129/31; *pret. ind.* 2 *sg.* luvedest,
11/14; 33/1; 3 *sg.* luvede, 25/20;
43/7, 9; 125/5; *pl.* luveden, 69/
21; *part.* ʒeluved, 57/6; 123/26;
131/18; 147/21; *pl.* iluvede, 73/
32.

M.

ma, *adj. adv. more*, 7/20; 11/22;
15/16; 19/5, 8, 33; 21/25; 49/
24; 87/20; 103/31; 117/4; 129/
10, 16; 139/32; 145/19; 151/21;
mo, 17/21; 19/3; 31/13; 35/11;
43/1; 55/6, 15, 21; 59/14; 89/
12, 23; 93/10; 97/4; 105/24;
113/14; 115/27; 121/3, 25; 123/
14.
mai, see muʒen.
maiden, *sb. maiden, sg. nom.* 55/18;
117/35; 129/16; 131/8, 10–13;
d. ac. 5/24; 25/24; 119/1; 131/
24.
maidenhad, *sb. maidenhood, sg. nom.*
129/13; 131/14; *d. ac.* 55/6, 14;
129/12, 17, 20, 23, 28; 131/21.
maini, *adj. mighty*, 107/1.
maister, *sb. master, d. sg.* maistre,
73/28.
makien, *v. to make*, 75/30; 91/22;
145/18; makie, 75/26; maken,
145/18; *pres. ind.* 2 *sg.* makest,
135/27, 30; 3 *sg.* makeð, 3/12;
29/33; 109/3, 13, 14; 125/25;

238 GLOSSARY.

139/14, 21; 149/28; *pl.* makieð,
37/4; 85/13; 87/32; 95/30; 105/
7; 137/31; *opt. 2 sg.* make, 125/
22; *imp. sg.* make, 83/8, 23; 115/
19, 20; *pl.* makieð, 123/33; *pret.
3 sg.* makede, 33/34; 49/26; 81/
26; *2 sg.* makedest, 145/28; *part.*
ȝemaked, 11/4; 43/24; imaked,
3/24; 83/21; 93/12; 95/19; 97/
20; maked, 55/12.
man, *sb. man, sg. nom.* 5/2, 22; 15/
20; 31/14; 37/11, 27; 59/4; 67/
34; 127/13; 133/15, 18; 149/5,
11; *ac.* 3/12; 99/13; 101/1; 149/
28; mann, *nom.* 3/2; 15/6, 7; 19/
6; 25/22; 27/1, 16; 29/17, 20;
33/17; 37/5, 30; 39/14, 30; 41/
11; 43/4; 45/20, 27, 28; 51/7,
11; 57/15, 19, 33; 61/33; 65/27;
67/3, 18; 69/2-4, 8, 30; 73/4;
77/19; 85/11; 89/2; 93/30; 97/
4; 99/10; 101/2, 9, 24, 31, *etc.*;
d. ac. 5/22; 13/31; 39/19, 28;
43/16; 63/18, 29; 65/18, 24; 67/
1, 3; 99/18; 101/3; 109/3, 8, 13;
139/11, 15, 21; manne, 5/20; 13/
13; 29/2, 21, 23, 33; 33/15, 17;
35/18, 20, 27, 29; 37/10; 41/8;
45/20; 47/27; 51/4, 9; 57/13;
61/1, 24; 63/11, 20; 69/6; 71/
10, 24; 77/10, 12; 79/7, 25; 105/
20; 107/24; 109/15; 113/15, 33;
117/31; 123/29; 127/13; 133/9,
16, 19, 24, 30; 135/2, 8; 139/18,
23; 143/18; 149/25; *g.* mannes,
11/3; 19/34; 27/25; 33/18; 35/
16, 28; 39/24, 29, 33; 41/2, 24,
33; 49/17; 65/22, 23; 67/23;
107/20; 117/7, 14; 135/27; 151/
17; manes, 15/23; *pl.* men, *nom.
ac.* 3/15; 57/12; 61/23; 77/4, 14;
79/28; 133/21; menn, 3/16; 7/4;
13/5; 15/3, 22; 25/9; 29/27;
33/8; 41/26; 51/2, 3; 57/11, 12;
59/10; 67/11, 22; 69/11; 75/1;
77/15, 27; 79/7, 12, 18, 28; 83/
30; 85/8; 91/30; 125/8; 137/12,
30; 139/25; 143/12; 149/17, 18;
g. manne, 65/31; 67/5; 121/22;
mannes, 3/5; *d.* mannen, 5/11, 32;
15/13; 31/6; 37/25; 39/17; 45/
25; 51/6; 55/7, 22, 25; 59/15;
73/31; 89/14, 15; 99/6, 32; 113/
8; 137/10; 141/23, 24; manne,
57/33; 63/30; 109/4; 143/15.
mang, *prep. among,* 5/18; 43/25;
51/6; 55/7, 8, 12; 75/1; 77/7;
85/20; 91/17; 117/30; 141/22;
149/9.
mani, *pron. many,* 13/9, 23; 39/28,

30; 115/10; maniȝe, 3/7, 24; 23/
18; 25/3; 29/25; 31/16; 39/24;
41/21; 43/23, 31; 47/11; 53/6;
59/12; 61/23; 67/10; 69/22; 71/
9; 79/34; 87/24; 97/5; 113/34;
129/18; 149/20; manie, 23/27;
149/21; *g.* maniȝes, 43/31; 73/11;
95/25; 151/17; manies, 9/8; 129/
8, 19; 149/18.
manifealde, *adj. manifold,* 81/29;
85/12; 87/18; 103/3; -felde, 79/
23; 93/16.
manikennes, *adj. various,* 71/27.
manken, *sb. mankind, sg. nom. ac.*
53/14; -kenn, 7/19; 49/12; 51/
19; 115/26, 32; 117/16, 22, 35;
119/2; mannkenn, 25/27; 109/26;
mankynn, 55/15; mannkyn, 49/6;
mannkynn, 25/20; mankinn, 109/
1; *d.* mankenne, 11/12; 81/29;
115/21.
mann, *see* man.
manniscnesse, *sb. manhood, humanity, ac. sg.* 25/23; mannischnesse,
97/9; mannisnesse, 25/25; 49/4.
mann-kenn, -kyn, *see* manken.
mannliche, *adj. human,* 43/29.
mantel, *sb. mantle, ac. sg.* 127/
31.
mare, *adj. adv. more,* 3/29; 9/6,
32; 11/15; 23/11; 37/20; 39/31;
69/21, 29 (2); 123/20; 127/6;
133/17; 141/25; 149/23; more,
5/26; 9/13; 11/15; 13/23; 29/
13, 20, 22; 33/13; 33/18; 39/9;
53/20; 59/6, 7; 61/24; 69/7, 23,
28, 31; 73/7, 16; 75/4; 77/22,
83/5; 109/33; 115/30; *superl.*
mæst, 45/16; 69/26; mest, 101/4;
mast, 101/9; 111/16, 18; mæste,
69/27.
mare, *sb. mark, ac. sg.* 57/31; 71/
34.
martirdom, *sb. martyrdom, ac. sg.*
129/19.
martirs, *sb. martyrs,* 33/32.
masses, *sb. masses,* 65/2.
mæst, mast, *see* mare.
mæðe, *sb. moderation, sobriety, sg.
ac.* 107/12; *nom.* maðe, 139/14.
mæðfull, *adj. sober,* 139/15.
maðliche, *adv. moderately,* 31/8.
me, *pron. one,* 3/29; 9/15, 16; 27/
10; 33/33; 53/8, 34; 61/18; 65/
3; 67/8; 71/13; 73/33; 75/1;
77/4, *etc.*
me, *see* ic.
mealten, *v. to melt,* 145/33.
mede, *sb. meed, reward, sg. nom. d.
ac.* 11/29; 77/20, 21; 79/6, 9;

GLOSSARY. 239

81/6; 139/32; miede, 77/24; 105/28; *pl.* nnedes, 79/24.
mehrþe, *see* **merhþe.**
men, *see* **man.**
menezen, *v. to admonish, remind,* 3 *sg. ind. pres.* menezeð, 19/13; 35/32; 113/3; 121/9.
menezinge, *sb. admonition, sg. d. ac.* 89/25; 101/2; 119/17; *pl.* menezinges, 51/12.
menster, *sb. minster, monastery* (?) *d. sg.* menstre, 7/3.
merhþe, *sb. mirth, joy, d. ac. sg.* 31/2, 14; 103/30; 113/16; merhðe, 41/10; 45/12; 57/6; 95/34; merchþe, 151/12; mehrþe, 87/25.
meri, *adj. merry, ac. sg. m.* merigne, 103/28.
mest, *see* **mast.**
mete, *sb. meat, sg. nom.* 89/7; *d.* 57/26, 27; 87/29; *pl.* metes, 43/10, 13; 137/17, 20, 35; 139/9.
mi, *see* **min.**
michel, *adj. adv. much, great,* 5/14, 27; 11/19; 17/9; 23/29; 29/19; 33/22; 37/17; 39/25, 27; 41/20; 47/15; 55/29; 59/7, 11; 61/15; 63/21; 67/18, 20; 69/15; 71/12, 13, 16, 17; 73/11; 77/17, 30; 79/26, 30; 81/28; 83/27; 85/30; 87/8, 27, 28; 91/31; 93/4; 99/4, 11; 105/34; 107/11, 13, 14, 15 (2), 16 (2); 111/11; 115/17, 22, 25; 125/5; 127/4, 5; 129/9; 135/23, 29; 137/18, 20, 21, 27; 139/31; 143/27; 147/27; 149/5, 6, 23; 151/18; muchel, 7/15; 25/20; 27/19; 47/4; 103/12, 15; 117/9; 141/25; miche, 113/26; michele, 17/32; 21/17; 25/7; 29/12, 14; 31/2, 9, 12; 37/1; 39/10, 28; 41/20; 43/1, 18; 45/7, 9, 12, 30; 49/5; 55/8, 21, 25; 57/8; 59/12; 65/16, 17; 67/13; 69/11, 14; 79/14, 27; 81/4, 28, 30; 83/10, 15, 18, 32; 85/1; 87/25, 27; 89/19; 93/16; 95/34; 97/11; 103/29, 30; 111/14; 119/19, 20, 24; 129/15; 135/21, 22; 137/19, 28, 29; 139/2, 30; 141/24; 145/17, 21, 31; 147/28; muchele, 9/10; 11/18; 15/1; 19/2, 12, 29; 21/6, 13, 19; 27/20; 29/5; 43/22, 24; 51/9, 13; 55/17; 63/7; 89/34; 95/24; 97/6; 103/4; 113/25; 115/1, 13; 137/4; michelere, 41/18, 20; micheles, 23/3; mucheles, 3/29.
mid, *prep. adv. with,* 3/19 (2); 7/1 (2); 9/24, 25; 11/12, 17, 23, 24; 13/16, 20; 15/19; 17/10, 14, 20; 19/5, 8, 29, 33; 21/1, 2, 4, 12, 23 (2), 24; 23/13, 25, 30-32; 25/12, 31; 27/19; 29/21, 22, 25, 26, 33; 81/13, 30; 33/3; 35/21, *etc.*; mide, 109/34; 125/23; 139/6; mit, 27/31; 75/6.
middaiz, *sb. mid-day, d. ac. sg.* 125/13.
midden, *sb. middle, d. sg.* 101/20.
middeneard, *sb. earth, sg. nom. ac.* 43/25; 117/11; middenard, 105/26.
mide, *see* **mid.**
midniht, *sb. mid-night, ac. sg.* 125/13.
miede, *see* **mede.**
miht, *see* **muzen.**
mihte, *sb. might, power, virtue, sg. nom. d. ac.* 9/2; 21/7, 17; 25/6, 10; 27/14; 29/15, 18, 21, 30, 33; 33/6, 34; 35/18, 20; 37/3; 39/7; 41/23; 47/14, 29; 49/4, 6, 7, 16, 24; 51/18; 53/20, 22, 31, *etc.*; *pl.* mihtes, 23/16, 25, 30; 35/9; 47/2, 10, 26; 49/28; 53/16, 23; 63/14; 71/2; 77/6; 87/2; 91/12, 25; 93/18; 95/6; 99/22, *etc.*; mihten, 43/32; 93/7; 149/21.
mihti, *adj. mighty,* 55/19.
mildce, *sb. mercy, pity, sg. nom. d. ac.* 9/4; 15/2; 21/5, 19, 22; 23/1; 55/17, 21; 65/6; 67/10; 81/28, 32; 83/27, 33; 97/11; 111/28; 113/1, 9, 11, 12, 27, 32; 115/5; mildse, 15/16; mildsce, 123/12, 13, 17, 19; 131/18; 145/21, 32; mildze, 21/6, 10, 20; milce, 19/21; 55/26; 111/23, 24; 113/7, 33; 115/6, 8, 13, 19, 29; milsce, 57/24; 59/14; *pl.* mildces, 81/29; milcen, 113/2.
mildciende, *part. pres. merciful,* 113/4.
milde, *adj. mild, merciful,* 81/30; 118/6; 145/22.
mildse, mildsce, mildze, *see* **mildce.**
milen, *sb. miles,* 127/31.
milsce, *see* **mildce.**
min, *pron. my, mine, sg. nom. m. f. and nom. ac. n.* 13/20; 17/2; 27/2, 22; 47/13; 71/29, 30; 83/5, 9, 12, 32; 87/10; 91/20; 93/15; 97/1, 2; 105/31; 145/30; 147/10; mi, 55/10; 79/22; 93/15; 119/30; *nom. f.* mine, 143/23; *g. m.* mines, 15/10; 17/12; *d. ac.* mine, 7/7; 11/24; 17/3, 11; 19/31; 21/8, 29, 31; 23/8, 12; 27/4; 39/18; 55/12, 14; 65/34; 71/29, 31;

81/28 ; 83/22, 34; 87/17, 19; 91/5; 93/17; 97/5, 9; 103/3; 125/2; 127/29; min, 7/31; 11/23; 15/15; 55/14; *d. f.* mire, 8/23; 15/10; 81/27; 97/3; 145/32; *pl. nom. d. ac.* mine, 7/30; 9/8; 13/25; 15/23; 17/13; 19/32; 21/6, 28; 27/5; 71/31; 83/4; 87/2; 91/20; 93/17; 103/4; 127/18; 147/7, 10.

misbileave, *sb. misbelief, d. sg.* 53/7.

misdade, *sb. misdeed, sg. nom.* 79/18 ; *pl.* misdædes, 65/2 ; misdades, 105/10 ; 125/29, 31.

misdon, *v. to misdo,* 107/25; *pres. ind.* 2 *sg.* misdest, 125/31 ; 3 *sg.* misdoð, 81/20 ; *opt.* 3 *sg.* misdo, 127/5 ; *pret. part.* misdon, 7/15 ; 13/23; 63/21; 71/13; 127/6.

misferen, *v. to fare amiss,* 3 *sg. pret.* misferde, 149/26.

misleven, *v. to misbelieve, pl. ind. pres.* misleveð, 27/19.

mislikien, *v. to mislike, displease, pres. ind.* 3 *sg.* mislikið, 123/31 ; *opt.* 3 *sg.* mislikie, 81/31 ; misliki, 101/31; 129/11.

misþenchen, *v. to think amiss,* 2 *sg. ind. pres.* misþencst, 133/11.

misunderstonden, *v. to misunderstand, pl. ind. pres.* misunderstondet, 37/14.

mit, *see* mid.

mo, *see* ma.

mod, *sb. mood, sg. ac.* 129/6 ; 131/6.

moder, *sb. mother, sg. nom. d. ac.* 9/25; 21/5; 25/14; 35/3; 51/4; 53/30; 55/18; 63/28; 81/24; 87/22; 117/5, 6; 149/10.

modi, *adj. proud, haughty,* 5/11, 14; 41/26 ; 55/29 ; 57/4.

modinesse, *sb. pride, haughtiness, sg. nom. d. ac.* 5/6, 8, 17 ; 7/17 ; 59/12 ; 65/23; 73/18; 89/28.

molde, *sb. mould, d. sg.* 57/22 ; 69/13.

mone, *sb. moon, sg. nom. d. ac.* 27/23, 26 ; 125/23.

moneþes, *sb. months,* 143/32.

more, *see* mare.

moten, *v. to be forced, obliged (I must), pres. ind.* 3 *sg.* mot, 71/13 ; 2 *sg.* most, 85/6 ; 107/1 ; *pl. ind. and opt.* moten, 9/2 ; 21/18, 23, 24; 43/16; 97/31; 141/8; 143/25; mote, 91/27; *opt.* 1 *and* 3 *sg.* mote, 57/9 ; 85/6 ; 97/13 ; *pret.* 3 *sg.* moste, 85/21 ; most, 123/18.

muchel, *see* michel.

muȝen, *v. to be able (I may), pres. ind.* 1 *and* 3 *sg.* mai, 3/2 ; 7/25 ; 13/13; 15/20, 30; 19/8; 25/7 ; 27/10, 11, 13, 17, 33 ; 29/14 ; 31/14; 33/8, 27 ; 37/11; 39/20, 22 (2) ; 41/11, 12, 13; 45/21 ; 47/29 ; 49/22 ; 51/1 ; 53/12, 20; 55/3; 57/24; 59/4, 28; 61/5, 30; 67/17, 28; 69/7, 8, 13, 17, *etc.* ; maiȝ, 129/1 ; 2 *sg.* miht, 29/13 ; 31/30; 35/19; 37/24, 25 ; 39/32; 49/7, 19, 24 ; 53/21 ; 57/10; 63/25, 33 ; 65/11, 31 ; 67/7, *etc.* ; *pl. ind. and opt.* muȝen, 13/7 ; 15/4 ; 23/31, 32 ; 27/8 ; 29/3 ; 31/18, 20 ; 49/11; 61/30; 67/24; 71/32, *etc.* ; *pl. ind.* mai, 69/19 ; *opt.* 1, 2, 3 *sg.* muȝe, 3/18 ; 59/3; 61/2 ; 71/1, 12 ; 73/17; 81/33; 83/8 ; 93/12, 13 ; 95/10; 99/23; 111/17; 125/11, 19; 127/22-24; 137/32, 34 ; 147/29 ; muge, 149/26 ; muȝen, 31/17; *pret.* 1 *and* 3 *sg.* mihte, 3/28; 15/32; 21/31; 23/2; 33/33; 41/23, 29 ; 43/11, 23 ; 53/28 ; 67/28; 95/27; 97/30; 105/15; 113/2 ; 123/15 ; 125/5 ; 137/12 ; 139/18; 145/33; 147/23; 149/14; 2 *sg.* mihtest, 17/22 ; 23/15 ; 33/22 ; 65/5; 91/2; 99/24; 103/17; *pl.* mihten, 9/24 ; 43/32 ; 45/27 ; 51/7, 14; 55/4; 69/20; 143/12 ; mihtin, 149/23 ; mihte, 57/29.

mule, *sb. mule, d. sg.* 89/31.

munec, *sb. monk, sg. nom. ac.* 29/9 ; 73/24 ; *pl.* munekes, 85/2 ; 45/25 ; 109/14.

munt, *sb. mount, d. sg.* munte, 79/2, 8 ; 137/14.

muð, *sb. mouth, sg. nom.* 101/8 ; *d.* muðe, 3/2 ; 11/19 ; 19/9; 29/18; 53/12; 55/32; 59/27 ; 79/32 ; 89/4; 119/15, 16; 121/31; muþe, 19/28.

N.

n-, *adv. not (with verbs), see* ne.

na, *pron. see* nan.

na, *adv. not,* 65/25 ; 31/1 ; 69/7 ; 109/33 ; 133/17 (?); 139/12 ; no, 97/16 ; 99/9 ; (*cf.* naðelæs, nauhwer, *and* ne).

nabben, *v. to have not, pres. ind.* 1 *sg.* nabbe, 15/27; 67/33; 3 *sg.* nafð, 57/19; *opt.* 3 *sg.* nabbe, 113/26 ; *pret.* 1 *and* 3 *sg.* nafde, 29/10; nadde, 13/1; 57/23; 111/33; 127/6.

næddre, *sb. adder, sg. g.* 101/19 ; *pl. nom.* 101/18.

nædle, *sb. needle*, g. *sg.* 69/9.
nafde, *see* nabben.
nafte, *sb. poverty*, d. *sg.* 41/20.
nafð, *see* nabben.
naht, *see* nawht.
næi, nai, *adv. nay*, 9/13.
nailes, *sb. nails*, 119/12.
naiðer—ne, *conj. neither—nor*, 9/12; neiðer, 27/33; 61/18; naðer, 129/19.
naked, *adj. naked*, 23/21.
nam, *see* nemen.
name, *sb. name*, d. ac. *sg.* 9/7, 22; 23/4, 8, 10; 27/31; 101/26.
namnen, *v. to name, call, mention, pres. ind.* 3 *sg.* namneð, 35/8; *pret.* 1 *sg.* nænnede, 91/1; *pl.* namden, 149/18; *part.* ʒenamned, 91/8; 125/12; inammned, 25/12; inamned, 95/3; 99/26; ʒenamd, 27/3; inamde, 149/21.
nan, *pron. no, none*, 8/4; 9/13, 31; 19/3; 23/15; 29/2; 39/21; 41/23; 49/31; 61/5; 63/29; 67/33; 71/32; 77/33; 79/5; 87/4; 89/22; 91/16; 129/11, 29; 131/28; 133/6 (2); 137/23; na, 27/16, 32; 39/31; 43/26; 61/6; 109/33; 127/5; non, 3/28; 7/25; 13/23; 15/2, 14; 27/1, 10 (2); 43/6; 47/29; 65/31; 67/34; 69/13, 17; 79/15; 81/15, 19, 20; 85/4; 89/11, 20, 23, 31; 93/6; 95/30; 99/7, 8, 13, 31; 103/6, 25, 26; 105/19; 107/13; 109/23; 111/21; 113/2, 17; 115/2; 117/8, 13; 121/22; 123/10; 125/18; 129/4; 133/22; 135/1; 137/16; 139/23; 149/4; no, 15/20; 17/10; 29/27; 31/14; 61/34; 79/18; 89/16; 93/30; 123/20; 135/4; 137/11; 141/4; nane, 41/28, 29; 79/33; 141/14; nanne, 99/13; 111/13; none, 5/2; 27/8, 18; 39/5, 20; 43/29; 45/18; 47/30; 51/18, 19; 53/17, 21; 61/1; 63/6; 65/7; 73/16; 79/5, 6, 7, 33; 85/4; 87/13; 89/10; 93/5; 97/18; 101/15, 23; 103/16; 105/28, 32; 109/5; 113/20; 123/26; 125/9; 129/11; 133/18; 143/7; 151/5; nanes, 31/29; 131/4; nones, 33/14.
nare, *see* ne.
nart, *see* ne.
nas, *see* ne.
naðelæs, *conj. nevertheless*, 5/18; 43/9; 115/20; 119/8; naþelæs, 55/5; naðelas, 27/17; 37/30; 97/24; 127/32; 137/12; naþelas, 131/11; naðeles, 97/2.

naðer, *pron. neither*, 43/11; noðer, 89/30; 97/26.
naðer—ne, *conj. see* naiðer.
nauht, *see* nawht.
nauhwer, *adv. nowhere*, 139/31; nawher, 147/14.
naust, *see* aʒen, *v.*
nævre, *adv. never*, 5/15, 25; 11/25; 13/20; 15/4; 17/30; 19/3, 21; 25/8, 10; 33/31; 39/23; 43/1, 5; 45/18, 25; 59/3; 67/6; 81/14, 30, 32; 83/18, 28; 87/14, 24; 89/12, 23; 91/14; 93/10; 99/4, 5; 103/22; 105/24; 111/33; navre, 7/30; 13/6; 19/33; 25/2; 29/8; 31/31; 39/4; 43/5; 53/11; 75/24; 81/25; 99/12; 113/23; 115/27; 121/25; 123/14, 19; 125/20, 23; 127/13, 18; 129/10; 131/1, 3; 139/2, 3, 32; 149/11, 25; 151/22; nevre, 5/34; 87/31; 77/25; 79/9; 119/8; 121/19; navere, 113/14; naver, 7/31; 133/5, 8; 145/19.
nawher, *see* nauhwer.
nawht, *pron. adv. not, naught, nothing*, 133/31; nauht, 17/10 (nauth *MS.*); 57/25; 81/18; 95/18; 121/24; 123/30; 133/19; 135/2; nohutt, 7/11; naht, 13/2; 15/21; 21/18; 25/30; 29/7, 10; 31/27; 33/14; 35/8; 37/21, 32; 39/19, 30; 41/8, 13, 25; 43/31; 49/21, 22, 23; 51/35; 53/16; 55/5; 57/27, 29, 32; 59/32; 61/29; 63/5, 9, 33; 65/24, 26; 67/2, 20; 71/10, 18, 23; 73/2, 5, 6, 16, 19, 23; 75/23, 27, 31, 33, 35; 77/2, 5, 26; 79/4, 6; 81/16; 89/3, 7; 91/5; 93/3, 7, 8; 101/3, 25; 103/11, 20; 109/11, *etc.*; noht, 9/16; 15/9; 29/5, 28; 31/17; 37/19, 26; 41/2; 59/1; 61/22; 75/7, 13; 77/14; 89/34; 101/10; 105/14; 113/26; 115/1, 16, 21; 119/7; 135/27; 139/10.
ne, *adv. not, neither, nor*, 3/28; 5/2, 15, 26; 7/1, 25, 30, 31; 9/12, 16; 11/9, 28; 13/6, 10, 13, 14, 19, 24; 15/3, 4, 9, 20, 21, 27, 30; 17/10, 29, 30, *etc.*; n- (*before verbs*), *see* aʒen, agrisen, acovren, ʒesen, nabben, nellen, not, ondraden, ortriwien. *With* bien *the following contractions occur:* pres. ind. 2 *sg.* nart, 139/10; 3 *sg.* nis, 8/4; 9/31; 11/18; 15/14; 19/28; 31/27; 37/21; 41/8, *etc.*; pret. ind. 3 *sg.* nas, 13/2; 133/6; opt. 3 *sg.* nare, 137/6; nere, 7/11 (*cf.* bien).

GLOSSARY.

ned, *see* nied.
neih, *adj. adv. near*, 5/19; nieh, 123/31; *superl.* necst, 123/16; neȝest, 129/14 (*cf.* nexte).
neihen, *v. to approach*, 3 *sg. ind. pres.* neiheð, 121/8; neihȝeð, 19/16.
neihibures, *sb. neighbours*, 75/32.
neiðer, *see* naiðer.
necst, *see* neih.
nellen, *v. to be not willing, pres. ind.* 2 *sg.* nelt, 73/5; 3 *sg.* nele, 61/8; *pl.* nelleð, 19/21, 25; *pret.* 1 *and* 3 *sg.* nolde, 5/16; 11/32; 51/18; 55/5, 13; 69/7; 125/3; 145/20; 2 *sg.* noldest, 17/24; *pl.* nolden, 19/31; 55/3; 61/16.
nemen, *v. to take*, 17/27; 125/27; *pres. ind.* 2 *sg.* nimst, 77/21; nemst, 103/17; nemest, 135/7; 3 *sg.* nimþ, 5/1; 109/5; nimð, 53/8; 79/6; 105/28; 129/4; 135/4; nemð, 129/6; *pl.* nimeð, 5/33; 57/31; 71/33; 81/6; nemeð, 27/22; 79/9; nemeeð, 73/22; *opt.* 2 *sg.* neme, 87/27; 125/30; 3 *sg.* nime, 11/19; 75/10; neme, 5/4; 129/24; *imp sg.* nim, 71/10; 89/19; 91/3; 111/11; nem, 65/30; *pl.* nimeð, 121/7; nemeð, 19/15; 89/31; 125/29; *pret. ind.* 3 *sg.* nam, 21/8; 25/21, 23; 49/17; 113/30; 119/28; 137/14; *pl.* namen, 119/13; *opt.* 3 *sg.* name, 5/2; *part.* inumen, 5/30; inomen, 77/33; *pl.* ȝenomene, 79/10.
nere, *see* ne.
net, nett, *see* nieden.
neten, *sb. animal, d. sg.* netene, 151/1.
neðer, *adj. adv. low, down, nether*, 5/13; 57/2; niðer, 45/17; 57/4; 145/9; niþer, 5/9; 105/26.
neðerin, *v. to humble, lower, cast down*, 49/20; neþerin, 49/21; *pres. ind. pl.* neðerið, 57/30; *opt. pl.* neðerien, 55/30; *pret. part.* ineðered, 57/3; *pl.* ineðerede, 5/13.
neuliche, *adv. soon*, 17/13.
nevre, *see* navre.
newe, *adj. new*, 27/23, 24, 25; 51/25; 151/3; niewe, 7/28.
newe, *v. to renew, sg. imp.* 83/9.
nexce, *adj. soft, weak*, 63/26; nexse, 87/29.
nexin, *v. to soften*, 45/18; nexxin, 145/33.
nexte, *sb. neighbour, sg. nom. d. ac.* 37/25; 39/13; 43/8; 67/5, 6; 79/4; 101/23; 133/16; *d.* nexten, 63/24 (*cf.* neih).

nied, *sb. need, sg. nom.* 23/29; 31/21; 39/27; 87/8, 32; 91/32; 129/9; 139/32; niede, 151/24; *d. ac.* niede, 11/30; 39/10; 65/29; 83/5; 85/4, 23, 25; 101/11; 137/29; 141/27; 148/7, 9; 147/23, 28; 151/23; nede, 137/28; *pl.* niedes, 143/18; nedes, 137/6.
nieden, *v. to compel, force, pres. ind.* 3 *sg.* nett, 9/15; 73/2; net, 9/16; 127/31; *opt.* 3 *sg.* niede, 9/15.
niedfull, *adj. needful, necessary*, 63/11; 81/13; 99/3; 107/6; 133/23; nedfull, 53/21; 77/19; niedfulle, 111/26; 147/5; niedfullen, 41/19.
nieh, *see* neih.
nielnesse, *sb. abyss, depth, d. sg.* 45/17.
niewe, *see* newe.
niht, *sb. night, sg. ac.* 31/31; 83/19; 137/32, 34; 147/8; *g.* niht, 49/27; nihtes, 17/31; *d.* nihte, 3/27; 19/17; 35/32; 39/10; 85/26; 137/26; 151/23.
nim, *see* nemen.
nis, *see* ne.
nith, *sb. envy, nom. d. ac. sg.* 7/11; nið, 41/4; 89/27.
niðer, *see* neðer.
no, *see* na.
nohutt, *see* nawht.
nolde, *see* nellen.
non, *see* nan.
non, *sb. noon, d. ac. sg.* 137/26, 29; none, 137/25, 28.
not, *v. I know not*, 1 *sg. ind. pres.* 11/31.
notien, *v. to eat, use, taste, pres. ind.* 3 *sg.* noteð, 53/11; *pl.* notieð, 51/33; 119/23; *imp. pl.* notieð, 51/29, 34.
nu, *adv. now*, 9/30; 17/17; 19/6; 21/12, 26, 29; 23/8, 28, 29; 35/18; 87/9, 10, *etc.*

O (see A).

o, *see* an.
obedience, *sb. obedience*, 7/3, 31.
of, *prep. of, from*, 3/6, 9, 11, 21, 28, 29; 5/1, 2, 6, 8, 10, 14, 23, 25, 33, 34; 7/2, 3, 4, 14, 19, 22, 25, 27; 9/5, 6, 8, 14, 17, 20, 25, 28; 11/1, 2, 18, 19, 21, 30, 32; 13/1, 3, 11, 16, 28; 15/2, 10, 11, 17, 24, 25; 17/1, *etc.*; os, 17/22, 26; 101/13 (*cf.* ut of).
ofdradd, *pret. part. afraid*, 11/18; -drad, 19/25; 27/21; 61/30.
ofearniȝen, *v. to earn, deserve, merit*, 75/5; -earnin, 25/8; 33/22; *pres.*

GLOSSARY. 243

ind. 2 *sg.* -earnest, 77/23; 3 *sg.*
-earned, 63/22; *pl.* -earniȝeð, 19/20; -earniþ, 19/10; *pret.* 3 *sg.*
-earnede, 83/23; 51/31; *part.*
-earned, 17/10; 29/12; 63/27; 83/13; 113/26; 119/7; 127/10; 145/15.

offeruht, *pret. part. affrighted, afraid,* 105/21.

offrin, *v. to offer, sacrifice,* 149/30; ofrien, 85/2, 23; 111/20; ofrin, 85/6, 11; *pres. ind.* 2 *sg.* offrest, 87/19; 3 *sg.* offreð, 151/2; *opt.* 2 *sg.* ofri, 111/19; *imp. sg.* offre, 111/11, 15; *pret.* 1 *and* 3 *sg.* offrede, 85/14, 17; 117/14; ofrede, 55/14; 85/19; 119/28.

ofne, *see* oven.

ofrende, *sb. offering, sg.* 3/4; 85/8; 117/13; 119/27; *pl.* offrendes, 139/30.

ofrien, *see* offrin.

ofslean, *v. to kill,* 61/30.

ofspreng, *sb. offspring, sg. ac.* 115/2; -spring, 9/23; *d.* -sprenge, 113/14; 115/27.

ofsteand, *pret. part. stoned,* 111/29.

oft, *adv. often,* 9/21; ofte, 3/14, 25, 26; 5/16, 19, 28; 9/6; 11/3, 13, 25; 13/15, *etc.*; *superl.* oftest, 101/4.

ofðanch, *sb. displeasure, d. sg.* ofðanche, 3/19.

ofþenchen, *v. to regret, displease,* 3/14; 71/9; 3 *sg. ind. pres.* -þingþ, 3/11.

ofþerst, *adj. thirsty,* 93/15.

olvende, *sb. camel, nom. sg.* 69/9.

on, *see* an.

on-, *see* an-.

onalen, *v. to kindle, inflame,* 3 *sg. ind. pres.* onalð, 35/21; anald, • 35/31.

onbuten, *see* abuten.

ondraden, *v. to fear, pres. ind.* 3 *sg.* ondrat, 61/21; -dratt, 63/9; n'ondratt, 61/22; *pl.* ondradeð, 55/22; -dreadeð, 55/26.

onfald, *adj. simple,* 41/17.

onȝeanes, (1) *prep. against,* 15/29; 89/1; 105/15; 133/12; ongeanes, 63/18; aȝeanes, 5/22; 7/7; 9/32; 11/4, 6, 8; 13/15; 15/6, 7; 23/25; 31/1; 39/7, 11; 41/5; 55/33; 59/32; 77/22; 83/28; 87/19; 89/13, 15; 91/2; 119/19; 125/3; aȝenes, 75/7; 89/13; (2) *conj.* aȝeanes ðat, 119/9, 11, 12-16.

onlepi, *adj. single,* 67/1; 115/17; anlepine, 39/19.

onuven, *prep. above,* 65/34.

opene, *adj. open,* 61/5; 101/32.

openin, *v. to open, reveal, pres. ind. pl.* openieð, 59/17; *imp. sg.* opene, 127/17; *pret.* 3 *sg.* openede, 27/2; *part.* iopened, 119/31.

openlicor, *adj. comp. more open,* 123/28.

ore, *see* are.

orefull, *adj. merciful,* 145/16.

orelease, *adj. merciless,* 83/28.

orliche, *adv. honourably,* 73/33.

ortrewnesse, *sb. despair,* 19/2.

ortriwien, *v. to mistrust,* 3 *sg. opt. pres.* n'ortriwi, 123/19.

oðe, *see* oððe.

oðer, *adj. pron. other,* 3/7, 17, 28; 5/7; 9/13, 21 (oder *MS.*); 11/2; 13/12, 18, 23, 29; 15/18, 21; 17/7; 19/27; 27/23; 29/9, 30; 37/15; 47/17; 53/18, 19; 59/19; 63/2, 11; 65/10; 71/6; 77/33; 81/2, 12; 85/28; 87/11; 91/8, 16; 93/30; 101/1, 2, 27; 103/9; 105/2; 107/5, 11, 27; 111/24; 117/2, 8, 13; 121/29; 123/25; 125/9; 127/30; 133/18, 23; 135/10; 137/2, 23; 139/14; 141/2; oþer, 125/27; oðður, 133/4, 6; oðre, 3/7; 5/18, 32, 34 (odre *MS.*); 7/15, 25; 21/2; 23/18, 27; 33/5; 35/5, 7, 11, 12; 53/22; 57/21, 31, 33; 59/10, 12; 63/1; 65/16, 20; 67/31; 73/20; 77/5, 29; 79/3, 10; 89/11; 93/19; 135/3, 5; 139/25; 143/7, 15; 149/9; oðres, 67/23; 149/2; oþres, 147/8; oðren, 83/29; 105/34; 107/3 (odren *MS.*).

oðer, *conj. or, either, or,* 3/17 (3); 5/20, 23, 24, 27, 28; 7/2, 3, 21; 9/8, 23; 11/26, 32; 13/1 (2); 19/11; 23/20, *etc.*; oððer, 123/18; 125/31, 32 (2); 127/1 (3), 2; 129/29; 133/11, 12; 135/6 (2); 139/4; 141/8, 30.

oðer, *pron. see* aiðer.

oðerhwile, *adv. sometimes,* 53/18; 57/16; 81/20; 87/20, 24, 25, 26; 89/29; -hwille, 57/16.

oðerlicor, *adv. otherwise,* 11/24; -liker, 59/9; 133/12.

oðerman, *pron. other people, g.* oðermannes, 3/25.

oððe, *conj. or,* 3/19; oðe, 39/34; 77/28.

oððer, *see* oðer, *conj.*

ouht, *see* awht.

oven, *sb. oven, d. sg.* ofne, 73/13, 29.

over, *prep. over,* 7/23; 17/8; 33/4,

244 GLOSSARY.

5; 35/11; 43/9; 53/29; 67/10; 77/18; 83/32; 89/32; 97/28; 105/34; 127/20; 135/3; 143/15.
overdon, *pret. part. overdone,* 107/13.
overgan, *v. to overflood,* 3 *sg. pret.* -ʒiede, 43/25.
overcumen, *v. to overcome,* 131/3; *pres. ind.* 2 *sg.* -cumst, 135/29; 3 *sg.* ovorcumþ, 129/5; *pret.* 3 *sg.* overcam, 43/5; 49/6; 51/17; 91/5; 115/24; 119/4, 5; 2 *sg.* -come, 103/2; *part.* -cumen, 145/1.
overmuʒen, *v. to overpower,* 3 *sg. ind. pres.* overmai, 13/13.
owh, *see* aʒen, *v.*

P.

pais, *sb. peace,* 59/32; 89/15; 95/11; 97/17, 24, 28; 99/5, 18, 19.
paneʒes, *sb. pennies, money,* 79/11.
paradise, *sb. paradise, d. sg.* 7/18, 27; 51/20, 26; 53/5; 89/22; 105/17; 113/1.
patriarches, *sb. patriarchs,* 115/10.
pesen, *sb. pease,* 43/13.
pett, *sb. pit, d. sg.* pette, 109/19.
pilegrimes, *sb. pilgrims,* 35/5.
pine, *sb. pain, sg.* 7/19; 33/22, 28, 29; 63/2, 6; 103/25; 115/11; 121/17; 147/12; *pl.* pinen, 19/9, 10; pines, 33/33; 63/27; 65/2.
pinen, *v. to pain, imp. sg.* pine, 33/28.
pineres, *sb. tormentors,* 17/26; 75/11.
pisteles, *sb. epistles,* 31/3.
pleiʒen, *v. to play,* 139/6; *pres. part.* pleiʒende, 135/1.
postes, *sb. posts,* 91/11; 95/2.
pott, *sb. pot, nom. sg.* 78/13.
pottere, *sb. potter, nom. sg.* 78/15.
prest, *see* priest.
pride, *sb. pride,* 5/6; priede, 89/28.
priest, *sb. priest, sg. ac.* 29/8; prest, 123/15, 17; *g.* priestes, 45/31; 53/12; *d.* prieste, 109/9; *pl.* priestes, 45/25.
prime, *sb. prime, morning prayer,* 19/27.
profiete, *sb. prophet, sg.* 19/23; 31/16, 32; 43/4; 59/21; 63/16; 77/34; 79/19, 28; 85/22, 32; 87/9; 93/14; 97/19; 99/10; 105/12; 107/7; 109/20; 117/23, 28; profete, 123/10; prophete, 125/28; 127/17; 137/15; 143/22; 147/6, 16, 24, 31; *pl.* profietes, 115/10.
prud, *adj. proud,* 5/14.
prudeliche, *adv. proudly,* 107/17.

R.

rad, *sb. counsel, sg. nom. ac.* 19/31; 23/2, 12; 45/5, 29; 71/10, 29; 75/6, 28; 77/6; 97/11; 113/13; ræd, 45/31; 69/7; 71/7; 73/22; 75/13; 77/7; 107/14; 109/18 (?); *d.* rade, 71/5, 8; 101/30; 127/2; ræde, 75/6.
ræden, *v. to counsel, ind. pres.* 3 *sg.* ratt, 61/6; 75/17, 21; *imp. sg.* ræd, 101/12.
ræden, *v. to read, ind. pres. pl.* radeð, 7/21; 141/20; radeþ, 19/11; *imp. sg.* ræd, 85/25.
radʒive, *sb. counsellor, ac. sg.* 75/4.
radinge, *sb. lesson, d. sg.* 27/13.
raftres, *sb. rafters,* 95/6.
ratt, *see* ræden.
raðe, *adv. soon, quickly,* 101/28; 145/24.
reaven, *v. to reave, rob, pres. ind.* 3 *sg.* reaveð, 11/2; *imp. sg.* reave, 67/30.
recchen, *v. to care, pres. ind.* 2 *sg.* recst, 125/20; *pl.* reccheð, 67/12; 137/23; *pret.* 3 *sg.* rohte, 43/7.
regule, *sb. rule, d. sg.* 73/28.
rein, *sb. rain, sg. d.* reine, 145/2; *pl.* reines, 143/31.
reinin, *v. to rain,* 143/30.
recst, *see* recchen.
religiun, *sb. religion, religious order, d. sg.* 5/33; 43/3; 71/11, 34; 121/26.
religiuse, *adj. religious,* 3/12.
rentes, *sb. rents,* 77/29.
reste, *sb. rest, nom. d. ac.* 13/24; 41/28; 49/11; 71/28; 87/32; 89/18; 95/11; 97/29; 115/14; 137/8; 143/6; 147/12.
resten, *v. to rest,* 41/30; 79/1, 9; 91/27, 33; 93/13; 107/15; *pret.* 3 *sg.* reste, 51/10.
reuhðe, *sb. ruth, pity, nom. d. ac. sg.* 63/13, 14, 22, 23; rewðe, 65/6; 101/13; 115/7, 20; rewhþe, 115/5; rewðhe, 91/31; 115/8.
reuliche, *adj. rueful,* 17/17.
reunesse, *sb. pity, grief, nom. d. sg.* 39/27; rewnesse, 95/28; *pl.* reunesses, 57/19.
rewen, *v. to rue, repent,* 65/3; 87/20; 107/23; *pres. ind.* 3 *sg.* rewð, 103/11; *pl.* reweð, 21/3; 115/14; *opt.* 3 *sg.* rewe, 121/23; *pret. ind.* 3 *sg.* rewh, 145/24.
rewliche, *adv. piteously,* 9/19.
rewnesse, *see* reunesse.
rewsende, *pres. part. repenting,*

GLOSSARY.

121/10; riewsiende, 63/26; riwsinde, 121/23.
rewŏe, *see* reuhŏe.
riche, *sb. kingdom, nom. d. ac. sg.* 69/18; 87/34; 89/4, 7, 9; 115/1, 3, 17, 27; 121/9; 129/10.
riche, *adj. rich,* 5/24; 65/25; 67/25; 69/6, 8, 11; 77/27; 141/23.
richeise, *sb. riches, nom. d. ac. sg.* 69/12; 75/24; 147/19.
riewsiende, *see* rewsende.
riht, *sb. right, justice, sg. nom. ac.* 75/19; 95/14; 105/10, 27, 28; 115/22; 125/31; rihte, 105/4; *d.* rihte, 9/24, 25; 51/34; 53/25; 69/24; 97/1; 99/26; 115/11; 133/7; 139/27.
riht, *adj. right, true,* 9/17; 77/18; 83/3; 115/29; 131/25; 141/18; 151/19; rihte, 15/27; 17/15; 25/5, 6, 31; 29/31; 39/1; 45/15; 51/20, 29; 53/34; 67/10; 81/5, 6; 83/11, 25; 93/27; 105/24; 111/13; 115/28, 30; 125/30; 127/3, 8; 129/29; 131/27; 137/5; rihtne, 83/9.
riht, *adv. rightly, just,* 31/24; 37/19, 20, 21; 93/5; 101/29; 145/10; *superl.* rihtist, 149/14.
rihtes, *adv. rightly, justly,* 53/14; 65/29.
rihtliche, *adv. rightly,* 31/8.
rihtwis, *adj. righteous,* 15/21; 61/3; 77/27; 89/13; 99/8; 101/24; 107/2; 145/18; rihtwise, 15/4; 77/1; 79/25; 115/32; rihwise, 41/17; rihtwises, 41/33; 105/8.
rihtwisen, *v. to justify, pres. ind. pl.* rihtwisiŏ, 79/24, 27; *pret. part.* irihtwised, 105/15; 123/3.
rihtwismann, *sb. righteous man, g. sg.* rihtwismannes, 143/28.
rihtwisnesse, *sb. righteousness, sg. nom. d. ac.* 11/15; 15/20; 33/2; 79/24; 89/7; 105/1, 2, 7; 113/28; 115/22; 117/23; rihwisnesse, 115/19; 117/17.
rimen, *v. to number,* 15/30.
ripe, *adj. ripe,* 135/2.
riwsinde, *see* rewsende.
rixin, *v. to reign,* 57/10; 149/11; *pres. ind.* 3 *sg.* rixeŏ, 57/15; 151/21; rixiŏ, 131/3; 149/11; rixit, 89/12; *pl.* rixit, 49/27; *opt.* 3 *sg.* rixi, 39/5; *part.* rixende, 57/13; 95/12; rixinde, 75/23.
rode, *sb. cross, nom. d. ac. sg.* 33/24, 27, 28, 31; 51/15, 28; 83/2; 103/1; 113/1; 119/3, 5, 8, 13, 14, 22.

rof, *sb. roof, sg. nom.* 95/7; *d.* rove, 95/5.
rohte, *see* recchen.
ropes, *sb. ropes,* 45/14.
rotien, *v. to rot,* 91/14.
rove, *see* rof.

S.

sa, *see* swa.
sad, *sb. seed, sg. nom.* 69/13; *d.* sade, 9/6; 27/28; *g.* sades, 27/28.
sæde, sade, *see* seggen.
sahtlin, *v. to reconcile,* 21/31; *pres. ind.* 2 *sg.* sahtlest, 39/34; *imp. sg.* seihtle, 3/4; *pret. part.* sahtled, 89/19.
sai, *see* seggen.
saide, *see* seggen.
sæinte, *adj. saint,* 9/24; sainte, 21/5; 25/24; 53/26; 55/24, 31; 57/7; 59/15'; seinte, 25/31; 129/16; 145/23, 32; seintre, 111/31.
saiŏ, *see* seggen.
sacleas, *adj. guiltless,* 9/14.
sal, *sb. room, d. sg.* 149/12.
sæli, *adj. blessed,* 67/22; sali, 127/33.
salm, *sb. psalm, ac.* 81/26; selm, 61/7.
saltere, *sb. psalter, d.* 113/8.
sand, *see* senden.
sånde, *sb. messenger, message, dish, sg. nom. ac.* 89/29; sande, 125/1; sonde, 55/16; *pl.* sonden, 17/13; sondes, 43/14.
sanden, *see* senden.
sang, *sb. song, ac. sg.* 15/12; song, 103/28.
sant, *see* senden.
sare, *sb. sore, wound, d. sg.* 89/33.
sare, *adj. sore, bitter,* 3/26; 21/2; 125/32.
sare, *adv. sorely, bitterly,* 21/3; 65/3; 151/8; sore, 137/30.
sari, *adj. sorry, sorrowful,* 3/13; 69/3, 7; 83/18, 34; 85/13; 103/18; 131/6; 137/8; 141/11; 147/18; sori, 95/25; 107/18; 127/6.
sariliche, *adv. sorrily,* 141/9.
sarinesse, *sb. sorrow, pain, sg.* 3/8-10, 19; 19/2; 87/26; sorinesse, 3/6; *pl.* sarinesses, 33/8; 57/19; 103/4.
sate, *see* sitten.
sate, *sb. seat, sg. nom. ac.* 105/7, 8.
saule, *see* sawle.
sawen, *v. to sow,* 27/28.
sawle, *sb. soul, sg. nom.' g. d. ac.* 135/15; 147/11, 12; saule, 3/7; 7/22, 29; 9/19; 11/17; 13/29;

17/18, 24, 31; 21/26; 23/5, 10, 22; 25/21; 31/28; 37/4, 22, 28, 30; 43/29, 32; 45/2; 47/7, 17; 49/11; 53/4, 19; 55/14, 33; 57/7; 61/14, 26, 31; 63/27, 32; 69/12, 18, 32; 71/28; 73/11; 79/14; 85/24; 89/10; 91/23; 93/1, 6, *etc.*; soule, 115/9; *pl.* saules, 23/19; 25/2; 115/10; soules, 103/23.

scadewe, *sb. shadow, d. sg.* 101/34.
scadwis, *adj. rational*, 15/3.
scadwisnesse, *sb. discernment, reason, discretion, sg. nom. ac.* 28/11, 23; 47/19; 125/15; 149/22.
scafte, *sb. creature, sg. nom.* 15/2; *pl.* scaftes, 69/31; 105/10.
scal, *see* sculen.
scame, *sb. shame, sg. nom. d. ac.* 61/25; 123/5, 6; *pl.* scames, 51/16; 59/4.
scameleas, *adj. free from shame*, 139/22.
scandliche, *adv. shamefully*, 99/31.
scarpe, *adj. sharp*, 23/30; 63/17; 65/18; 79/23.
sceaweres, *sb. watchmen*, 103/13.
sceawien, *v. to view, spy, to show*, 31/10; sceawin, 31/18; 45/11, 12; 109/29; 111/8, 12; *pres. ind.* 2 *sg.* sceawest, 59/11; 3 *sg.* sceaweð, 103/15; *pret.* 3 *sg.* sceawede, 31/6; 49/5, 12; 51/9; 111/25; 143/8; *part.* isceawed, 15/22.
sceawinge, *sb. sight, nom.* 103/12.
scechen, *see* sechen.
sceld, *sb. shield, nom.* 39/11.
sceldih, *adj. guilty*, 51/24; sceldi, 13/8.
scelie, *v. to depart*, 2 *sg. opt. pres.* 57/10.
scene, *adj. bright*, 95/30.
sceppen, *v. to create, shape, pret. ind.* 3 *sg.* scop, 97/3; 2 *sg.* scope, 113/23; (*cf.* ȝesceppen).
sceppend, *sb. creator, sg. nom. d. ac.* 63/21; 69/31; 95/18; 97/30; 115/23.
scette, *v. to shut, sg. imp.* 143/3; scete, 143/6.
schele, *see* skele.
sciften, *v. to divide, pres. ind.* 2 *sg.* sciftst, 37/20; 3 *sg.* scift, 77/7; *pret. part.* iscift, 37/21.
scilden, *v. to shield*, 23/31; 87/3; 107/6; *pres. opt.* 3 *sg.* scilde, 89/16; *imp. sg.* scild, 103/1.
scile, *see* skele.
scinen, *v. to shine*, 31/13; *pres. part.* scinende, 49/23.

scincles, *sb. shingles*, 95/8.
scip, *sb. ship, sg. nom. ac.* 45/3, 19; *g.* scipes, 43/33.
scolde, *see* sculen.
scop, *see* sceppen.
scorte, *adj. short*, 9/1; 21/24; 23/2; 59/26; 61/25; 75/15.
screden, *v. to shroud*, 149/17; *pret. part.* iscredd, 107/17.
scrift, *sb. penitence, penance, repentance, d. ac. sg.* 19/15; scrifte, 77/34; 105/23; 121/4, 7, 19, 26.
scrifte, *sb. confessor, d. sg.* 121/31; 127/2.
scrud, *sb. shroud, ac. sg.* 95/31.
sculen, *v. to be obliged, have to, pres. ind.* 1, 3 *sg.* scal, *I shall*, 9/26; 11/12, 16; 17/9, 17, 29; 27/32; 31/12; 35/11; 41/10; 51/30; 53/14; 55/32; 61/13, 17, 18; 63/3, 12; 67/3; 71/9; 75/24, 35; 93/10, 26; 97/9, 21, 26; 105/19, *etc.*; scall, 17/13; 61/34; 69/30; 87/19; 93/9; 95/14; 103/26; 105/18; 107/15; 133/29; 2 *sg.* scalt, 11/11; 25/13; 39/14; 45/25; 53/28; 59/5; 63/25; 65/13, 14; 73/12; 75/4, 14, *etc.*; scaltu, 125/22; *pl. ind. and opt.* sculen, 5/13; 7/24; 11/28, 29; 19/3, 4; 25/29, 30; 27/5, 6; 43/20, *etc.*; scule, 43/27; 87/31; *opt.* 2 *sg.* scule, 111/6; 115/6; *pret.* 1 *and* 3 *sg.* scolde, 3/27; 5/16; 13/10; 15/28; 19/7; 21/28; 53/16, 29; 55/7, 17; 57/23; 63/21, *etc.*; 2 *sg.* scoldest, 17/25; 75/26; 83/13; 127/16; 139/11; 141/23, 25; *pl.* scolden, 81/6; 37/6; 99/16; 101/17; 121/10; 139/26; 141/32; scolde, 13/22; 143/9.
scunien, *v. to shun*, 123/32; *pres. opt. pl.* scunien, 7/23; *pret.* 1 *sg.* scunede, 5/15.
se, *pron., art. and rel. the, that, who, which, sg. nom. m. f.* 13/18; 15/6; 17/30; 19/22; 31/3; 51/31; 67/4; 105/25; 113/31; 117/32; 147/12; 151/4; se ðe, 5/4; 9/33; 11/19; 29/28; 33/26; 37/12; 41/7; 45/5, 6; 47/22, 26; 53/15; 61/8, 20, 21; 63/9; 77/21; 77/9; 79/3-6; 81/21; 89/33; 91/20; 93/25; 97/4; 99/7, 9; 107/13; 123/13; 125/19; 127/10, 29, 31; 129/23, 24; 139/20; 145/4, 14; 149/26; 151/20, 21; se þe, 127/30; *nom. ac. n. and com.* ðat, 8/23; 5/26, 29, 31; 9/22, 29; 11/3, 14, 18; 13/18; 15/14; 19/16, 34; 23/13,

GLOSSARY. 247

24; 25/1; 27/9, 17, 30; 29/14, 31; 31/24; 35/1, 23, 26; 37/7, 23, 26; 39/2, 14, 17; 41/14; 43/4, 13; 45/3, 20, 24; 47/17, 21; 49/ 18, 27, 31; 51/28, 32; 53/5, 6, 9, 34, 35; 59/6, 25; 61/16, 19, 26; 63/10; 65/33; 67/28; 69/2, 4, 24, 30; 71/15, 18, 19; 75/13; 77/25, 33; 79/33, 34; 81/5, 14, 31; 85/ 11; 87/22, 23, 32; 89/14; 91/30; 95/20, 31; 97/18, 28; 101/8, 20, 21, 22, 24, 25; 103/7; 105/14; 111/9, 15; 113/10; 117/11, 18, 30; 119/9, 15; 123/5; 125/10; 127/29; 133/20; 135/15, 22; 137/ 4; 139/26; 148/9, 24; 145/28; 149/3; 151/21; ðatt, 109/30; *as pl.* 59/4; 61/24; 79/10; 87/28; 99/7; 105/11; þat, 147/5; *sg.* þat, 3/8; 5/1, 7, 19; 7/16; 9/13; 11/ 25; 13/12, 30; 17/3, 4; 23/11; 25/6; 27/13; 29/10, 12, 31; 31/2, 5, 11, 17; 35/8, 16, 21; 37/21, 24; 39/1, 23; 41/24; 43/10; 47/28; 59/ 24, 25; 61/16; 83/20; 85/11; 95/ 20; 133/13; 135/22; 137/25; 145/ 8; 147/5, 11, 13, 20; 149/19; 151/ 9; ðat ðe, 5/16; 27/14; 75/10; 93/31; 125/16; ðat te, 77/11; þat ðe, 59/19; þat þe, 125/6; *nom. com.* ðe, 5/21; 7/16; 9/25, 27; 13/4; 15/7; 17/6, 7; 21/15; 23/ 13, 18; 25/13; 27/19, 29; 29/16, 20, 26, 31; 31/15; 33/16; 35/8, 24, 30, 33; 37/3, 11, 22, 27, 30; 39/15; 41/6, 29; 43/4; 45/3, 28; 49/3, 13; 47/7; 51/19, 27, 31, *etc.*; þe, 5/1; 17/28, 29; 25/13, 15; 37/5; 39/30; 59/20; 73/12; 89/5; 93/1; 127/18; 129/3, 19; 131/15, 19; ð', 113/3 (*note*); *gen. m. n.* ðas, 5/17; 9/18; 17/16, 31; 27/ 28; 33/33; 41/31; 69/29; 75/4; 105/8; 119/13; 145/23; þas, 15/ 25; 143/28; ðes, 29/12; 35/28; 41/7, 26, 30; 83/31; 89/29; 95/ 23; 103/2; 107/20; 111/2, 3; ðe, 15/23; 69/9; 115/8; ðas þe, 47/ 20; 49/12; ðas ðe, 61/2; *f.* ðare, 41/3; 61/25; 65/4; 89/33; 101/ 19; 121/19; 127/19; þare, 87/16; 125/9; ðar, 19/26; 47/16; 53/2; 75/9; 111/1; 125/20; 137/19; ða, 31/18; *dat. ac. m. and d. n.* ðan, 9/15, 16, 27; 11/30; 13/31; 19/3, 31; 25/29 (dan *MS.*), 30; 33/21; 41/8; 45/20; 47/8; 53/4; 55/4; 65/13, 34; 69/14; 78/29; 83/2; 89/18; 98/10; 103/4; 109/ 19 (?); 119/4, 24; 125/17; 135/3;

ðan ðe, 9/17; 31/19; 53/10; ðen, 135/3; ten, 25/3; 89/26; *f.* ðære, 41/15; ðare, 5/9; 7/28; 17/19, 28, 32; 19/2, 28; 21/8; 25/12; 27/26, 29; 29/34; 31/1, 9, 28; 33/23; 35/7, 12, 22; 39/10, 32; 41/12 (?), 18, 33; 43/1, 18, 20, 22; 45/9, 15; 47/14; 49/5, 6; 51/27, 30; 53/7, 8, 34; 55/11; 57/22; 61/25; 63/4, 15, 19; 65/27; 67/ 16; 73/2, 5, 21, 22, 34; 75/2; 77/ 5; 79/17; 81/8; 83/2, 6, 34; 93/ 2; 95/27; 101/34; 103/1, 11, 21, 27, 31; 109/16; 111/9, 12, 21, 29; 113/1, 24; 115/1, 3; 119/3, 13, 20; 123/6; 129/10; 133/27; 135/ 15, 16; 137/4; 143/12; 149/4, 6, 29; þare, 23/5; 129/15; 131/6; 141/4; tare, 83/2; tare ðe, 91/13; ðere, 63/1; 71/21; 83/1; *ac. m.* ðane, 3/12; 5/9; 15/12; 31/9; 37/2; 41/17; 43/21; 47/9; 51/ 13, 14, 17; 53/2; 63/17; 65/18; 67/3, 14; 79/24; 81/9, 26, 31; 83/22, 33; 99/15, 18; 109/3, 13; 111/30; 117/33; 119/6; 123/17; 127/10; þane, 31/11; ðanne, 149/ 28; þanne, 139/15, 21; ðene, 61/ 7; *d. ac. com.* ða, 13/18; 17/23; 19/19; 21/20; 31/6, 8; 33/3; 35/ 18, 20, 21; 48/23, 28; 55/1, 8; 57/13; 63/31; 67/7, 10, 25; 69/6; 71/24; 73/12; 75/9, 17, 26, 28; 79/34; 85/22; 103/14; 119/1, 14, 21, 22; 121/17, 23, 25; 125/30; 127/3; 137/9; 141/11; 151/20; ðo, 21/13; 37/16; 47/27; 75/14; 77/12; 95/4; 109/29; 111/8; 115/33; 133/16; 145/14; 149/1; þo, 113/34; ðæ, 53/9; ðe, 5/20, 33; 7/4, 19, 22, 27, 32; 9/3, 6, 18; 13/13; 17/27; 19/1, 22; 21/ 20, 30; 25/13, 24; 27/15, 25, 26; 29/19, 21, 33; 33/29; 35/31; 37/ 3, 10, 21; 41/9, 10, 11, 22, 26; 43/3, 14, 24, 28, 32; 45/2, 12, 18, 26; 47/22, 27; 49/12, 22, 23; 51/ 4, 9, 25, *etc.*; þe, 19/12; 27/25; 97/14; 127/18; 131/14, 17; 133/ 28; 137/13, 15; 143/3; 147/10, 11, 15, 25, 31; the, 115/32; te, 11/17; 141/21; *pl. nom. d. ac.* ða, 11/12; 13/5; 15/11; 17/1, 2, 5, 20; 19/5, 33; 23/26; 25/9; 27/8; 31/18; 43/27; 45/7; 57/ 18; 65/2; 69/34; 73/32; 77/27, 28; 79/6; 87/7, 28; 89/3; 109/ 19; 119/19; 125/8, 10, 14, 18; 133/6; 139/25, 27, 29; 149/19; þa, 135/15; ðo, 8/16; 15/13, 30,

GLOSSARY.

31; 17/10; 19/9, 10; 21/12; 27/7, 9; 29/16, 34; 31/11, 13; 33/8, 32; 43/8, 14, 19; 45/18; 49/25; 55/8, 22; 59/15; 63/27; 67/25; 69/19; 75/6, 33; 77/15; 83/26, 34; 87/5; 89/23; 91/11; 93/16; 95/27; 99/6, 23; 103/23; 107/9; 113/16; 127/11; 135/12; 137/6; 139/29; 143/18; þo, 3/15; 51/12; 133/26; to, 75/34; 83/28; ðe, 3/9, 29; 5/33; 7/5; 17/11, 20; 23/15, 20, 25; 33/34; 35/1, 31; 41/27; 43/5, 15, 19; 45/4, 12, 13; 47/2, 11; 51/8, 16; 55/23; 67/10; 69/31; 75/11, 12, 34; 77/1, 6, 7, 14–16, 18, 24; 79/11; 81/22, 33; 85/14, *etc.*; þe, 41/27; 75/34; 77/24; 139/19; te, 41/27, 28; ða ðe, 19/21, 25; 79/9; 99/9; 121/26; 139/26; 141/10; þa ðe, 89/34; 105/29; ðo ðe, 5/12; 15/14; 33/13; 43/2, 20, 21; 55/33; 57/5, 29; 73/17; 91/31; 107/21 (ðo ne *MS.*); ðo þe, 129/20; 143/15; þo ðe, 25/29, 30; 55/27; 79/26; *g.* ðare, 29/2; 43/6; 85/5; 99/13; 121/22; 129/11 (*note*); *d.* ðan, 147/5; ðan ðe, 81/19.

se, *see* swa.

sea, *sb. sea, d. sg.* 45/9.

sealde, *see* sellen.

sechen, *v. to seek,* 3/17; scechen, 143/9; seken, 5/27; siechen, 89/5; *pres. ind.* 3 *sg.* secð, 139/32; sehþ, 101/11; *pl.* secheð, 89/21; *opt. pl.* siechen, 99/27; *imp. sg.* siec, 59/32; siech, 39/4; 93/18; *pl.* secheð, 87/34.

seggen, *v. to say, tell,* 9/16; 11/31; 17/18; 19/9; 23/9; 27/13; 55/16; 59/5, 16; 69/23; 75/25; 77/8; 93/12; 95/1; 99/17; 141/28 (?); *pres. ind.* 1 *sg.* segge, 103/16; 145/8; 2 *sg.* seiest, 117/4; seist, 31/20; 59/27; 3 *sg.* seizeð, 29/32; 39/16; 105/30; seieð, 37/7; seið, 3/3; 5/12, 29; 9/11; 11/6; 13/4, 26; 15/8; 19/13, 14, 22, 29; 27/29; 29/15; 31/4, 5, 23, 32; 37/11, 18, 26; 39/21, 30; 41/6, 14; 45/3, 5, 16, 24, 29; 47/7, *etc.*; seiþ, 59/21, 25; seid, 45/7; 47/24; saið, 87/34; syeð, 23/5; seggeð, 35/10; 55/15; *pl.* seggeð, 11/7; 29/8, 9; 31/17; 57/32; 59/17; 77/4; 79/27, 30, 32; 141/21; 149/10; siggen, 125/11; *opt.* 3 *sg.* segge, 123/20; 2 *sg.* seggen (?), 141/28; *pl.* seggen, 141/19; *imp. sg.* seize, 91/3; 101/33, 34; 145/11; seih, 127/16; sei, 25/31; 113/13; 123/2; sai, 147/25; 1 *pl.* (*adhort.*) segge (we), 147/30; *pret.* 1 *and* 3 *sg.* sæide, 13/22; 55/8; saide, 13/24; 135/14; seide, 53/27; 59/19; 67/26, 29; 69/1; 71/7; 117/29; sæde, 27/21; 29/25; 53/31; 55/24; 63/17; 69/26; 77/34, 35; 79/3; 93/13, 15; 101/17; 105/12; 109/30; 113/32; 115/16; sede, 17/8; 51/23; 115/22; sade, 9/26; 13/18; 25/9; 27/19; 29/18; 31/15, 17; 33/1, 25; 35/23, 26; 53/26; 55/31; 61/29; 65/17, 32; 69/6; 79/19; 87/8; 91/24; 93/31; 101/7, 18; 105/13; 107/7; 109/20; 111/4; 113/17, 27; 115/7, 29; 117/3, 12, 17, 21; 119/29; 121/6; 123/1, 3, 10, 12; 125/7, *etc.*; 2 *sg.* sadest, 113/21, 22; *pl.* seiden, 23/22; *part.* zesæd, 71/24; isæd, 105/18; iseid, 133/15.

seizen, *v. to sift, pl. ind. pres.* seizeð, 105/23.

seizen, *see* seggen *and* sien.

seihte, *sb. reconciliation, ac. sg.* 115/19.

seihtþe, *sb. sight, d. sg.* 29/19.

seihtle, *see* sahtlin.

seinte, *see* sainte.

seke, *adj. sick,* 149/17.

seken, *see* sechen.

self, *pron. self, same, sg. nom.* 15/8; 29/15; 35/15; 109/15, 19; 125/27; 127/27; 137/8; 141/32; *with pron.* meself, 7/6; meselv, 53/17; himself, 5/12; 19/29; 33/20; 37/16, 18; 101/7; 113/5; 117/34; 119/7; 141/28; 145/6; himselv, 111/25; hireself, 55/25; 59/15; ðe selve, *the same,* 9/25; *d. ac.* selven, 5/2, 12, 14, 25; 9/8; 13/14, 16; 23/7; 25/19; 31/10; 33/28; 37/21, 25, 26; 39/28; 41/2; 45/6, 7; 49/16, 20; 51/1; 53/15, 30; 57/1, 2, 20; 59/9; 63/20, 23, 26, 33; 65/4, 7, 20; 67/5; 69/27; 81/10, 16; 83/24; 97/3; 103/17; 107/2; 115/25, 27; 125/31; 133/6, 11; 135/4, 27, 29; selve, 41/22; self, 105/21; 137/14; *as nom.* ðu ðeselven, 65/7; *pl. d. ac.* selven, 5/12, 34; 7/2, 5; 51/2; 53/33; 55/29, 30; 57/32; 59/2; 65/15; 73/20; 79/11, 21; 83/29; 87/32; 95/29; 105/23, 24, 29; 123/5; 139/24; *as nom.* zeuselven, 93/23; zewselven, 123/5 (*dat.*?) (*cf.* ic).

GLOSSARY. 249

selcuð, *adj. strange, remarkable,* 29/15; 55/18; 97/16.
selcuðliche, *adj. wonderful,* 137/16.
selcuðliche, *adv. wonderfully,* 25/23.
sellen, *v. to sell, pres. ind.* 3 *sg.* selð, 121/18; *imp. sg.* sell, 69/2; *pret.* 1 *and* 3 *sg.* sealde, 11/26; 29/10.
selver, *sb. silver, d. ac. sg.* 33/14; 67/19.
senden, *v. to send,* 85/23; sanden, 145/34; *pres. ind.* 3 *sg.* sent, 77/8; 85/8; sant, 17/17; 35/30; 101/1; 149/28; *opt.* 2 *sg.* send, 115/13; *imp. sg.* sand, 145/32; *pret.* 1 *and* 3 *sg.* sente, 75/25; 99/14; sænte, 21/21; 25/21; sante, 55/16; 147/15; *part.* ȝesænt, 83/33; ȝesant, 143/21; isænt, 85/7.
senderlic, *adj. private, ac. sg. m.* senderlicne, 143/9.
seneȝin, *v. to sin,* 15/32; 123/20, 21; 125/3; 145/20; *pres. ind.* 2 *sg.* senegest, 37/20; *pl.* seneȝin, 123/4; *pret.* 1 *sg.* sineȝede, 83/21.
senevei, *sb. mustard, g. sg.* seneveies, 29/19.
senfulle, *adj. sinful,* 15/31; 21/26; 23/1; 51/6; 77/14; 83/33; 137/7; 145/13, 18, 28; *sup.* senfullest, 57/33.
senne, *sb. sin, sg. nom. d. ac.* 3/7, 22, 28; 5/1, 21; 7/15, 23, 25; 9/14, 15, 21, 30; 11/2; 13/29; 15/18; 19/16; 27/10; 61/23; 75/19; 81/28; 83/6; 85/16; 93/26; 119/8; 121/11, 14; 123/8; 129/1; 137/27; 141/14; sennne, 13/12; 39/5; 109/11; *pl.* sennes, 5/8, 18, 27; 7/25; 15/29, 30; 21/6, 8, 29; 27/12; 33/8; 63/24; 65/1; 69/34; 71/28; 83/4; 87/12, 14, 27; 97/19; 101/6; 119/21; 121/8, 24, 31; 127/11; sennen, 3/15; 7/1; 25/22; 51/11; 85/18; 93/17; 103/20; 111/32; 121/10; 123/11, 16; sennnen, 87/1; sinnen, 111/30.
senneleas, *adj. sinless,* 139/22.
sente, *see* senden.
sermuns, *sb. sermons,* 35/29.
servin, *v. to serve, pl. ind. pres.* servið, 43/3.
servise, *sb. service, d. ac. sg.* 3/27; 33/18; 85/9; 151/2.
sete, *see* setten.
setle, *sb. throne, d. sg.* 117/1.
setten, *v. to set, put,* 17/9; 117/1; *pres. opt.* 2 *sg.* sette, 47/15; *imp.*

sg. sete, 93/18; *pret.* 3 *sg.* sette, 97/6.
seððen, *adv. conj. since, afterwards,* 7/19; 13/16; 15/32; 23/23, 26; 43/24; 65/7; 75/11; 105/4, 19; 115/26; 119/26; 129/21; 137/11; siððen, 87/34; siðþen, 129/22.
seven, *num. seven,* 91/11.
sibbe, *sb. relations, sg. nom.* 65/6; *d. ac.* 13/9; 19/4; 41/22.
sibsumnesse, *sb. peace,* 15/13; 61/2; 89/8; 95/12; 97/20; 99/5, 11, 17; 101/16; 115/16, 17; 117/23; 129/31.
side, *sb. side, d. ac. sg.* 21/16; 83/3; 101/32; 103/5.
siechen, *see* sechen.
sien, *v. to see, pres. opt. pl.* 127/8; *pret. pl.* seiȝen, 25/10; *part. (cf.* ȝesen).
siggen, *see* seggen.
sihten, (!) *v. to sigh, pl imp.* sihteþ, 19/18.
siker, *adj. sure, certain,* 25/31; 31/23, 30; 103/6; sikere, 43/31; *comp.* sikerere, 67/24.
sikerest, *adv. sup. most surely,* 149/14.
sikerliche, *adv. surely,* 37/32; 39/8; 51/32; 53/13; 151/13; *comp.* sikerliker, 147/30.
sikernesse, *sb. certainty, ac. sg.* 81/21.
sineȝede, *see* seneȝin.
singen, *v. to sing, pres. ind. pl.* singeð, 19/26; *pret. pl.* sunge, 15/12.
sinken, *v. to sink,* 43/32.
sinnen, *see* senne.
sitten, *v. to sit,* 67/21; 135/2; *pres. ind.* 3 *sg.* sitt, 25/26; 133/18; sitteð, 79/15; *pret. ind.* 2 *sg.* sate, 11/6; *opt.* 3 *sg.* sate, 141/22.
sið, *sb. way, time, sg. g.* siðes, 69/29; *pl. ac.* 3/24.
siððen, *see* seððen.
six, *num. six,* 143/32.
skele, *sb. reason, discretion, discernment, distinction, sg. nom.* 125/14; 149/22; *d. ac.* 139/30; schele, 139/25; scile, 107/12.
sckelewisnesse, *sb. discretion,* 149/8.
skelien, *v. to separate, discern,* 17/25; skilien, 125/15.
skentinges, *sb. amusements,* 69/18.
scile, *see* skele.
skilien, *see* skelien.
slap, *sb. sleep, d. sg.* slape, 87/30.

GLOSSARY.

slæpen, *v. to sleep*, 8/27; slapen, 107/15; *pres. part.* slapinde, 127/19; *pret. ind.* 3 *sg.* sliep, 51/10.
slauþhe, *sb. sloth, d. sg.* 5/2.
slaw, *adj. slow*, 3/24.
slean, *v. to slay, pres. ind.* 3 *sg.* slecð, 129/6; *pl.* sleað, 61/26; *imp. sg.* sleih, 67/30; *pret. ind.* 3 *sg.* slou, 115/25; *part.* islaȝe, 5/22.
slider, *adj. slippery*, 21/15.
sliep, *see* slapen.
slou, *see* slean.
smac, *sb. taste, nom. sg.* 17/4.
smekes, *sb. smokes*, 129/8.
smec-hus, *sb. smoke-house, d. sg.* huse, 129/7.
smell, *sb. smell, nom. sg.* 17/5.
smiten, *v. to smite, pres. ind.* 3 *sg.* smit, 18/18; 127/29; *part.* smitende, 135/25.
smið, *sb. carpenter, d. sg.* smiðe, 51/4.
snaw, *sb. snow, nom. sg.* 83/4.
so, *see* swa.
sobben, *v. to sob, pres. ind.* 3 *sg.* sobbeð, 57/16; *part.* sobbiende, 85/13.
softe, *adj. soft, meek*, 49/10; 71/30.
softin, *v. to soften*, 127/23.
softnesse, *sb. softness*, 41/29; sofnesse, 115/18.
sonde, *see* sande.
sone, *adv. soon*, 5/33; 19/7; 53/31; 57/34; 73/14; 85/20; 97/28; 99/30; 109/12; 111/27, 28; 113/32; 141/15; 145/24.
song, *see* sang.
sore, *see* sare.
sorhfull, *adj. sorrowful*, 83/18; 95/25.
sori, *see* sari.
sorwȝe, *sb. sorrow, nom. sg.* 19/2.
sothade, *sb. folly, foolishness, sg. nom.* 127/32; *ac.* 67/18; *pl. ac.* sothades, 101/6.
sott, *sb. fool, sg. nom.* 67/17; *d. ac.* 79/26; 127/32.
sotwordes, *sb. foolish words*, 101/15.
soð, *sb. sooth, truth, sg. nom. ac.* 5/4; 9/16, 32; 28/9; 69/24; 79/4; 93/12; 113/9, 12, 13, 17, 26; 115/29; 117/12, 21; soðh, 9/24; soþ, 11/31; *d.* (+to, te) soðe, 27/32; 41/32; 49/21; 53/1; 55/24; 59/11; 63/1; 65/22; 75/16; 89/28; 113/12; 123/5; 135/26; 147/4; soþe, 25/1; 69/28.
soð, *adj. true*, 25/18, 22 (2); 51/6, 7, 11; 93/3; 97/4 (2); 105/20; 115/30; 117/4, 7, 19, 25, 31 (2); 119/27; 125/10; 151/20; soþ, 25/11; soðe, 15/27; 35/26; 39/2, 30; 45/15; 51/30, 33; 59/3; 63/4; 71/34; 85/13; 105/23; 121/16, 19; 127/18; 145/19, 29; soðre, 7/1; *sup.* soðeste, 69/24.
soðliche, *adv. truly*, 21/20, 21; 31/15; 33/20; 53/2, 3, 5, 6, 13; 55/31, 32; 97/7, 8, 9; 121/1; 139/2.
soule, *see* sawle.
spaches, *sb. speeches*, 11/5; 79/16, 24; 81/6; 123/29, 30; 131/5; speches, 15/21.
spak, *see* speken.
speden, *v. to speed, pl. imp.* spedeð, 19/16.
speken, *v. to speak*, 9/21, 23; 47/1, 5; 49/31; 61/18; 87/15; 125/21; 133/29; 141/23, 25; *ger.* spekene, 11/15; 53/25; *pres. ind.* 2 *sg.* spekest, 133/12; 3 *sg.* spekð, 59/21; 61/7; 85/32; 87/10; 101/6, 8, 10; spekeð, 141/20; *pl.* spekeð, 41/24; 49/2; 53/23; 81/6; 99/3; speked, 147/4; speke (we), 141/21; *opt.* 2 *sg.* speke, 125/21; 3 *sg.* 101/4; 113/12; *pl.* speken, 47/28 (?); 59/30; *part.* spekende, 101/15; 107/16; spekinde, 49/31; 149/13; specinde, 131/5; *pret. ind.* 3 *sg.* spak, 109/20, 27; spac, 117/3; 2 *sg.* spake, 11/8; *pl.* spaken, 23/21; 73/29; *part.* ȝespeken, 11/23; 91/12; ispeken, 69/22.
spell, *sb. gospel, d. sg.* spelle, 125/18; 127/28.
spellen, *v. to preach*, 121/5.
spelleres, *sb. preachers*, 45/24.
spottes, *sb. spots*, 95/29.
spraden, *v. to spread*, 3 *sg. ind. pres.* sprat, 45/32; spratt, 105/26.
sprængen, *v. to besprinkle, sg. imp.* spræng, 83/1.
springen, *v. to spring*, 69/17; 3 *sg. ind. pres.* springþ, 63/11.
spus, *sb. spouse, husband, sg. nom.* 131/25.
spuse, *sb. spouse, wife, d. ac. sg.* 111/13; 129/29.
stampen, *v. to stamp*, 3 *sg. ind. pres.* stampeþ, 29/20.
stan, *sb. stone, d. sg.* stane, 27/3.
stand, *see* stonden.
stan-roches, *sb. stone-rocks*, 45/18.
stant, *see* stonden.
stede, *sb. stead, place, d. ac. sg.* 81/2; 95/7; 117/2; 143/9.
stedefast, *adj. steadfast*, 135/2.
stedel, *sb. stead, place, nom. sg.* 97/20.

steih, *see* stien.
stelen, *v. to steal, sg. imp.* stell, 67/30.
steren, *see* stieren.
stervin, *v. to starve, die*, 137/20 (?).
stiefne, *sb. voice, d. sg.* 71/25.
stien, *v. to ascend, descend, pres. ind.
pl.* stieð, 45/11; stikð, 45/16;
pret. ind. 3 *sg.* steih, 25/26; 143/
11.
stieren, *v. to steer, direct, guide*, 43/
20; 95/16; steren, 43/27; *pres.
opt. pl.* stieren, 97/13; *pret.* 3 *sg.*
stierde, 43/24.
stieresman, *sb. steersman, sg. d. ac.*
45/9; -mann, 43/21; -manne, 45/
1; *pl. nom.* -menn, 43/27; -mannen, 45/4, 7.
stikke, *sb. stick, d. sg.* 135/1.
stikð, *see* stien.
stille, *adj. still*, 11/9.
stinkende, *part. pres. stinking*, 15/
24; 63/30.
stonden, *r. to stand*, 11/11; *pres.
ind.* 3 *sg.* stant, 49/22; 51/25;
imp. sg. stand, 73/11.
stor, *sb. incense, nom. sg.* 143/24.
storfat, *sb. censer, d. sg.* -fate, 143/24.
storm, *sb. storm, d. sg.* storme, 43/
30; *pl.* stormes, 43/25; 45/13.
strænges, *sb. strings*, 45/14.
straw, *sb. straw, d. sg.* strawe, 135/1.
strengere, *see* strong.
strengþe, *sb. strength, force, sg. nom.*
81/13; 105/25; 107/5, 9; strencþe,
129/4; *d. ac.* 25/17; 27/8, 11;
29/20; 39/7; 51/18, 19; 81/15,
18, 23; 83/23, 24; 91/5; 105/34;
107/8; 113/20; strencþe, 93/5;
115/24; stregþe, 93/4, 6; strenðe,
81/11; 107/4; *pl.* strengþes, 49/
28.
strong, *adj. strong*, 83/23; stronge,
43/25; 83/25; 129/3; *comp.* strengere, 29/21, 23; 53/24; 129/5.
sue-, *see* awe-.
sull, *sb. plough, d. sg.* 71/21.
sum, *pron. some*, 3/17; 7/3; 29/6
(2), 9; 35/13; 41/11; 47/17; 57/
33; 67/3; 81/16; 93/19; 101/
11; 141/19; 149/14, 15 (3), 16
(2), 17; sume, 5/32; 7/2; 9/8,
14; 29/7; 35/29; 37/13, 16; 53/
7; 57/11, 12, 27, 31, 34; 65/14;
73/33; 75/1 (2); 79/10, 12; 87/
30; 115/13; 137/20, 26; 139/18,
23; 145/34; 147/29; 149/12, 23,
24; sumen, 65/16; sumere, 33/9;
121/17; sumes, 11/32.
sumþing, *pron. something, ac. sg.* 27/
23; 135/28.

sune, *sb. son, sg. nom. d. ac.* 18/21;
21/7; 25/11, 13, 21; 27/2, 4, 11;
31/5, 10; 35/26; 37/1; 49/15; 51/
17; 53/28; 57/9; 63/5, 28; 73/
9; 83/34, *etc.*; *g.* sunes, 55/18.
sunge, *see* singen.
sunne, *sb. sun, sg. nom. d. ac.* 31/13;
49/23; 89/18; 125/23.
suster, *see* swuster.
swa, *adv. conj. so, as*, 3/4 (2), 16; 5/
25, 29; 7/17; 9/3, 28; 13/5, 14;
15/15, 25; 17/7, 18; 19/5; 21/11
(2), 20, 23, 29; 23/6, 8; 25/20;
27/6; 29/13, 27; 31/13 (2); 33/
4, 5, 7, 20-23, 27, 31, 32, 34;
35/2, 5, 19, 31; 37/17; 41/9, 23;
43/24, 27; 49/7, 11, 26; 53/2, 3,
5, 6, 8, 20, 21, 33; 55/31, 32; 57/
24, 29; 59/2, 10, 26; 61/15; 63/
21; 65/25-27; 67/2, 6, 14, 17, 24,
33; 69/3, 11, 16; 71/34; 73/18,
33; 75/16; 77/9, 11, 14-16, 30;
81/14, 32, *etc.*; swo, 3/14; 7/27;
9/14; 19/5; 29/26; 33/27; 35/6;
11; 43/31; 45/30; 49/27; 55/27;
57/21; 61/18; 65/20; 67/9, 20;
93/9; 95/30; 99/4; 101/24, 29
(2); 105/26 (2), 33; 109/13; 113/
34; 115/2, 17; 117/9 (2); so, 81/
14; 101/25; 125/18; 145/24; sa,
9/19; 21/21; se, 51/23; 65/26;
95/30.
swaint, *pret. part. troubled* (*cf.*
ȝeswæint), 29/22.
swanc, *see* swinken.
swaswa, *conj.* (1) *as*, 5/16; 11/10;
15/28; 39/27; 53/17; 59/15; 83/
14; 119/7; 127/16; 137/18; 145/
31; 147/1; swase, 101/16; (2)
if, swaswa, 41/16; 43/18; 45/2;
107/3; (3) *although*, 43/11; swoswo, 113/7; 117/7, 25.
swaðelbond, *sb. swaddling bands, d.
sg.* -bonde, 49/29.
swellen, *v. to puff up*, 3 *sg. ind.
pres.* swelð, 65/18, 19.
sweord, *sb. sword, ac. sg.* 91/3.
sweriȝen, *v. to swear*, 9/9; *pres. ind.*
3 *sg.* swereð, 79/4; *pl.* sweriȝeð,
9/13; *imp. pl.* sweriȝeð, 9/12.
sueriingge, *sb. swearing, d. sg* 9/5.
swete, *adj. sweet*, 41/10; 57/17; 63/
5, 6; 71/32; 81/32; 83/34; 89/
25; 119/15; 137/22, 35; 139/9;
145/32; 149/1, 4, 5, 7; swiete, 33/
34.
swiche, *see* swilch.
swieten, *v. to sweeten*, 3 *sg. ind.
pres.* swieteð, 33/32.
swigende, *part. pres. silent*, 107/16.

swikedom, *sb. fraud, guile, deceit, sg.
ac.* 59/30; *d.* swicedome, 11/21.
swikele, *adj. deceptive, deceitful,
treacherous,* 8/22; 15/19; 29/34;
41/10; 43/2; 51/17; 81/6; 89/
25.
swiken, *v. to cease, imp. sg.* swic, 31/
31.
swilch, (1) *pron. such,* 3/28; 19/6;
57/29; 71/15; 91/14; 105/32;
127/23; swulch, 75/7; 77/31;
swilche, 5/28; 9/9; 13/22; 43/
13; 65/19, 21; 79/19; 127/22;
swiche, 27/19; (2) *conj. as if,*
swilch, 57/28; 113/12; 119/8;
145/10; swilche, 81/7.
swinches, *see* **swink.**
swingen, *v. to chastise,* 13/20.
swink, *sb. toil, labour, sg. ac.* 3/26;
d. swinke, 13/21; 79/15; 127/1;
pl. swinkes, 95/25; swinches, 93/
16.
swinken, *v. to work, toil, labour,* 97/
31; *pres. ind. pl.* swinkeð, 33/9,
13; 71/27; *part.* swinkende, 93/
13; *pret. ind.* 3 *sg.* swanc, 43/23;
pl. swunken, 151/18; *part.* iswun-
ken, 91/32; 99/4.
swinkfulle, *adj. toilful, -some,* 33/9;
137/8.
swiðe, *adv. very, much, strongly,* 5/18,
19 (2); 7/5, 7; 21/2, 29; 25/23;
29/13; 35/15; 41/9; 43/22; 45/
32; 47/11, 21; 53/21; 55/4, *etc.
comp.* swiðere, 93/16.
swiðer, *adj. right (dexter),* 97/7; swiðere, 28/8; swiþere, 145/27; swi-
ðre, 25/26; 77/2.
swo, *see* **swa.**
swot, *sb. sweat, d. sg.* swote, 93/17.
swulch, *see* **swilch.**
swunken, *see* **swinken.**
swuster, *sb. sister, sg. d.* 63/29; suster, *nom. ac.* 3/22; 29/31; 131/8.

T.

ta, *see* **to.**
tachen, *v. to teach,* 59/23; 99/15;
tache, 88/26; *pres. ind.* 3 *sg.* tachþ,
27/29; takð, 31/3; takd, 65/12;
opt. 2 *sg.* tæche, 47/10; *imp. sg.*
tach, 31/21; 127/21, 22; *pret.* 3
sg. 27/1; 31/6; 127/27; 141/32;
143/8; *pl.* tahte, 27/15.
tail, *sb. tail, nom. sg.* 151/1.
taken, *v. to take,* 3 *sg. ind. pres.*
takð, 105/25.
tacne, *token, nom. d. sg.* 31/25; 57/
13; tocne, 135/1.
tacnien, *v. to betoken, pres. ind.* 3 *sg.*
tacneð, 147/10; tacnieð, 33/28;
tocneð, 151/1; *pl.* tacniþ, 17/5;
pret. part. tokned, 103/12.
tactþe, *sb. touch, nom. sg.* 17/5.
tare, *see* **se.**
te-, *see* **to-.**
te, *see* **se, ðe,** *and* **þu.**
tear, *sb. tear, sg. ac.* 145/34; 147/
26; *pl.* teares, 21/2; 57/16, 17;
81/33; 85/1, 14; 95/27, 30, *etc.*
teiþin, *v. to grant, yield, give way,* 141/
15; *pres. ind.* 2 *sg.* teiðest, 89/25;
teiþest, 135/26; *imp. sg.* teiþe,
135/24; *part.* teiþinde, 75/10;
teiðinde, 75/16; *pret.* 2 *sg.* teiðe-
dest, 85/21; 3 *sg.* teiþede, 119/18;
part. iteiþed, 29/17.
teiþinge, *sb. granting,* 119/19.
teld, *sb. tent, d. sg.* telde, 79/8.
teli3en, *v. to till,* 75/3.
tellen, *v. to tell, think, account,
reckon,* 15/30; *pres. ind.* 3 *sg.* telþ,
31/1; *pl.* telleð, 53/33; *pret. part.*
iteld, 77/24.
temple, *sb. temple, nom. d. ac. sg.*
83/3; 93/21, 23, 26, 27; 95/9;
97/29; 99/4, 24; 105/5; 107/6;
111/22; 123/27.
temple-rihtwisnesse, *sb. temple-
righteousness, nom sg.* 105/9.
tempren, *v. to regulate,* 3 *sg. ind.
pres.* tempreð, 107/18.
ten, *see* **se.**
tes, *see* **ðes.**
tetreden, *pret. part. trodden down,*
89/35.
tidinge, *s^h. tiding, sg. ac.* 17/17; *pl.*
tidinges, 101/14.
ti3eþes, *sb. tithes,* 139/30.
timber, *sb. timber, nom. ac. sg.* 27/26;
91/14, 24.
timbringe, *sb. timber, d. sg.* 91/17.
time, *sb. time, d. sg.* 23/2; 35/2;
39/25; 55/1; 121/25.
to, (1) *prep.* (*with sb. and pron.*) *to,
until,* 5/3; 7/5, 32; 9/3, 15, 22;
11/7, 9, 23, 31; 15/13, 28; 19/13,
14; 21/3, 5, 7, 8, 12, 18; 23/1, 5,
26, 32; 25/1, 29; 27/20, 23, 32;
29/31; 31/28; 33/14, 18, 21, 29;
39/12, 18, 25; 43/1, 18, 26, 27;
45/2, 3, 4, 20; 47/2, 13; 49/21;
51/3, *etc.*; ta, 131/25; te, 23/22;
29/14; 33/14, 15, 17, 18; 39/6,
12; 41/32; 45/15, 30; 47/29, 30;
49/6, 11; 51/26; 53/1; 55/23;
57/9, 26; 59/11; 63/28, 29; 65/
16, 22; 69/28; 75/16; 79/6, 13;
81/5, 6; 89/18, 32; 99/17; 111/
29; 113/15, 24, 29; 115/3; 117/

GLOSSARY.   253

27; 119/4, 14; t, 101/2; (2) *with verbs (ger. and inf.)* 3/17; 9/8, 9, 29; 11/15, 31; 15/1, 10; 17/3, 19; 19/6, 11; 21/10, 15; 23/15, 16; 25/27; 27/14, 23, 24, 26, 31; 31/10; 33/12, 30; 35/6, 22; 87/15; 39/3, 7, 18; 43/12, 13, 27; 47/4, 5, 8, *etc*. te, 3/11, 15, 16, 17; 5/27; 7/11; 9/16; 11/20; 15/3, 9, 16; 21/1, 7, 27; 27/24, 28; 31/2; 33/24; 35/23; 37/3, 17, 31; 41/17; 43/8; 47/17, *etc*.; (*cf.* forto). (3) *adv. (with verbs)*, 13/18; 25/1; 27/33; 29/11; 35/28; 63/25; 89/32; 103/15; 127/30; 143/6; 149/18, 28; (4) *adv*. *too*, 7/4; 13/15; 15/18; 23/27, 28; 25/2; 29/27; 43/31; 47/4, 12, *etc*.
tobrecen, *v. to break*, 41/25; *pres. ind*. 2 *sg*. tebrecst, 39/4; 89/18; 3 *sg*. tobrecþ, 45/23; tobrecð, 95/13; tobrekð, 45/19; tobrekd, 45/21; *opt. pl*. tobreken, 45/14; *imp. sg*. tebrec, 67/31; *pret. opt*. 3 *sg*. tobreke, 113/18; *part*. tobroken, 133/20; tebrocen, 67/33; tebroken, 117/20.
to-daiȝ, *adv. to-day*, 145/23.
toforen, *prep. adv. before*, 49/17; 79/21; 103/11; 123/29; 131/11, 13; 135/7; 137/29; 139/22; 141/7, 10, 11, 23, 26; 143/23; 145/10; tofore, 9/29; 95/33; teforen, 5/32; 7/24; 9/30; 11/11; 17/13; 21/16; 27/15; 59/12; 103/19; 113/32; tefore, 9/30; 11/11; 17/25; 101/24; 113/27.
togedere, *adv. together*, 35/9; 113/10; 115/20; 117/24; 131/20; 133/2; 149/13; tegedere, 97/14.
tocyme, *sb. coming, arrival, ac. sg*. 31/9.
tocne, *see* tacne.
toterinde, *pres. part. tottering*, 135/3.
toð, *sb. tooth, d. pl*. toðen, 19/1.
to .. ward, *prep. towards*, 75/23.
tresor, *sb. treasure, ac. sg*. 135/23.
treu, *sb. tree, sg. nom. ac*. 7/27; 51/27, 29; trew, 53/5, 6; *d*. treuwe, 119/10, 12; trewe, 51/23, 25; 53/11; trowe, 119/1, 2, 4; *gen*. trewes, 119/13.
treuwe, *adj. true*, 111/10; trewe, 17/8; 45/27; *comp*. trewer, 75/25.
trewðe, *sb. fidelity, d. sg*. 103/31.
trukien, *v. to fail, cease, relax*, 61/34; 75/24; *pres. ind*. 1 *sg*. truke, 75/24; 3 *sg*. trukeð, 81/32; *pl*.

trukieð, 91/29; *pret*. 3 *sg*. trukede, 149/22.
tu, *see* þu.
tunes, *sb. towns, pl*. 77/28.
tunge, *sb. tongue, sg. ac*. 59/29; 133/28; *pl*. tungen, 49/30.
tur, *sb. tower, nom. sg*. 107/8, 9.
twa, *num. two*, 39/22, 23; 51/15; 73/30; 119/19, 20; 125/14; 127/31; tua, 111/28; two, 113/11.
twammen, *v. to divide, separate*, 131/28; *pres. ind. pl*. twameð. 87/14; *pret. part*. ȝetwamd, 63/30; i-twamd, 75/18.
twene, *sb. doubt, d. sg*. 151/12.
twifeald, *adj. twofold, double*, 11/28, (2); 15/21.
twifealden, *v. to double, ind. pres*. 3 *sg*. 5/21.
two, *see* twa.

Ð, þ.

ða, (1) *adv. then*, 15/11; 23/13, 15, 21; 53/29; 113/16; 115/29; 117/3; 121/6; 149/19; þa, 113/20; ðo, 99/15; 117/12; þo, 147/19; (2) *conj. when (rel.)* 23/20; 58/31; ðo, 117/24; ðaðe, 15/11; 23/12; 81/23; 83/10; 121/5; 187/12; þaþe, 147/23; ðoðe, 49/15 (*though!*) 99/14; 111/32; 121/5; þoþe, 103/24; 137/9; ðaða, 9/26; 85/15; ðaþa, 115/24.
ða, ðan. *see* se.
ðan, *see* ðanne.
ðane, *see* se *and* ðanne.
ðanen, *adv. whence (rel.)*, 25/26.
þanc, *sb. thought, mood, imagination, sg. ac*. 55/30; *d*. þanke, 53/9; 131/8, 10, 14; *g*. þankes, *voluntarily*, 111/7.
þankin, *v. to thank*, 151/15; *pres. ind*. 1 *sg*. þanki, 83/31; 3 *sg*. þankeð, 81/2; *pl*. ðankieð, 21/16; *opt*. 2 *sg*. ðanki, 87/28; þanke, 151/22; *pl*. þankin, 151/19; *imp. sg*. þanke, 29/4; ðanke, 29/13; *pret. part*. ȝeþanked, 23/6; 93/5; iþ nked, 97/5; iþankked, 73/33.
ðanne, *adv. conj*. (1) *then*, 5/22; 17/26; 25/29; 33/31; 37/2, 24; 39/8, 13, 19; 41/1; 53/17; 59/5, 11; 61/3, 4; 63/24; 65/3; 67/1; 71/13; 73/4, 20; 75/35, *etc*.; þanne, 35/30; 37/29, 33; 63/25; 99/18; 111/18; 137/6; 141/21; 147/28; ðane, 25/31; 31/30; 75/33; 137/25; ðan, 51/32; (2) *when (rel.)*, ðanne, 17/29; 19/29; 29/6; 37/

28; 39/12, 34; 61/2; 63/29; 65/23; 75/17 (2), 30; 77/1, etc.; þanne, 29/3; 81/10; 39/9; 73/9; 111/3, etc.; ðane, 87/25; þan, 143/20; (3) *than, than that*, ðanne, 7/20; 9/18, 32; 11/15, 27; 15/22; 17/21; 23/12, 19; 81/1; 33/18; 39/9, 31; 43/14; 55/30; 57/21; 59/9; 65/1; 67/22; 69/8, 21, 23, 31; 73/17, 21; 75/25, etc. ðannne, 55/7; þanne, 69/5; 98/31; 105/11; 127/6; 129/3, 6; 133/12, 17; ðane, 15/2; 47/1; 61/24; 65/24; 83/4; ðan, 27/23, 24; 37/20, 22; 57/20; þan, 149/23.

ðanne, *see* se.
ðar, *see* se.
ðær, *adv. conj.* (1) *there*, 99/5; þær, 69/25; ðar, 9/28; 17/32; 19/1, 2; 25/2; 53/14; 69/26; 75/5; 79/9; 85/18; 91/26; 95/30; 99/5, 28, 31; 101/11, *etc.*; þar, 147/12; ðer, 115/18; ðe, 67/33; (2) *where (rel.)*, ðar, 3/27; 11/12; 13/2; 17/30; 19/33; 21/15; 33/28; 41/29; 71/1; 99/16; 129/10; 139/32; 141/22; þar, 131/3; 145/29.
ðar after, *adv. thereafter*, 27/12; 29/27, 28; 37/2; 45/30; 61/9; 65/8; 71/10; 93/24; 99/33; 109/4, 17; ðer after, 71/8.
ðar aȝean, *adv. at it*, 13/21.
ðare, *see* se.
ðar embe, *adv. thereabout*, 47/4; 101/10.
ðare mide, *see* ðar mide.
ðarfore, *adv. therefore*, 55/5; 129/19.
ðarinne, *adv. therein*, 17/31; 41/15; 45/4; 49/17, 26; 73/13, 32; 97/30; 99/18; 107/10; 117/11; ðerinne, 99/9; þerinne, 137/5.
ðar mide, *adv. therewith*, 17/6; 59/13; 79/10, 13; 81/27; ðare mide, 133/27.
ðarof, *adv. thereof*, 5/24, 29, 31; 21/9; 29/4; 31/1; 43/26, 28; 65/32; 77/17, 31; 79/15; 93/4; 95/14; 101/8; 127/11; 141/10; 143/22, 28; þarof, 137/21; ðerof, 11/32; 29/13; 73/8; 111/4, 17; 141/6.
ðarof ðe, *adv. whereof (rel.)*, 69/26; þar of ðe, 147/13.
ðær on, *adv. thereon, therein*, 41/13; ðar on, 119/3; þar on, 151/2.
ðar over, *adv. thereover*, 91/25; ðer over, 91/15.
ðar to, *adv. thereto*, 5/26; 23/32 *f.*; 39/24; 45/19; 47/5; 75/31; 89/32; 113/25; þar to, 109/11; 137/21; ðerto, 78/3; 75/23.
ðar to ðe, *adv. whereto (rel.)*, 73/15.
ðar ðe, *adv. where (rel.)*, 29/33; 69/25; 89/22; 149/10; ðar þe, 139/31; þar ðe, 93/31; 137/13; 139/10; 147/11.
ðar uppe, *adv. thereupon*, 77/30; ðar uppen, 39/18; þærupen, 103/13.
ðar ut (*MS.* dar), *adv. there out*, 119/22.
ðas, *see* se, *and* þes.
ðat, *conj. that*, 5/1, 2 (2), 3, 12, 21, 23, 28 (2); 7/6, 7; 9/1, 2; 11/28, 32; 18/4, 8, 13; 15/15 (2); 19/6; 21/3, 6, 14, 18, 23, 24, 28, 30; 23/6, 21; 25/8, 10; 27/4, 18 (2), 21, 32; 29/5, 11, 14, *etc.*; ðatt, 19/10; þat, 3/14; 7/22; 11/8, 10, 26; 13/1, 6; 17/13, 24; 21/29; 23/29; 25/13, 21; 27/1, 5, 11; 29/8, 9, *etc.*
ðat, *see* se.
ða ða, ða ðe, *see* ða.
ðe, *see* se *and* ðu.
ðe, *conj.* (1) *rel. who, which, that, as, when, etc.*, 3/3, 7, 11, 12, 15, 16, 22, 23, 29; 5/7, 18, 19, 21, 22, 24, 31, 32, 34; 7/21, 24, 29, 32; 9/3, 6, 9, 11, 17, 23, 24, 27, 32; 11/2, 4, 7, 9, 12, 18, 23, 30; 13/5, 7, 10, 13, 16, 23, 30, 31; 15/2, 6, 7, 13, 18, 31, 32; 17/2, 6, 7, 10, 16, 21, 23, 29, 31; 19/2-5, 10, 11, 14, 19, 24-26, 27, 31, 34; 21/2-4, 7, 8, 12, 14, 17, 22, 26, 31; 23/10, 14, 16, 19, 25, 30; 25/9, 20, 21, 23, 29; 27/3, 4, 12, 19, 22, 25, 26, *etc.*; de, 135/22; þe, 7/15; 15/24; 27/19; 53/11 (*cf.* se); (2) *than*, 69/28; (3) *or*, 109/5; ðe—ðe, 109/6.
ðe, *adv. the* (*with comp.*), 8/29; 5/24; 23/3; 29/20 (2), 22, 23; 49/19; 53/24; 67/24; 87/19; 109/23; 139/12; 143/19; 147/30 (2); þe, 49/20; 133/30; te, 75/4; ð, 133/29.—ðe las te, *conj. lest*, 109/18; þe las te, 125/29 (*cf.* laste).
ðe, *see* ðær.
þearvan, *adj. needy ones*, 57/31.
ðeawes, *sb. manners*, 95/29; 107/20 109/34; þeawes, 57/32; 65/12; 87/1.
ðeih, *conj. though, although*, 3/9; 5/17; 53/16; 57/19; 59/12; 77/25; 95/18; þeih, 9/15; 25/19; 87/23; 97/1; 101/3; 103/6; 127/

GLOSSARY. 255

5; 131/10, 21; 133/19; 149/6; þei, 113/25.
þeihhweðere, *conj. yet*, 57/20.
þeink, *see* þenchen.
ðelliche, *pron. such*, 35/20; 51/17; 65/27; 67/10; 89/1; 117/6; 137/29; 143/28; þelliche, 45/23; 91/17; 143/9.
ðen, *see* se.
þenchen, *v. to think*, 17/24; 19/8; 61/19; 85/26; 87/12; þenken, 69/17; 125/5; 143/13; þennken, 47/4; *pres. ind.* 1 *sg.* þenche, 97/1; 2 *sg.* þencst, 9/29; 125/16; þenkst, 69/26, 29; ðencst, 87/20; ðenchst, 87/15; þenst, 39/9; 3 *sg.* þencþ, 41/12; 103/10; þencð, 135/4; þengþ, 57/17; ðenþ, 57/21; þincþ, 81/17; ðingþ, 45/29; *pl.* þenceð, 137/21; þenken, 137/18; *opt.* 2 *sg.* þenke, 69/28; þenche, 125/21; *pl.* ðenchen, 21/14; *imp. sg.* þench, 29/11; 133/13; 139/8; 147/21; ðench, 93/17; þenc, 67/9; 133/11; ðenc, 101/22; þenk, 139/5; þinc, 145/10; *pl.* ðencheð, 5/32; þeinkeð, 139/33; *part.* þenchinde, 47/15; þenkinde, 131/5; þeinkinde, 137/32, 34; *pret.* 1 *sg.* ðohte, 13/22; þohte, 83/7; *part.* ʒeþouht, 47/1; iþoht, 33/12; 53/16.
þenchen, *v. to seem, pres. ind.* 3 *sg.* þincþ, 47/3, 20; ðincð, 79/17; þincð, 127/32; 137/22; þingþ, 47/28; þingð, 65/23; ðingþ, 89/25; ðingð, 109/6; *pl.* þencheð, 29/34; *opt.* 3 *sg.* þinche, 33/31; þenche, 97/16; *pret.* 3 *sg.* ðuhte, 13/1; 119/15; *pl.* þouhten, 147/8.
ðen(e), *see* se.
ðenin, *v. to serve*, 73/10; *pres. ind.* 3 *sg.* ðeneð, 63/7.
þenken, *see* þenchen.
ðeof, *see* þief.
ðer, *see* þær.
ðere, *see* se.
ðerniðer, *adv. down*, 63/19.
ðes, *see* se.
ðes, *pron. this, sg. nom. com.* 3/12; 19/28; 33/6, 21; 57/19; 98/14; 105/9; 107/21; þes, 3/8; 131/1; 137/7; tes, 31/32; ðies, 3/22, 28; 5/17, 20; 7/6 (ðie *MS.*); 23/7; 25/18; 29/32; 33/7; 49/2; 51/5; 63/5, 8; 69/3; 85/29; 95/9; 103/14; 107/8, 24, 28; 109/3, 8; 117/3; 129/15; 137/33; 139/14, 21; 143/20; 145/2; 147/10, 22; þies, 33/32; 35/10; 53/31;

95/12; 99/2; 131/2; 139/26; ðis, 5/4, 26; 7/21; 9/1, 10, 27; 25/10; 33/33; 53/3, 6; 57/9; 65/18; 71/24; 85/25; 91/18; 97/1, 29; 105/6, 15, 34; 107/19; 111/3, 33; 117/24; 135/17; þis, 57/13; 65/7; 77/6; 91/14; 105/20; 115/16; 119/30; 127/32; 133/19; *gen. m. n.* ðeses, 41/33; ðies, 127/8; *f.* ðesere, 127/14; þessere, 127/14; ðese, 81/3; *dat. m. n.* ðesen, 35/23; 95/9; 99/17; ðese, 9/22; 11/18; 15/2; 19/12; 21/14; 23/2; 35/2 (?), 27; 47/16; 49/21; 51/5, 23, 33; 53/3, 10; 55/31; 57/8; 61/14, 21; 67/24; 75/15; 85/34; 89/19, 34; 91/13; 93/27; 97/27; 117/4, 31; 139/32; 151/16; þese, 27/3; *f.* ðesse, 43/6; 63/1 (desse *MS.*); 109/24; ðesere, 121/9; ðesere, 63/10; ðessere, 5/1; 7/18; 9/14, 30; 13/29; 19/25; 21/17; 23/22; 27/8, 11, 13, 14; 29/15, 18; 33/9, 13; 35/3, 12; 37/4; 41/9; 45/8; 47/29; 49/20, 24; 51/9, 18, 33; 53/19; 65/15; 69/33; 71/32; 87/5; 105/25, 32; 111/22; 113/3, 8; 141/17; 151/2; *ac. m.* ðisne, 43/16; þisne, 135/28; *f.* ðas, 41/23; 99/5; ðes, 7/23; ðese (*d. ac.*) 5/15; 25/22; 29/21; 31/14, 29; 35/16, 18, 19; 41/4, 7; 43/2, 15; 47/15; 49/7; 53/23; 55/21; 61/2, 8; 63/25; 81/15, 18, 22, 23, 30; 99/9, 25; 101/4; 107/1; 109/12; 121/20; 125/24; 127/33; 131/12; 133/10, 21; þese, 31/27; 129/9; 131/10; 149/25; *com.* ðis, 5/26; 7/21; 9/1; 13/19; 19/8, 11; 21/23; 25/2, 18; 27/1, 4; 37/3, 14; 41/2, 11, 24; 45/29; 49/19; 51/15 (dis *MS.*) 53/10; 55/18; 59/26; 61/4; 63/22; 65/30; 69/20, 21; 75/12; 79/16; 85/14, 17, 19, 23, 24; 87/30; 93/12; 95/3, 27; 99/24; 103/5; 109/30; 111/6, 20; 121/15; 137/9; 143/27; 149/9; 151/8; þis, 9/10; 17/9, 16; 45/7; 61/33; 77/4; 93/3; 95/1; 111/18; 129/20; 139/3, 11; 145/20; *pl. nom.* ðas, 17/5; ðese, 25/16; 53/23; 73/30; 79/8; 113/11; 125/12; 133/1; þese, 23/30; 137/15; 147/4; *d. ac.* ðesen, 75/32; 149/20, 21; ðese, 19/21; 23/31; 35/8, 10; 47/9; 53/16; 63/14; 67/32; 69/16; 71/2; 81/8; 87/1; 89/1, 12; 91/24; 93/7, 18; 107/21; 109/14; þese, 15/29; 45/25; 125/

16, 17; 131/20; 149/4; 151/13; ðase, 125/23.
þesternesse, *see* þiesternesse.
þewdom, *sb. thraldom, d. sg.* -dome, 23/28.
pief, *sb. thief, sg. nom.* 19/17; ðeof, 111/33; *d.* þieve, 145/26; *pl* þieves, 51/15.
ðies, *see* ðes.
ðiester, *adj. dark*, 139/6.
þiesternesse, *sb. darkness*, 17/28, 30; 63/31; þəsternesse, 17/28; ðester-, 113/34.
ðin, *pron. poss. thy, thine, sg. nom.* 33/2, 18, 23; 67/6; 69/25–27; 75/13, 25; 81/27; 85/10, 22; 97/29; 109/32; 113/13; 115/16, 17; þin, 39/11; 63/29; 69/25; 85/5; 109/32; 115/21; 145/29; 147/29; tin, 89/20; ði, 117/20; *f.* þine, 143/6; *gen. m. n.* ðines, 39/25; 109/28, 32; 111/7; þines, 111/1, 8; ðine, 17/9; 39/8; ðinne, 71/14; *d. ac. com.* ðine, 3/4; 11/6; 17/24; 21/5; 23/2; 29/4; 31/29; 33/24, 30; 37/25; 39/4, 12, 13; 47/13; 53/28; 57/10; 59/10, 29; 63/27; 67/5; 73/10; 75/18, 23, 32; 79/1; 81/32; 83/3, 12, 14, 15, 17; 85/21, 31; 87/6, 13, 17, 26, 29; 89/11; 91/27; 97/28; 99/12; 101/23, 32, 33; 103/5; 105/14; 109/28, 31, 33; 111/11, 20, 29; 113/23, 24, 33; 115/1, 9, 17, 31; 117/1, 15, 18, 27, 30; 129/7; 145/20; ðinne, 73/6; þine, 21/7; 27/3; 33/19; 75/9; 83/30, 32; 111/15; 123/34; 125/22; 127/2, 23, 30, 31; 143/2, 3, 5, 7; 145/17; 147/17, 21, 22, 26, 27; ðin, 23/3, 11, 17, 32; 29/5; 39/5, 14; 57/9; 69/28; 71/13; 75/26; 77/19, 20; 79/1; 91/3; 111/18; 115/5; 117/10; 135/26; þin, 33/31; 67/8; 133/12; tin, 45/27; ði, 65/23; 123/27; þi, 147/28; *d. f.* ðire, 83/21, 23; 87/6; 97/17; 113/25; 115/12; 123/28; þire, 145/21, 27, 31, 32; ðiere, 141/27; *pl. nom.* ðine, 63/17; 81/30; 87/14; 109/34; *d. ac.* ðinen, 77/21; 85/7; ðine, 9/31; 17/26; 19/24; 59/30; 61/5; 65/1, 2, 6; 75/31, 32; 81/29; 83/26; 85/18; 87/12, 18, 26; 91/4; 101/34; 103/1, 17, 20; 115/9, 10; þine, 77/16; 87/1; 123/2; 125/3; 145/19.
þinchen, *see* þenchen 2.
þing, *sb. thing, sg. nom. ac.* 11/26; 27/27, 33; 29/15; 37/23; 39/32;
41/4; 45/28; 71/32; 77/21; 85/3; 89/19, *etc.*; ðing, 9/13, 31; 11/31; 101/22; 141/19; *d.* þinge, 39/9; 53/18; 59/8; 65/27; 67/10; 89/20; 135/24; ðinge, 79/5; —*pl. nom. ac.* þing, 7/23; 13/9; 17/8, 9; 21/3; 29/16; 43/8, 9; 49/25; 53/29; 69/19; 71/8; 75/6, *etc.*; þinng, 69/32; ðing, 25/20; 51/10; 71/31; 89/12; þinges, 29/34; 43/17; 57/18; 71/9; 77/29; 79/3; 85/30; 101/5; 135/12; 139/25, 29; ðinges, 139/27; *g.* þinge, 29/2; 99/14; 121/9; 129/11; ðinge, 43/6; 47/28; ðing, 143/19; *d.* þinge, 101/26; 107/12 (*sg.*?)
ðingþ, *see* þənchen.
þinc, *see* þenchen.
þirə, *see* þin.
ðis, *see* ðes.
ðo, *see* se, *and* ða.
poht, *sb. thought, sg. nom. ac.* 99/28; 115/18; þouht, 143/13; *pl.* þohtes, 15/25; 17/13, 22; 33/12; 39/26; 45/11; 83/6; 85/13; 87/24; 89/32; 95/8; 133/27; ðohtes, 45/17; 79/16; 87/5, 7, 28; 89/1, 24, 26; 91/1; 99/26; þouhtes, 13/14; 123/29; 133/10; ðouhtes, 11/32; 123/28; þauhtes, 143/7; þoutes, 133/9; 139/17; 141/7; þowtes, 131/5.
ðohte, *see* þənchen.
þolemode, *adj. patient*, 129/3.
ðolemodnesse, *sb. patience*, 19/12; 41/24; 81/1; 127/25, 26; þolemodnesse, 33/30.
polien, *v. to suffer*, 7/24; 59/6; 73/17; 117/18; 137/18; ðolien, 123/30; þolizen, 9/18; 15/16; 19/8; 29/3; 59/4; 73/7, 16; 113/18, 21; ðolizen, 105/19; 107/12; 117/19; þoliezen, 129/1; *pres. ind.* 2 *sg.* þolest, 65/2; 103/7; 3 *sg.* ðoleð, 81/1; 115/22, 23; *pl.* þolieð, 115/11; *opt.* 3 *sg.* þolize, 105/32; *imp. sg.* ðole, 39/4; þole, 127/29; *pret.* 2 *sg.* þoledest, 33/22; 3 *sg.* ðolede, 7/19; 33/29; 115/24; 119/18; þolede, 25/25; 59/7; 97/6; 119/8, 10; *pl.* ðoleden, 35/1; ðolede, 129/19; *part.* iþoled, 59/6; iðoled, 113/34.
ðorften, *see* ðurve.
popə, *see* ða.
pouht, pout, *see* þoht.
pouhten, *see* þenchen.
powt, *see* þoht.
prall, *sb. thrall, slave, sg. nom. ac.*

GLOSSARY. 257

17/7; 135/27; ðrall, 17/8; þreall, 109/14; d. þralle, 17/6; 83/16; 105/14; g. þralles, 49/17.
þralle, *sb. servant, hand-maiden, sg. nom. ac.*? 53/32; *d.* 55/11.
þreades, *sb. threads*, 39/24.
þreatt, *sb. threat, sg. d.* 87/25.
ðridde, *num. third*, 89/19.
þrie, *num. three*, 25/11; 33/3; 35/9, 10; 45/14; 51/6; 89/12; 127/32; 131/2, 20; 137/15; 143/32; ðrie, 23/14; 25/16; 137/4.
þrihti, *num. thirty*, 51/6.
ðrinnesse, *sb. trinity*, 25/12; þrinnesse, 93/2; 151/20.
prist, *adj. bold*, 123/20.
þruh, *sb. coffin, tomb, sg. nom.* 15/23.
ðu, *pron. thou, sg. nom.* 9/28 (3), 29; 11/6, 8, 9, 11, 12, 16, 17; 13/19; 17/8, 18-20, 22, 23 (2); 21/26, 29; 23/3, 8, 11, 12, 15, 17, 21, 30, 32; 25/1, 2, 13, 31 (2); 27/3, 16, 32; 29/7, 11-13, *etc.*; þu, 17/17; 23/29; 25/33, *etc.*; tu, 9/29; 17/24; 21/6, 30; 23/6; 27/5, 18 (2); 33/1; 39/1, 13; 41/2; 45/24; 47/3, 10, 15; 49/21; 53/20, 21; 59/3, 5, 10, 32; 61/3; 63/25, 33; 65/4, 28; 69/2, 29, 33; 71/3, 15, 18; 75/7, 13, 20, 26, 27, 35; 77/2, 3, 5, 21; 81/14, 15; 83/8, 15; 85/34; 87/4, 8; 89/10, 13, 14, 16, 19; 91/26; 99/22; 101/20, 25; 103/7, 17, 18, 25; 109/23, 33; 111/6; 115/6, 20, 30; 117/4; 125/22 (scal tu); 145/34; 147/18; *d. ac.* ðe, 11/10-13; 13/18, 19; 17/8, 9, 19, 23; 21/5, 9, 30; 23/6, 9-12, 14-17, 26, 32; 25/10; 27/1, 29, 33; 29/4, 6, 11, 14, *etc.*; þe, 17/21; 21/28; 23/27, 29; 29/4, *etc.*; ðie, 23/31; te, 9/31; 33/31; 41/4; 71/16; 75/18, 25, 35 (2); 77/19; 85/25; 87/18, 19; 101/21, 31; 111/7; (*cf.* self).
ðuhte, *see* þenchen.
ðþunresleiȝ, *sb. thunderclap, d. sg.* 11/18.
þurȝhali, *adj. thoroughly holy*, 145/28.
ðurh, *prep. through*, 3/22, 23, 24, 25; 5/16, 21; 7/15, 26, 28 (2), 29; 9/1, 4; 13/29; 15/1; 17/11; 19/15, 22; 21/10, 27; 23/1, 8, 29; 25/24, 25; 27/9; 29/1 (2), 2 (3), *etc.*; þurh, 13/15; 17/11; 91/5; 95/23; 115/31; 119/2, 5; 137/5; 143/25; 149/15 (2), 16; þurȝh, 143/25.

ðurhborede, *pret. part. bored through*, 119/12.
ðurhnailed, *pret. part. nailed through*, 119/14.
þurhstingen, *v. to sting through*, 3 *sg. ind. pret.* -stong, 119/18.
ðurhut, *adv. perfectly*, 69/1; 73/4.
ðurhwuniȝen, *v. to continue, endure, remain*, 55/18; 87/12; *pres. ind.* 3 *sg.* -wuneð, 121/20; þurwuneð, 149/29; durȝwuneð, 151/4; *opt.* 3 *sg.* þurȝwunie, 151/2.
ðurst, *sb. thirst, sg. d. ac.* 145/1; *pl.* ðurstes, 95/24.
ðurve, *v. to need, want, pres. opt.* 3 *sg.* 121/14; *pret. pl.* ðorften, 67/14.
ðus, *adv. thus, so*, 3/3; 11/5, 9, 13; 23/18; 33/30; 37/4; 39/12, 15, 34; 59/21; 61/6, 27; 65/8; 71/25; 75/8; 87/11, *etc.*; þus, 31/3; 37/7; 41/6; 47/19; 119/25; 131/22.
þusend, *num. thousand, pl.* 115/10; 129/18; ðusend, 7/20; ðusende, 17/21.

U.

unakenned, *part. pret. unbegotten*, 25/13.
unaseiȝenliche, *adj. invisible*, 53/24.
unbehealdene, *part. pret. intemperate*, 41/25.
unbecnawe, *part. pret. unknown*, 47/11.
unberinde, *part. pres. barren*, 85/19.
unbiliefde, *part. pret. unbelieving*, 45/20.
unbleðeliche, *adv. unblithely*, 3/19.
unbuhsumnesse, *sb. disobedience*, 7/14.
unbunden, *part. pret. unbound*, 53/12.
under, *prep. under*, 13/18; 43/9; 63/29; 89/35; 101/34; 121/26; 127/29.
underfeng, *see* underfon.
underfinden, *v. to find out*, 99/32.
underfon, *v. to receive, accept*, 97/10; *pres. ind.* 3 *sg.* underfoð, 85/33; 37/2; -fengð, 99/33; -fonȝð, 141/8; *imp. sg.* -foh, 103/29; *pret. ind.* 3 *sg.* -feng, 97/8; 119/16; *opt.* 1 *sg.* -fenge, 21/11; 117/13.
undernemen, *v. to reprove, undertake, receive, understand*, 11/12; 87/11; *pres. ind.* 2 *sg.* -nimst, 71/

258   GLOSSARY.

15; 87/2; -nemest, 95/17; 3 sg.
-nimþ, 57/34; -nimð, 141/11;
-nemð, 11/5; -nemeð, 141/13.
understanden, v. *to understand*, 45/
21; 47/6; 61/9; 81/33; 87/10;
-stonden, 19/11; 47/20; 49/13;
85/29, 30; 151/11; *pres.* ind. 2
sg. -stancst, 23/6; -stanst, 125/14;
pl. -standeþ, 25/2; -ð, 137/27;
opt. 2 *sg.* -stande, 23/30; 69/33;
-standen, 87/8; *pl.* -stande, 127/8;
imp. sg. -stand, 69/27; -stond, 35/
17; 111/16; *pl.* -standeþ, 19/10;
pret. part. -stonden, 93/21.
undetten, v. *to open*, 3 *sg.* ind. pres.
undett, 121/31.
uneaðe, *adv. scarcely*, 137/25; unneaðe, 95/26.
uneilinde, *part. pres. harmless*, 79/
7; 133/5.
uneilindnesse, *sb. harmlessness*, 133/
3, 4.
unforʒolden, *part. pret. unrewarded*,
37/32.
unfrið, *adj. in discord*, 97/18.
unʒelimp, *sb. mishap, misfortune*, *sg.
nom.* 13/23; 29/6, 11; *pl.* -ʒelim-
pes, 13/22; 63/24.
unʒemæte, *adj. immeasurable*, 17/32.
unʒesali, *adj. unhappy*, 13/29; 137/
34; -ʒesælie, 17/18.
unʒewares, *adv. unawares*, 19/17.
unʒewill, *sb. obstinacy, ac. sg.* 15/16.
unhale, *sb. sickness, d. ac. sg.* 29/1;
71/14, 15; -hæle, 41/20.
unhersum, *adj. disobedient*, 75/21;
77/3; 115/23.
unhersumnesse, *sb. disobedience*, 7/
16, 18, 26, 29; 9/1; 109/1; 115/
11, 26; 119/4.
unc, *see* **wit**.
unker, *pron. our (of two)*, 11/27.
unclannesse, *sb. uncleanness*, 123/27.
uncuðe, *adj. unknown*, 23/3.
uncwemer, *adj. disagreeable, comp.*
133/30.
unlawliche, *adv. unlawfully*, 121/
18.
unlust, *sb. listlessness, displeasure*,
sg. 3/21; *pl.* -es, 107/23.
unmate, *adj. immeasured*, 19/1.
unmihte, *sb. powerlessness, impo-
tence, nom. d. sg.* 107/22; 129/5.
unmihti, *adj. unmighty, weak*, 5/13;
15/29; 75/34.
unne, *v. to grant*, 3 *sg. opt. pres.* 21/
22.
unneaðe, *see* **uneaðe**.
unofearned, *part. pret. undeserved*,
3/26; 51/16; 59/7.

unorne, *adj. coarse*, 43/13.
unorneliche, *adv. coarsely*, 57/25,
27; 107/17.
unpined, *part. pret. unpunished*,
103/27.
unriht, *sb. injustice, wrong, sg. nom.
ac.* 105/28; 113/17; unrihte, 51/
13; 77/33; 79/33; 105/29; *pl.*
unrihtes, 79/34; 105/27.
unriht, *adj. unjust*, 121/22.
unrihtwis, *adj. unrighteous*, 37/29;
-rihwisen, 83/26.
unrihtwisnesse, *sb. unrighteousness,
sg.* 11/15; 15/18; 33/2; 37/27,
29; 55/26; 77/26; 79/31; (-irht-,
MS.) 81/30; -ritwis-, 121/19; hun-
rihtwisnesse, 15/17; *pl.* unrihtwis-
nesses, 123/2.
unsali, *adj. unhappy*, 79/33; 137/30.
unstrang, *adj. weak*, 91/28; -strong,
15/29.
unþank, *sb. reluctance, g. sg.* -es, 69/
6; 111/8; -ðankes, 131/11.
unðeaufulle, *adj. illmannered*, 131/
4.
unþeaw, *sb. vice, sg. d.* -e, 57/34;
pl. -ðeawes, 11/22; 15/19, 30;
47/11.
unþolemod, *adj. impatient*, 13/21.
unðolemodnesse, *sb. impatience*, 13/
11; -þole-, 13/12; 129/8.
unware, *adj. unguarded*, 45/28.
unwilles, *unwillingness, pl.* 107/23.
unwine, *sb. enemy, sg. nom. d.* 5/23;
75/13; *pl.* -wines, 21/16; 77/16;
103/14, 17; 107/6, 8.
unwise, *adj. unwise*, 45/20.
unworðere, *see* **unwurð**.
unwraste, *adj. frail*, 31/6.
unwurscipe, *sb. irrererence, unworthi-
ness, humiliation, d. sg.* 53/8; *pl.*
-wurðscipes, 97/5.
unwurð, *adj. unworthy, worthless,
despised*, 5/34; 29/34; 55/4, 12;
85/19; 97/1; *comp.* -wurþere, 109/
23; -worðere, 133/29.
unwurðen, *v. to despise, disdain,
pret.* 3 *sg.* -wurðede, 115/23; *part.*
-wurðed, 55/7.
unwurðliche, *adv. unworthily*, 53/8.
unwurðscipes, *see* **unwurscipe**.
up, (1) *prep. upon*, 85/31; (2) *adv. a.
with prep.* upan, 95/7; up fram,
95/3; up in, 75/26; up to, 45/11;
119/27; *b. with verbs*, 95/2, 5;
101/15; 105/25; upp, 41/27; 49/
25; 69/17; 143/23.
upbreides, *sb. upbraidings, pl.* 41/
21.
uppon, *prep. upon*, 31/24; 33/19;

GLOSSARY. 259

71/34; 79/8; 123/15; 127/3;
143/3, 11; upen, 75/27; 111/32;
uppe, 11/24; 27/3; 51/24; 61/4,
12; 71/30; 77/27, 28; 85/1; 87/
3; 89/11; 93/2; 117/1; 137/14;
upe, 63/19; 79/1; 85/18; 89/10,
11; 97/2; 103/14, 24; 111/12,
20; uppe on, 93/22.
ure, *pron. poss.* our, 7/18, 32; 15/
28; 21/5, 12, 17, 19; 25/8, 21;
27/14; 31/12; 33/19; 43/3; 45/
9, 14, *etc.*
ure, *see* we.
us, *see* we.
ut, *adv. out*, 51/21; 53/18; 63/11;
73/14, 19, 24; 85/16; 105/16 (2);
109/27; 111/4, 6; 119/22; 145/
34.
ute, *adv. without, outside*, 43/21.
ut of, *prep. out of*, 5/27; 7/17, 18;
11/19; 19/7, 27; 51/19; 73/2;
83/2, 11, 16; 87/18, *etc.*
uttreste, *adj. uttermost*, 17/18, 30.

V.

virgines, *sb. virgins, pl.* 35/1.

W.

w-, *cf.* hw-.
wa, *int. woe*, 5/17; 15/25; 19/9;
41/8; 49/22; 69/10; 79/20, 29,
32; 81/3, 4; 139/11.
wæcche, *sb. watching, vigil, sg. d. ac.*
89/11; *pl.* wacches, 95/24.
wacchen, *v. to watch, to keep vigil*,
33/29; 149/15.
wæiȝe, *sb. weight, d. ac. sg.* 11/28;
17/15.
waitin, *v. to wait, pl. ind. pres.*
waitið, 103/23.
wake, *sb. watching*, 125/32.
wakien, *v. to watch, to be awake*, 3/
26; *imp. pl.* wakieð, 19/17; 139/
17.
walawa, *int. welaway, alas*, 15/15;
127/14; walewa, 69/29; waleawa,
89/21; weilawei, 15/14.
walde, *see* willen.
wallende, *part. pres. boiling*, 63/32.
walte, *sb. power, sg. d.* 115/2.
wan, *see* hwa.
wåndede, *see* wonde.
wænden, *v. to turn, wend*, 27/24;
47/2; 83/29; wanden, 29/14; 31/
12; 99/20; 145/5; *pres. ind.* 3 *sg.*
want, 33/17; 53/7; 103/7; 145/
5; *pl.* wændeð, 81/5; wandeð,
57/31; want, 65/15; *opt.* 3 *sg.*
wande, 101/23; *imp. sg.* wænd,

59/31; wand, 127/30; 147/25;
want (to) 13/18; *pl.* wændeð, 89/
22 (2); wandeð, 19/14; *part.*
wændinde, 71/23; *pret.* 1 *and* 3 *sg.*
wante, 147/19; wænte, 23/12;
wente, 23/13; *pl.* wanten, 23/16;
145/1; *part.* iwant, 19/14; 27/20.
wændinge, *sb. turning*, 23/7.
wanien, *sb. to wail, pres. ind.* 3 *sg.*
woneð, 63/20; *pl.* wonið, 115/12;
imp. pl. wanið, 19/18; wanieð,
21/1; *part.* woninde, 95/26.
wann, *see* winnen.
wante, *see* wænden.
wapman, *sb. man, g. sg.* wapmannes,
55/13.
war, *adj. aware*, 9/32; 53/15; 59/
2, 8; 61/8; 71/1; 73/10; 81/8;
139/20; warr, 39/13; 71/16.
ward, *see* toward.
ware, waren, *see* bien.
wariȝing, *see* werȝinge.
hwarliker, *adv. cautiously, comp.*
49/20.
wærnen, *v. to deny*, 61/6; *pret.* 3 *sg.*
wernde, 147/14.
warnien, *v. to warn*, 11/13; 57/11;
warniȝen, 55/25; warnin, 45/13,
17; 73/8; 151/9; *pres. ind.* 1 *sg.*
warni, 7/22; 69/32; 89/10; 103/
19; 125/19; 3 *sg.* warneð, 39/15;
61/27; 73/1; 75/7; *pret.* 1 *sg.*
warnede, 113/17; 2 *sg.* warnedest,
21/27; *pl.* warneden, 103/14;
part. ȝewarned, 27/18; iwarned,
51/21; 149/4.
warp, *see* werpen.
warr, *see* war.
warð, *see* wurðen.
was, *see* bien.
wascen, *v. to wash*, 147/13; *imp.* 2
sg. wassce, 125/10; 1 *pl.* (adhort.)
waschen, 95/29; *pret. part.* iwas-
cen, 119/21.
wast, *see* witen.
wastme, *sb. fruit, sg.* 51/28; 53/6,
10; 117/1; 119/1, 3, 9, 13, 15,
21; wasme, 51/33; 117/30; *pl.*
wastmes, 51/25.
wat, *see* witen, *and* hwa.
wæte, *adj. wet*, 85/14.
water, *sb. water, sg. nom. ac.* 29/2;
43/13; 119/20; *d.* watere, 45/19;
79/14; 83/2; 119/21.
wætes, *sb. liquids, pl.* 33/4.
watrien, *v. to water*, 147/10.
wauȝe, *see* wouh.
wauȝhe, *see* wohȝe.
we, *pron. we*, 7/24, 32; 9/1, 2, 13;
11/28, 29; 13/4; 15/5, 23; 19/19;

GLOSSARY.

21/1, 15, 16, 18, 23. 24; 23/22, 24; 27/6, 17, *etc.*; *d. ac.* us, 7/24, 26; 9/2, 4; 11/27, 30, 31; 19/12, 13; 21/14, 22 (2); 23/14, 25; 27/15; 31/3, 6, 11, *etc.*; hus, 121/11; *gen.* ure, 131/26.
wealden, *v. to rule, control*, 13/13; 51/1; 61/2; 117/10; *pres. ind. pl.* welden, 51/2; *pret. part.* iwelt, 23/28.
weapne, *sb. weapons*, *pl.* 121/18.
webb, *sb web, nom.* 39/22.
weddede, *pret. part. wedded*, 41/16.
weder, *sb. weather, d. sg.* wedere, 43/30.
wei, *sb. way, sg. nom. ac.* 21/15; 99/15; wei3, 127/3; *d.* wei3e, 75/9, 15, 17; 83/11; 85/34; 125/30; 127/8; *pl.* wei3es, 83/26.
wei3en, *v. to lift, to weigh, pres. ind.* 3 *sg.* wei3þ, 49/25; *pret. part* iwæi3en, 17/15.
weilawei, *see* walawa.
wel, *adv.* (1) *well*, 5/23; 7/2, 31; 9/29; 13/2, 8; 17/8, 15 (2), 16, 19; 21/27; 23/6; 27/32; 29/4, 8, 12. 16; 31/15, 17, 25; 33/8; 35/18; 39/13, *etc.*; (2) *very, quite,* 29/11; 57/16; 59/6; 67/11; 73/10; 81/16; 89/26; 97/7; 135/24; 147/29; well, 93/18; wiel, 123/9; wol, 125/10.
welden, *see* wealden.
wele, *sb. weal, wealth, right, d. ac. sg.* 29/1; 31/19; 85/4; 41/20; 67/19; 69/14; 81/4.
welcume, *adj. welcome*, 99/29; 141/9.
well, *see* wel.
welle, *sb. source, nom. sg.* 115/8.
well-riðe, *sb. well-spring, d. sg.* 95/27.
well-stream, *sb. stream, sg. ac.* 81/31; *d.* -streme, 103/4.
wene, *sb. assumption, nom. sg.* 31/19.
wenen, *v. to ween, hope, fancy, assume, presume, pres. ind.* 3 *sg.* wenþ, 39/28; *pl.* weneð, 9/14; 37/14; 69/22; *pret.* 1 *sg.* wende, 9/9; 83/23; 2 *sg.* wende3t, 11/10; *pl.* wenden, 149/24.
wente, *see* wanden.
weork, *sb. work, sg. ac.* 93/3; weorc, 95/3; *d.* weorke, 61/1; 123/9; werke, 117/27; *pl.* weorkes, 3/18, 25; 11/24; 13/1, 14; werkes, 7/5; 29/23, 25, 26; 39/26, 31; 65/14; 71/27; 73/24; 81/19; 95/32; 97/14; 99/27; 103/24; woerkes, 9/2; 17/22; workes, 3/14;

workes, 123/31; 133/10; 141/7 143/8, 26.
weormes, *see* wermes.
wepen, *v. to weep*, 111/32; 149/6; *pres. ind.* 3 *sg.* wepð, 57/16; 63/20; *pl.* wepeð, 115/12; *imp. pl.* wepeð, 19/18, 34; 95/28 (2); *part.* wepinde, 95/26; 137/30.
wer, *sb. man, d. sg.* were, 131/24.
werchen, *v. to work*, 77/8; 109/17; 117/15; *pres. ind.* 2 *sg.* wercst, 65/8; *pl.* wercheð, 27/13; wercheþ, 29/28; *part.* werchinde, 39/2; 131/4; wurchende, 3/10.
werdles, *see* woreld.
were, *see* bien.
wer3inge, *sb. cursing, sg.* 19/25, 28; wari3ing, 19/27; *pl.* wer3inginges, 41/28.
weri3en, *v. to curse*, 9/8; wer3ien, 13/6; wer3i, 13/10; *pres. ind. pl.* wer3ieð, 13/7; wer3ið, 19/26; *part.* wer3inde, 13/5; wer3hinde, 13/3; *pret.* 3 *sg.* were3ede, 13/19; *part.* 3ewer3ed, 13/8; 33/16; 55/2; 117/25, 26; iwer3ed, 117/32; 3ewerwed, 19/24; 3ewere3ede, 23/31; 41/31; 3ewere3ede, 11/17; iwer3ede, 7/6; 19/30; wer3ede, 23/26; were3ede, 5/15; werewede, 23/20; 103/23.
weri3en, *v. to resist*, 3 *sg. opt. pres.* weri3e, 89/33.
weri3en, *v. to weary oneself*, 75/3.
weringe (*MS.* þeringe), *sb. wearying*, 125/32.
werk, *see* weork.
wermes, *sb. worms*, 15/24; 63/31; weormes, 139/8.
wernde, *see* wærnen.
werpen, *v. to throw, cast*, 17/27; 61/31; worpen, 135/3; *pres. ind.* 2 *sg.* werpest, 63/18; *pret.ind.* 3 *sg.* warp, 105/16; 111/4; *part.* 3eworpen, 73/14; iworpen, 73/19.
wers, *adv. worse*, 57/20; wurse, 57/23.
werse, *adj. worse*, 73/24; wurse, 65/24; *superl.* werste, 77/15.
werð, *see* wurðen.
werwen, *see* weri3en.
wexen, *v. to wax, grow*, 69/13.
wh-, *see* hw-.
wicchen, *sb. witches, nom. pl.* 121/21.
wid-, *see* wið-.
wide, *adv. wide*, 105/26.
wiel, *see* wel.
wif, *sb. wife, woman, sg. nom. ac.* 27/24; 85/4; 55/3; 67/19; 75/3; *d.*

GLOSSARY.

wive, 41/16, 18, 21; 111/29; *pl.* wives, 117/30.
wifman, *sb. woman, d. sg.* -manne, 127/12.
wike, *sb. office, ac. sg.* 99/25; 121/20.
wilde, *adj. wild,* 43/24.
wilderne, *sb. wilderness, d. sg.* 73/27; 137/9, 15.
wile, *see* hwile, *and* wille (v).
wilke, *see* hwilk.
wille, *sb. will, lust, sg.* 13/27, 31; 15/1, 5, 6, 10, 11, 13, 14; 23/13, 17, 19, 24, 28; 33/30; 35/33; 45/22; 47/5; 69/5; 77/8; 85/5, 23; 87/19, *etc.*; willen, 57/25; *pl.* willes, 87/18.
willen, *v. to will, wish, pres. ind.* 1 *sg.* 27/4, 17; 113/29; 117/1; 141/31; wile, 23/3, 9; 47/2, 12; 57/11; 59/16, 23, 27; 71/28; 73/8; 83/26; 85/33, 34; 87/3, 10; 97/11; 109/29; 111/12; 117/10; 149/3; 2 *sg.* wilt, 23/8; 25/31; 37/32; 41/16; 47/20; 49/7, 20, 21; 59/3; 65/28; 69/1; 73/3, 7; 75/2, 14, 27, 30; 77/5; 81/7, *etc.*; 3 *sg.* wile, 5/5; 9/33; 11/19; 15/6, 7; 17/15, 18, 29; 23/24; 29/3, 17, 28; 31/11; 33/4, 5, 6, 19, 26; 37/16; 45/18, 20, 31; 47/18; 53/15; 59/25; 61/6; 65/3; 71/22; 73/16; 75/10, 18, 19; 77/9, 13, 19; 79/34, *etc.*; wyle, 107/22; wille, 27/12; *pl.* willeð, 13/6; 23/19, 24; 35/12; 41/28, 30; 43/18; 45/2; 55/27; 59/23; 61/12; 71/29; 79/8; 91/21, 22, 31; 105/29; 119/32; 131/7; 143/16; willen, 5/12; 69/20; wile, 45/27; *opt.* 2 *sg.* wille, 75/12; 145/21; wile, 45/24; 61/8; *pl.* willen, 23/20; 99/28; 129/22; *pret.* 1 *and* 3 *sg.* wolde, 5/1; 9/17, 18; 13/20; 37/5; 55/6; 57/1; 85/2; 101/10; 113/19; 131/13; 137/12; 147/13; walde, 143/13; 2 *sg.* woldest, 17/20, 23; 23/4; 47/5; 67/8; 75/13; 77/11; 91/2; 103/18, 19; 117/13; 133/13; 141/21; *pl.* wolden, 45/26; 67/13; 129/20; wolde, 49/18.
win, *sb. wine, sg. nom. ac.* 51/35; 53/2; 149/4; *d.* wine, 149/6; *pl.* wines, 43/15.
wind, *sb. wind, d. sg.* winde, 43/29; 47/27; 73/19; *pl.* windes, 43/25; 45/12.
winne, *sb. joy, nom. sg.* 145/3.
winnen, *v. to strive, pres. ind. pl.*

winneð, 23/25; 97/26; 135/15; *pret. ind.* 3 *sg.* wann, 63/18.
wintre, *sb. years, pl.* 7/20; 43/23; 51/6; 113/34.
wipe, *v. to wipe, imp. sg.* 125/10.
wis, *adj. wise,* 39/29; 65/25; 67/16, 17; 71/11; 81/14, 16; 99/26; wise, 35/29; 65/14; 67/11, 17; 71/10; 79/11, 18, 21; *superl.* wisest, 149/20.
wisdom, *sb. wisdom, sg. nom. ac.* 25/23; 35/27; 47/28; 49/29; 59/20; 69/30; 91/7, 9, 10, 18, 25; 95/8; 117/34; 127/32; wisedom, 25/14; 37/1; *d.* wisdome, 25/17; 45/19; 61/32; 67/13; 91/13; 151/16; *pl.* wisdomes, 49/30.
wise, *sb. wise, manner, sg.* 3/18; 5/28; 9/9; 21/31; 29/7; 35/21; 39/20; 51/17; 53/22; 65/19, 21; 117/6, 19; 149/14; *pl. d.* wisen, 15/5; 25/18; 39/3; 49/16; 149/18.
wisliche, *adv. wisely,* 117/34.
wisliche, *adv. certainly,* 81/16.
wissin, *v. to instruct, teach,* 85/34; 95/16; 101/1; 109/18; 127/10; 151/9, 18; *pres. ind.* 3 *sg.* wisseð, 35/28; 59/28; 81/17; 89/5; *opt.* 2 *sg.* wissi, 21/30; *pl.* wissien, 97/12; *imp. sg.* wisse, 81/21; *pret.* 2 *sg.* wissedest, 21/27; 3 *sg.* wissede, 13/17.
wissinge, *sb. instruction,* 33/24.
wit, *pron. we two, nom.* 91/27; 95/18; 97/31; *d.* unc, 9/9.
witen, *v. to know,* 23/9; 53/29; 65/11; 89/4; 125/11; 141/5; witten, 113/2; *part.* witende, 51/26; witinde, 53/5; *pres. ind.* 1 *and* 3 *sg.* wat, 15/32; 21/3; 83/7; 97/18; 123/28; 143/4; 151/9; wot, 75/2 (2); 85/3; 95/26; 97/21; 115/20; 123/30; 145/22; 151/9; 2 *sg.* wast, 39/3; wost, 77/13; 109/23; *pl. ind. and opt.* witen, 45/28; 61/13; 141/29; *opt.* 1 *and* 3 *sg.* wite, 53/13, 18; 101/3; *imp. sg.* wite, 25/1; 27/32; 49/21; 55/23; 59/11; 65/22; 69/28; 75/16; 89/28; 135/26; 147/4; *pl.* wite (3e), 41/32; 53/1; 123/5.
witen, *v. to go, imp.* 1 *pl.* wuten, 23/22; hute, 151/15; 2 *pl.* witeð, 19/32.
witt, *sb. wit, understanding, reason, sense, sg. nom. ac.* 19/11; 65/11; 69/30; 79/23; *d.* witte, 23/30; 65/9; 81/17; 151/16; *g.* wittes, 41/9; *pl.* wittes, 17/1, 2, 5, 11; 49/30.

H

witten, *see* witen.
witti, *adj. cunning,* 81/14.
wiŏ, *prep. with, by, against,* 3/4; 7/20; 21/31; 45/17; 71/1; 83/16; 113/12; 133/29; 135/14; 141/20, 21.
wiŏealden, *see* wiŏhealden.
wiŏerwine, *sb. enemy, sg.* 75/9; 115/24; 139/17; *pl.* -winen, 5/11.
wiŏhealden, *v. to withhold, retain, restrain,* 71/3; 101/6, 10; -ealden, 61/9; 139/29; *pres. ind.* 3 *sg.* -halt, 107/24; 133/28; 135/11; *opt. pl.* -ealden, 135/19; *imp. sg.* wideald, 135/25; *pl.* wiŏhealdeþ, 135/14; *pret. ind.* 3 *sg.* wiŏeld, 143/31; *part.* wiŏhealden, 27/27; 47/29.
wiŏhealdnesse, *sb. continence, abstinence,* wiŏhealnesse, 43/10; wiŏealdnesse, 135/10, 16; widhealdnesse, 131/16; wideadlnesse, 131/17; wiŏhealdenesse, 43/17; wiŏhelŏnesse, 135/9.
wiŏinnen, (1) *prep. within, in,* 43/33; -inne, 73/17; (2) *adv.* -innen, 7/5; 95/10, 11; 147/11; -inne, 15/24.
wiŏseggen, *v. to contradict,* 3 *sg. ind. pres.* wiŏseiŏ, 101/25.
wiŏstanden, *v. to withstand,* 39/7; *pres. ind.* 3 *sg.* -stant, 5/11; *imp. sg.* -stond, 91/1.
wiŏuten, *adv. prep. without, outside, save,* 7/5; 9/24; 11/29; 15/22-24; 19/8; 21/9, 21; 25/1, 14, 15, 19, 22; 27/25; 29/25; 39/22, 23; 47/26; 51/11, 35; 53/30; 59/11, *etc.*; widuten, 47/29; 133/21.
wive, *see* wif.
woerkes, *see* weork.
wohȝe (*corr. into* wrohȝe), *adj. wrong,* 81/5; wauȝhe, 29/1.
wocnesse, *sb. weakness,* 83/22.
wol, *see* wel.
wolde, *see* wille (v.).
wolkne, *sb. welkin, clouds, d. sg.* 103/24.
wombe, *sb. womb, sg. nom. d.* 53/28; 87/23; 117/1, 30; 137/31; 139/8.
wonde, *v. to spare,* 105/21; *imp. sg.* 93/7; *pret.* 3 *sg.* wăndede, 105/20.
wonien, *see* wanien.
woninge, *sb. wailing,* 17/32.
wop, *sb. wailing, weeping, sg. nom.* 17/32; *d.* wope, 125/32.
word, *sb. word, sg. nom. ac.* 69/17; 75/12; 91/3, 19; 99/29; 125/1; *d.* worde, 41/25; 61/1; 75/20; 127/27; 143/8; *pl.* wordes, *ac.* 11/12, 23; 13/1, 14, 16; 17/22; 19/22; 29/25; 35/33; 37/5; 39/26, 30, 31; 41/28; 45/23; 47/23; 55/23; 59/1; 69/13, *etc.*
woreld, *sb. world, sg. nom. d. ac.* 17/19; 29/34; 33/21; 35/7, 12; 37/22; 39/10, 32; 41/5, 7, 10, 15, 18, 33; 43/2, 15, 21; 45/9, 26; 49/7; 63/3; 65/27; 67/16; 71/22 24, 33; 78/2, 4, 5, 21, 23, 34; 75/2; 77/5, 16; 103/21; 103/16; 111/6, 7; 151/21; world, 5/33; 7/4; 83/9; 41/12; 81/8; 99/15; 123/13; 137/11; 143/12; 149/5; *d.* worlde, 43/6; *g.* woreldes, 31/27, 29; worldes, 35/4; 43/5; 61/25; 67/19; 75/22; 139/33; werdles, 31/19; wordles, 79/33; 81/3; wordlles, 83/15; *pl. g.* worelde, 63/3.
woreldliches, *adj. worldly,* 31/7.
woreld-mann, *sb. worldling, nom. sg.* 57/14, 18; 67/17; world-mann, 81/9; *pl.* world-menn, 41/32.
woreld-þing, *sb. worldly things, pl.* 3/13.
workes, *see* weork.
world-eihte, *sb. worldly possession, d. sg.* 57/26.
worpen, *see* werpen.
woroŏ, *see* wurŏen.
worŏliche, *see* wurŏliche.
wost, wot, *see* witen.
wouh, *sb. wall, sg. ac.* 95/4; *d.* wauȝe, 147/20.
wraŏ, *adj. wroth,* 83/16; wroŏe, 99/12.
wraŏhin, *v. to become, make angry,* 99/10; *pres.* 3 *sg. opt.* wraŏþi, 125/30.
wraŏliche, *adv. wrathfully,* 61/11.
wraŏŏe, *sb. ire, anger, sg.* 21/1; 39/33; 41/4; 61/13; 77/23; 89/27; 127/3, 23; wraŏþe, 121/20; 127/4; 137/2, 3; wraŏ, 81/26; *pl.* wraŏŏhes, 41/27.
wrecchade, *sb. wretchedness, sg. d.* 21/18; *pl.* wrecchades, 95/25.
1. wrecche, *sb. wretch, poor, sg. nom.* 67/20; *pl. d.* wrecchen, 69/2; *ac.* wrecches, 75/33.
2. wrecche,*adj. wretched, poor,* 7/29; 15/31; 17/3; 39/17; 47/16; 69/16; 85/31; 91/27; 103/16; 115/8; 145/33; 149/17; wreche, 103/3; 119/24.
wrecchede, *part. pret. wretched,* 9/18.
wreiȝen, *v. to accuse,* 9/29; *pres. ind.* 1 *sg.* wreiȝe, 9/30; 3 *sg.* wreiŏ,

GLOSSARY.

17/2; wreiʒeð, 141/11; wreihð, 141/14; *pret.* 3 *sg.* wreiʒede, 147/14.
wreken, *v. to revenge*, 105/29. 31; wreke, 77/18; *pret. part.* iwreken, 5/23.
wrien, *v. to cover, pres. ind.* 3 *sg.* wrikð, 95/7.
wrihte, *sb. workmaster, carpenter, sg. nom. d.* 27/26; 91/15, 25; 95/9.
wrikð, *see* wrien.
writ, *sb. writ, sg. nom. ac.* 37/26; 61/19; 101/24; 133/14; writt, 37/14; 41/14; 67/9; 121/17; 151/8; *d.* write, 15/6; 47/15; 75/7, 14, 26; 85/22; 113/11; 123/14; *pl.* writes, 35/29; 59/17; 77/8, 24.
writen, *v. to write*, 53/16; 95/27; write, 19/9; *pres. ind.* 1 *sg.* write, 113/12; *pret. pl.* writen, 27/15; *part.* ʒewriten, 5/10; 45/9; 59/8; 65/12; 105/6; 145/3; iwriten, 29/24; 33/15; 39/1; 55/2, 23; 85/24; 113/8; writen, 59/14.
wrohʒe, *see* wohʒe.
wroðe, *see* wrað.
wulder, *sb. glory, nom. sg.* 5/20.
wunde, *sb. wound, d. sg.* 119/20.
wunder, *sb. wonder, sg. nom.* 117/18; *pl. ac.* wundren, 15/31.
wundien, *v. to wound, pres. ind. pl.* wundieð, 63/17; *pret. part.* ʒewunded, 71/2; iwunded, 63/15; iwundede, 63/15.
wune, *sb. custom, d. sg.* 59/31.
wuneliche, *adv. habitually*, 121/21.
wunien, *v. to dwell*, 19/5; 73/25, 28; 97/31; 123/32; 137/18; wuniʒen, 13/6; 21/24; 37/11, 24, 32; 41/13(2); 73/5; 79/3; 81/8; 83/8; 87/14, 17; 91/26; 95/34; 97/21; 121/3; 143/16; wunen, 79/1; *pres. ind.* 2 *sg.* wunest, 39/8; 41/15; 129/7; 3 *sg.* wuneð, 35/17-20; 37/10, 13(2); 39/33; 99/5; 141/4; wuniʒeð, 53/3; *pl.* wunieð, 61/15; 97/14; wuniʒeð, 45/1, 4; wuniʒið, 19/20; wunien, 33/6; wuniʒen, 109/16; *opt.* 3 *sg.* wuniʒe, 41/3; *part.* wuniende, 35/30; 37/7; 47/16; 67/26; 73/31; 95/5; wuniʒende, 21/4, 13; 41/17; 51/5; 97/18; 103/20; 107/10; wunende, 57/12; *pret. pl.* wuneden, 73/32.
wunienge, *sb. dwelling*, 37/4; 41/31; 73/18; 91/22; 101/15; wuniʒenge, 87/13.
wurchende, *see* werchen.
wurscipe, *see* wurðscipe.
wurse, *see* wers(e).
wurðe, *adj. worth, worthy*, 21/11; 29/11; 59/6; wurde, 71/23.
wurðen, *v. to become, pres. ind.* 1 *sg.* wurð (ic), 83/3; 3 *sg.* wurð, 5/25; 89/23; 117/4; 123/13; wurþ, 19/21; 37/32; worð, 151/5; *opt.* 3 *sg.* wurðe, 131/10; 133/28; *pret. ind.* 3 *sg.* warð, 51/11; 117/32; 119/1; 137/3; 147/18; werð, 119/2; *opt.* 3 *sg.* wurðe, 5/4.
wurðiʒen, *v. to honour, praise*, 85/2; wurðin, 65/24; *pret. part.* ʒewurðed, 25/12; 135/7; wurðed, 65/26.
wurðliche, *adv. worthily*, 21/11; 133/30; worðliche, 133/24.
wurðscipe, *sb. worship, sg. d. ac.* 55/8; 97/6; 103/30; wurdscipe, 85/6; wurscipe, 85/9; 135/21.
wuten, *int. let us!* (= Fr. *allons!*) 23/22; hute, 151/15 (*see* witen 2).

Y, *see* **I**.

LIST OF QUOTATIONS.

A. BIBLICAL QUOTATIONS AND ALLUSIONS.

I. OLD TESTAMENT.

GENESIS.

CHAP.		PAGE
i. 26 f.	. . .	23/9; 113/22.
27	. . .	95/22.
28	. . .	13/7.
ii. 7	. . .	95/20.
9	. . .	51/25.
17	. . .	51/22; 105/18; 113/18.
18	. . .	127/12.
iii. 3	. . .	51/25.
17	. . .	117/26.
iv. 7	. . .	37/18.
v. 31	. . .	43/23.
vi. 8 f.	. . .	43/21.
vii. 5 f.	. . .	43/23.
xii. 1	. . .	109/27.
3	. . .	109/24; 115/31.
xv. 6	. . .	109/24.
xxi. 5	. . .	111/13.
xxii. 2	. . .	111/10.
18	. . .	109/24; 115/31.
xxviii. 17	. . .	91/15.

EXODUS.

xxii. 25	. . .	77/21.
xxiv. 18	. . .	137/13.
xxxiv. 28	. . .	137/13.

LEVITICUS.

xix. 18	. . .	67/4.
35 f.	. . .	11/28.
xxii. 19 f.	. . .	149/29 f.
xxv. 35 f.	. . .	77/21.

DEUTERONOMIUM.

viii. 3	. . .	89/2.
ix. 9-18	. .	137/13.
xv. 21	. . .	149/29.
xvii. 1	. . .	149/29.
xxiii. 19 f.	. . .	77/21.
xxv. 13	. . .	11/28.
xxxii. 35	. . .	77/17.

I. LIBER SAMUELIS OR REGUM.

| i. 1 ff. | . . | 85/19. |

II. LIBER SAMUELIS OR REGUM.

CHAP.		PAGE
xi.	. . .	81/23.
xxii. 3, 31	. .	39/11.

III. LIBER REGUM (I KINGS).

| xvii. | . . . | 143/28. |
| xix. 8 | . . . | 137/14. |

IV. LIBER REGUM (II KINGS).

| xx. | . . . | 147/16 f. |

JOB.

| i. 1 | . . . | 41/17. |
| vii. 1 | . . . | 89/33. |

PSALMI.

ii. 7	. . .	117/2.
8 f.	. . .	117/8.
12	. . .	125/28.
iv. 6	. . .	31/16.
7	. . .	31/21, 26.
vi. 7	. . .	147/9.
x. 6	. . .	37/26.
xii. 4 f.	. .	127/17.
xiv. 1	. . .	77/34.
4	. . .	79/3.
5	. . .	77/21; 79/5.
xv. 2	. . .	85/4.
xvi. 8	. . .	101/33 f.
xviii. 10	. . .	63/2.
xxiii. 15	. . .	19/18; 65/13.
xxvi. 13	. . .	41/11; 45/2; 61/16.
xxxi. 8	. . .	85/32; 87/2.
9	. . .	89/30.
xxxiii. 12	. . .	59/21.
13	. . .	59/24.
14	. . .	59/29.
15	. . .	19/18; 59/30 65/13.
16	. . .	61/4.
17	. . .	61/10.
xxxix. 8	. . .	117/12.
xli. 4	. . .	147/6.
xliv. 6	. . .	63/16.
8	. . .	81/32.
xlix. 20	. . .	11/5.
21	. . .	11/9 f.
l. 3	. . .	81/25 f.
9	. . .	83/1 ff.

LIST OF QUOTATIONS.

CHAP.		PAGE
I. 12	. . .	83/5 ff 9.
13	. . .	83/12 ff. 17.
14	. . .	83/19 ff. 22.
15	. . .	83/25 ff. 28.
18	. . .	85/2.
19	. . .	85/9 ff. 11.
li. 5	. . .	11/13.
7	. . .	11/16; 41/11; 45/2; 61/16
liv. 12	. . .	77/21.
lx. 4	. . .	107/7.
lxi. 11	. . .	75/22.
lxii. 2	. . .	93/14.
lxxi. 14	. . .	77/21.
lxxii. 23	. . .	93/10.
lxxv. 3	. . .	97/19.
lxxvi. 11	. . .	23/7.
lxxix. 6	. . .	147/31 ff.
lxxx. 13	. . .	13/25.
lxxxiv. 2	. . .	117/28.
9	. . .	87/9.
11	. . .	113/8; 117/22.
12	. . .	117/24.
lxxxviii. 15	. . .	105/6.
xcvi. 2	. . .	105/6.
ciii. 25	. . .	45/8.
cv. 1	. . .	123/10.
cvi. 1	. . .	123/10.
26	. . .	45/10.
cx. 10	. . .	59/19.
cxvii. 1	. . .	123/10.
cviii. 11	. . .	125/1.
21	. . .	19/23.
66	. . .	127/20.
165	. . .	99/10.
cxxxi. 11	. . .	115/33.
cxxxv. 1	. . .	123/10.
cxxxvii. 8	. . .	13/7; 21/22; 115/5.
cxl. 2	. . .	143/22.
cxli. 6	. . .	41/11; 45/2; 61/16.
cxlii. 2	. . .	105/12.
cxlv. 4	. . .	33/11.

PROVERBIA.

i. 7	. . .	59/20; 91/13.
ix. 1	. . .	91/9.
10	. . .	59/20; 91/13.
xi. 1	. . .	11/28.
21	. . .	133/14.
xii. 23	. . .	105/7.
xvi. 32	. . .	129/2.
xx. 10	. . .	11/28.
23	. . .	11/28.
xxviii. 8	. . .	77/21.
9	. . .	145/3.
14	. . .	61/19.
xxx 5	. . .	39/11.

ECCLESIASTES.

CHAP.		PAGE
iv. 12	. . .	45/14 f.
vii. 19	. . .	63/8.
xii. 13	. . .	61/32.

LIBER SAPIENTIAE.

ii. 2 f.	. . .	129/7.
23	. . .	95/22.
24	. . .	7/12.

ECCLESIASTICUS OR JESUS SIRACH.

i. 16	. . .	59/20; 91/13.
ii. 1	. . .	73/8.
v. 5 f.	. . .	123/21.
x. 15	. . .	5/8.
xvii. 1	. . .	95/22.
xxvii. 6	. . .	73/12.
xxviii. 1	. . .	77/17.
xxxii. 24	. . .	71/7; 75/6.

ISAIAS.

v. 20	. . .	79/29.
21	. . .	79/19.
23	. . .	79/24.
vi. 10	. . .	127/6.
xi. 2 f.	. . .	91/11.
xiv. 14	. . .	9/26.
xxxviii. 1 f.	. . .	147/16 ff.
11	. . .	41/11; 45/2; 61/16.
xliii. 26	. . .	123/1.
xlix. 14 f.	. . .	87/20 f.
lii. 11	. . .	123/32.
liii. 8	. . .	41/11; 45/2; 61/16.
lvi. 10	. . .	109/21.
lviii. 9	. . .	145/7.

JEREMIAS.

xi. 19	. . .	41/11; 45/2; 61/16.
xvii. 5	. . .	33/15.

EZECHIEL.

xiv. 14–20	. . .	43/21 f.
xviii. 8, 13, 17	. . .	77/21.
30	. . .	19/13.
xxii. 12	. . .	77/21.
xxxii. 23 f.	. . .	41/11; 45/2; 61/16.
xlvii. 1 f.	. . .	88/2.

DANIEL.

i. 5–16	. . .	43/12 f.
ix. 23	. . .	43/4.

JONAS.

| iii. 1 ff. | . . . | 137/3. |

II. NEW TESTAMENT.

MATTHAEUS.

CHAP.		PAGE
ii. 16	. . .	133/7.
iv. 2	. . .	137/8.
4	. . .	89/2.
17	. . .	121/6.
v. 7	. . .	113/5.
8	. . .	125/7.
24	. . .	3/3.
25	. . .	75/8.
37	. . .	9/11 f.
39 f.	. . .	13/17; 127/28.
42	. . .	77/19.
44	. . .	77/16 f.
46 f.	. . .	77/14 f.
vi. 2	. . .	5/30.
6	. . .	143/1.
9	. . .	11/8.
19 f.	. . .	75/26.
21	. . .	69/24.
25 f.	. . .	87/30 f.
33	. . .	87/33.
vii. 23	. . .	11/17.
x. 5	. . .	99/14.
12	. . .	99/17 ff.
16	. . .	101/17.
22	. . .	151/3.
28	. . .	61/27.
xi. 28 f.	. . .	71/25.
29	. . .	49/8.
xii. 34	. . .	101/7.
xiii. 22	. . .	69/12.
42	. . .	17/32; 19/1; 63/32.
43	. . .	31/11 f.
50	. . .	17/32; 19/1.
xiv. 23	. . .	143/10.
xv. 14	. . .	109/19; 127/10.
xvi. 16 f.	. . .	25/32; 95/1.
17 f.	. . .	27/1 f. 7.
24	. . .	33/25.
26	. . .	37/22.
xvii. 5	. . .	119/29.
19	. . .	29/18.
xix. 12	. . .	129/19, 24.
16	. . .	67/26.
18	. . .	67/30.
19	. . .	67/4.
21	. . .	67/35; 73/2.
22	. . .	69/3.
24	. . .	69/7.
xxii. 1–14	. . .	95/31 f.
13	. . .	17/26, 32; 19/1.
39	. . .	67/4.
xiii. 12	. . .	5/12.
13	. . .	19/1.

CHAP.		PAGE
xxiii. 16, 24	. .	127/10.
27	. .	15/24.
xxiv. 30	. .	71/34.
51	. .	17/32; 19/1.
xxv. 14 f.	. .	17/5 f.
30	. .	17/26,32; 19/1.
33 f.	. .	77/2.
41	. .	11/17; 19/29.
46	. .	25/27.
xxvi. 39	. .	141/30.
58 f.	. .	111/31.
69 ff.	. .	85/14 ff.
75	. .	85/16.

MARCUS.

iv. 18 f.	. .	69/12.
viii. 33	. .	91/3.
36	. .	37/22.
ix. 22	. .	29/15.
x. 17 f.	. .	67/24 f.
19	. .	67/30 f.
25	. .	69/7.
xii. 31	. .	67/4.
xiv. 54 f.	. .	111/31.
66 f.	. .	85/14 f.

LUCAS.

i. 25	. .	55/3.
28	. .	53/26; 117/28.
31 f.	. .	53/28.
38	. .	53/31.
42	. .	117/28.
48	. .	55/8.
49 f.	. .	55/19 f.
51 f.	. .	55/28.
52	. .	57/3.
ii. 7	. .	49/28.
14	. .	15/12; 99/7.
19	. .	125/6.
51	. .	51/3.
iv. 2	. .	137/8.
4	. .	89/2.
vi. 24	. .	69/9; 81/4.
25	. .	81/2.
28	. .	13/19.
29	. .	13/17; 127/28.
30 f.	. .	77/9 f.
32 f.	. .	77/12 f.
35	. .	77/16 f.
36	. .	113/4.
39	. .	109/19; 127/10.
45	. .	101/7.
vii. 37 f. 48	. .	85/18; 145/27.
viii. 14	. .	69/12.
ix. 2	. .	71/19.
23	. .	33/25.
25	. .	37/22.
62	. .	71/19.

LIST OF QUOTATIONS.

CHAP.	PAGE
x. 1-16	99/14.
5	99/17 f.
6	99/18.
16	45/4.
xii. 22 f.	87/30 f.
31	87/33.
33	75/26.
49	35/21.
58	75/8.
xiii. 27	11/17.
xiv. 11	5/12.
12 f.	75/29 f.
14	77/1.
xvi. 9	79/32.
xvii. 6	29/18.
xviii. 13	145/12.
14	5/12.
15 f.	111/33.
20	67/29 f.
xxii. 54 f.	85/14 f.; 111/31 f.
61 f.	111/31; 145/24.
62	85/16.
xxiii. 27	11/17.
33	145/26.
39 f.	111/33.
43	113/1.

JOHANNES.

i. 4	49/18.
9	35/24; 49/18.
iii. 16	25/20.
iv. 6	5/10.
v. 29	25/27 f.
vi. 38 f.	15/8.
viii. 3-11	111/28.
12	49/18.
44	9/25.
47	47/22.
ix. 5	49/18.
xi. 3	111/27.
xii. 31	111/4.
46	49/18.
xiv. 3	121/1.
6	119/26.
23	37/7; 91/19, 21.
26	83/33.
xv. 26	83/33.
xviii. 15	85/14 f.; 111/31.
25 f.	85/14 f.
xx. 29	25/9.

ACTA APOSTOLORUM.

ii. 3	35/31.

EPISTOLA AD ROMANOS.

ii. 19, 21	127/10.
viii. 35	131/28.

CHAP.	PAGE
xii. 19	77/17; 105/30.
xiii. 9	87/4.
xiv. 17	89/5.

EP. I. AD CORINTHIOS.

i. 24, 30	25/14; 35/27; 91/18; 117/34; 127/32.
iii. 11	93/28.
17	93/22 f.
18	67/14.
vi. 10	13/4; 139/1.
15	27/5; 131/26.
vii. 1, 7 f., 25, 38	129/19 f.
28	75/2.
viii. 1	65/17.
x. 13	73/5.
xi. 3	27/5; 131/26.
27, 29	53/8-15.
xi. 31	105/22.
xiii. 3	39/16; 65/32.
8	35/11.
13	35/8.

EP. II. AD CORINTHIOS.

vii. 10	3/10.
ix. 7	139/28.
xi. 2	131/22.
xii. 9	49/3.

EP. AD GALATOS.

iv. 10	27/22 f.
11	27/20.
26	111/9.
v. 17	97/21, 25.

EP. AD EPHESIOS.

i. 22	27/5; 131/26.
iv. 15	27/5; 131/26.
26	89/17.
v. 23, 30	27/5; 131/26.
vi. 17	91/3.

EP. AD PHILIPPENSES.

ii. 6 f.	49/13.
8	7/32; 51/8; 109/7; 117/21; 119/6.
10	51/3.
iii. 8	31/1.
19	137/30 f.
20	31/11 f.

EP. AD COLOSSENSES.

i. 18	27/5; 131/26.
iii. 17	27/2.

LIST OF QUOTATIONS.

Ep. I. ad Thessalonicenses.

CHAP.	PAGE
iv. 4	135/19.
8	135/22.

Ep. II. ad Thessalonicenses.

iv. 3	135/16.

Ep. I. ad Timotheum.

vi. 15	95/10; 141/26.

Ep. ad Titum.

i. 16	29/25.
ii. 11 f.	31/4 f.

Ep. ad Hebraeos.

x. 7, 9	117/12.
30	77/17; 105/30.
xi. 1	25/8.
xii. 14	129/30.
22	111/9.

Ep. S. Jacobi.

ii. 19	29/26.
20, 26	29/24.
iv. 6	5/10.
v. 12	9/11.
16	142/26.
17 f.	143/28.

Ep. S. Petri I.

CHAP.	PAGE
ii. 11	135/13.
v. 5	5/10.
8	139/16.
10	5/10.

Ep. S. Petri II.

ii. 15	127/3.
iii. 10	19/16 (?).

Ep. S. Johannis I.

ii. 15	41/6.
iii. 21 f.	141/12.
iv. 8, 16	35/15.
9	25/20.
16	37/12.
21	39/12.
v. 6	9/24; 69/24; 113/9.

Apocalypsis.

iii. 12	111/9.
xiv. 4	129/14.
xvii. 14	95/10; 141/26.
xix. 16	95/10; 141/26.
xxi. 2	111/9.

B. OTHER QUOTATIONS.

Augustinus (*cf.* Liber), 121/15; 123/4, 6; 131/9 f., 12 f.
Boc (*unknown source*), 37/33.
Breviary prayer, 19/25 f.
Confiteor, 15/25.
Credo (Apost. and Athan.), 25/10 f.; 27/15; 49/15; 77/18; 97/7.
Evangelium de Nativitate Mariae, ch. ii. 55/2; vii. 55/5.
Evangelium Nicodemi, Pars I (Gesta Pilati), ch. x. 145/26.
Evangelium Nicodemi, Pars II (Descensus ad inferos), ch. ii, v, viii. 17/30; iii, xii. 7/20.
Evangelium Pseudo-Matthaei, ch. vii. 55/5.

Gregorius, expos. on Ps. xxxvii. 47/24.
Gregorius, hom. on Matth. ch. xxii. 1–13; 39/21.
Hieronymus (?) 121/12.
Liber de vera et falsa poenitentia (*Pseudo-Augustinean*), ch. x. 123/4, 6, 14; ch. xix. 121/15.
Nimia humilitas, &c., 59/8.
Nullum malum impunitum, 103/26.
Physiologus, (*The adder*), 101/19.
Rule of S. Benet or Isidor, 73/27.
Sobrietas est, &c., 139/20.
Veni creator, &c., 151/25.
Veni sponsa (Antiphona), 103/28.
Vitae patrum, 149/9 f.
Writ (*unknown source*), 15/6; 41/14; 67/9; 121/17 f

THE END.

The manufacturer's authorised representative in the EU for product safety is Oxford University Press España S.A. of El Parque Empresarial San Fernando de Henares, Avenida de Castilla, 2 - 28830 Madrid (www.oup.es/en or product.safety@oup.com). OUP España S.A. also acts as importer into Spain of products made by the manufacturer.
Printed and bound by CPI Group (UK) Ltd, Croydon, CR0 4YY

20/03/2026

02075329-0003